MORE PERIOD
DETAILS

MORE PERIOD DETAILS

JUDITH MILLER

CLARKSON POTTER/PUBLISHERS
NEW YORK

Copyright © 1999 by Octopus Publishing Group Ltd.

Text copyright © 1999 by Vista 2000

Chief Contributor **John Wainwright**

Contributor **Suzanne Woloszynska**

Published by Clarkson N. Potter, 201 East 50th Street, New York, New York 10022. Member of the Crown Publishing Group.

Originally published in Great Britain by Mitchell Beazley in 1999.

Random House, Inc. New York, London, Toronto, Sydney, Auckland, www.randomhouse.com

CLARKSON N. POTTER, POTTER, and colophon are registered trademarks of Random House, Inc.

Printed in China

Library of Congress Cataloging-in-Publication Data is available upon request.

ISBN 0-609-60410-4

10 9 8 7 6 5 4 3 2 1

First American Edition

CONTENTS

FOREWORD

We produced the first *Period Details* in 1987 and, judging from readers' comments and subsequent sales, it proved a major success as a source of reference and inspiration for homeowners wishing to restore their period houses or re-create period interiors. Much, of course, has happened since its initial publication.

First, and foremost, the substantial growth of interest in period architecture and ornament that began in the 1970s has continued unabated, as more and more people have come to recognize the decorative (and, indeed, financial) potential of their homes. Second, in response to the considerable demand, numerous designers and manufacturers have been making an evermore extensive and diverse range of high-quality reproduction architectural fixtures and fittings. As demand for salvaged original components has often outstripped supply, this has been a welcome development, and one that has made restoration not only easier, but also, generally, more affordable.

Third, and equally significantly, ongoing historical research has continued to unearth new examples of period styles and period details–mostly adding to our knowledge, but sometimes requiring a reassessment of previously held beliefs.

Because of these developments we feel that the time is right for a totally new *More Period Details*. Among the many improvements on the original title, you will find a comprehensive style guide to the prevailing fashions in architecture and ornament from the Middle Ages to the end of the First World War. This should make it much easier to match particular fixtures and fittings to their original historical context. In addition, all the illustrations are new, technically superior to their predecessors, and accompanied by far more detailed and useful descriptions. Empowered with all this information, I believe that you will find restoring and improving your home much easier, and also, as I have, even more rewarding.

Judith Miller

MEDIEVAL

During the Middle Ages–the period that began in the fifth century A.D., following the fall of the Roman Empire, and lasted until the Renaissance (*see* pp. 10–1)–architecture and interior decoration were the preserve of the seigneurial classes, who alone had the time and money to indulge in these "artistic" preoccupations. Consequently, what is now referred to as "Medieval style" was confined to their sparsely furnished stone-built or timber-framed castles and manor houses, rather than the primitive and often impermanent dwellings of the poor.

The prevailing vocabulary of architecture and ornament in the Middle Ages was Gothic. While exhibiting various regional variations, Gothic style was characterized by the use of architectural elements such as lancers (pointed arches); foils (lobed forms shaped like the outlines of grapevine, ivy, or strawberry leaves); cusping (decorative projections, mainly in the form of heads, animals, or leaves); tracery (decorative ribs applied to the upper sections of arched windows, and often consisting of foils and cusps); and arcading (linked arches supported by piers or columns). These forms were also applied (carved or painted) to furniture and artifacts, and were augmented with a rich vocabulary of decorative motifs and imagery, much of which was derived from illustrated medieval manuscripts or, simply, the architect's or artist's imagination. Notable examples included naturalistic representations of flora and fauna; the seasons; human figures, such as clerics, masons, and patrons of the arts; chevron and checker patterns; and heraldic emblems, such as cyphers, coats-of-arms, mythical beasts, and the "Tree of Life."

While the Middle Ages ended in the fourteenth century, with the flowering of the Renaissance and its revival of the classical Greco-Roman vocabulary of architecture and ornament, medieval style lingered on, especially in England, where Gothic and heraldic forms and motifs were, until the seventeenth century, often combined with their classical equivalents. Moreover, like its eventual successor, it was to enjoy a revival during the nineteenth century (*see* pp. 24–5).

1 In many single-story medieval houses, and in the upper rooms of two-story houses, ceilings consisted of the exposed skeletal structure–the wooden beams, trusses, purlins (horizontal timbers), and rafters–of the roof, and the underside of the roof covering, made of woven straw matting, wattled hazel twigs, or wooden boards. Ceilings in the first-floor rooms of two-story houses were the supporting beams and joists of the upper floors, the spaces in between being the undersides of the floor-boards or, as here, plaster panels. Decoration of the beams and joists ranged from simple chamfering to elaborate carvings, usually of organic motifs. Plaster infills were limewashed, either white or, as here, in earth tones, and sometimes hand-painted or stenciled with heraldic motifs.

2 Plastered wall surfaces above wainscoting (see 4) often featured heavy tapestry hangings, which provided pictorial decoration and insulated against the cold. These were usually suspended from metal or wooden rods, now used here to hang paintings, sculptures, and a mirror above the fireplace.

3 Internal door frames in medieval houses were often more elaborate than their external counterparts. They could be made of either wood or stone, and either flat-topped or "four-centered" (in the form of a shallow arch rising to a central point). Many were unornamented. However, some were carved with foliate and heraldic motifs. Most doors were battened planks, usually oak or elm, and occasionally the securing nailheads were left exposed as decoration. During the late Middle Ages, lighter paneled doors were sometimes installed in lieu of heavier battened ones.

4 Many timber-framed medieval houses had half-timbered walls. These consisted of an exposed framework of vertical wooden studs and horizontal cross-rails, filled in between with lath-and-plaster or wattle-and-daub. However, in stone-built and some grander timber-framed houses, the walls were uniformly plastered. As with the plaster infills

on ceilings (see 1), basic decoration took the form of limewashing, either in white, "natural" stone, or earth colors. Stenciled motifs, such as flowers and heraldic devices, were often applied over the limewash in contrasting colors, including gold. Yet, in the most flamboyant interiors, large murals of landscapes, or hunting, biblical, or mythological scenes, could also be applied.

5 In the wealthiest medieval households, plastered walls (see 4) were often lined with wainscoting–usually half-height, as here, but sometimes full-height. The paneling, mostly of oak or elm, but sometimes painted fir, was constructed in simple geometric patterns. The finest also featured decorative carvings and roundel paintings.

6 For most of the Middle Ages, open fires (from which the smoke drifted up through a hole in the roof) were universal. However, late in the period, the enclosed wall fireplace was gradually adopted. In many cases, as here, there was no fire surround–just an open hearth–although some hearths were topped with a carved wooden or stone lintel, usually in the shape of a four-centered arch. The painted checker pattern applied here to match the flooring (see 8) is a rather elaborate, but not untypical, form of decoration.

7 The hearth itself was either made of stone or brick, the rear of which was often protected by a wrought-iron fireback. Logs were the primary source of fuel, and burned on a pair of small brick walls, or on wrought-iron firedogs, or, very occasionally, in an iron firebasket.

8 While oak or elm boards were used in upper stories, at first-floor level beaten earth, bricks laid on edge, stone slabs, or tiles laid in geometric patterns were the most common types of flooring. Some floors were embellished with stenciled patterns. However, carpets were only laid on tabletops. Floor coverings, if used, were either strewn rushes or plaited rush matting–the latter loose laid, or fused to a thin plaster screed before it dried.

ℛENAISSANCE

Classical Greco-Roman architecture and ornament, largely dormant during the Middle Ages (*see* pp. 8–9), was revived during the fourteenth, fifteenth, and sixteenth centuries–a period known as the Renaissance. Beginning in Italy, following archaeological excavations of buildings and artifacts that had survived from Ancient Rome, and thereafter spreading across Europe, the Renaissance saw the reintroduction of the columns, pilasters, pedestals, capitals, and entablatures of the Cclassical Orders of architecture, as well as classical forms such as temple-front porticoes, curved arches, and rusticated masonry. Equally significant was the readoption of classical Roman motifs, such as acanthus leaves, scrolling foliage, swags and festoons, *pateras*, and scallop shells, which were applied not only as architectural ornament, but also to furniture, textiles, and decorative artifacts.

The impact of the Renaissance on subsequent styles of architecture and ornament was substantial. For example, the High Renaissance classicism of architects such as Andrea Palladio, who strove to preserve the integrity and purity of original Roman forms, provided the inspiration for early-eighteenth-century Palladianism (*see* pp. 12–5), while the Renaissance Mannerism of architects such as Michelangelo, who elaborated on Roman forms in a highly sculptural way, gave rise to the flamboyant, seventeenth-century Baroque style (*see* right). Interestingly, however, the influence of Renaissance classicism on contemporary sixteenth-century Elizabethan, and early-seventeenth-century Jacobean, houses in England wasn't all-embracing. As this room (*see* left) at Parham House reveals, the symmetry and proportion of classical forms is evident in the rectilinear configuration of the wall paneling and the paneled doors, in the scrolling arms and stretchers of the upholstered chairs, and in the gilt picture frames with their bands of bead and foliage moldings. However, in this example these features are characteristically and eclectically combined with lingering elements of Medieval style, notably the rush matting on the floor, the stretchered stool, and the barley-twist table legs.

1 Medieval-style, battened-plank oak doors were still hung in most Renaissance interiors. However, in the grandest houses they were increasingly supplanted by lighter paneled oak doors–the oak either a natural honey color, or limed. Carved, linenfold panels were very fashionable, although plain geometric panels defined by simple moldings were more prevalent. Most doors were secured with a simple wooden or iron latch; iron or brass box locks were the preserve of the wealthy.

2 The most common interior wall surface was limewashed flat plaster. However, full-height oak paneling, or dado-height paneling surmounted by tapestry hangings, were installed in the best houses. The configuration of the panels generally echoed those on the doors, with the most opulent featuring carved arabesques, strapwork, or foliate forms.

3 Where full-height paneling was used, ornate, gilt-framed paintings provided pictorial decoration previously supplied by tapestries.

4 Except in the poorest households, which were lit by rushes dipped in fat, and fire from the hearth, wax candles were the source of artificial illumination in Renaissance houses. Some were housed in lanterns, wall sconces, and, in the finest reception rooms, centrally hung chandeliers. However, most were fixed in candlestands made of, as here, turned and carved wood, or brass or pewter.

5 Stone slab floors were often laid on the first floor in Renaissance houses, sometimes in illusionistic, geometric patterns. However, as methods of damp-proofing improved, wide butt-jointed oak or elm boards were increasingly used, having once been confined to the upper stories. Where a floor covering was employed, as here, the near-universal choice was woven rush matting.

6 Imported Oriental carpets were considered too expensive to walk on, and thus only used as table coverings or, as here, placed under the best pieces of furniture.

BAROQUE

Emerging from the late-sixteenth-century Mannerist interpretation of classical Roman architecture and ornament (*see* left), the flamboyant Baroque style swept across Europe during the seventeenth century, and lasted until the Palladian Revival of the early eighteenth century (*see* pp. 12–3). This English Baroque fireplace exhibits many of the fundamental characteristics of this style, in which architectural fixtures and fittings–pediments, cornices, arches, columns, corbels, fire surrounds–and furniture, were voluptuously carved and, in some cases, embellished with figural ornaments (especially cupids and angels). When combined with an extensive use of exotically colored marbles, mirror-glass, extravagantly painted trompe l'oeil decorations and, as here, displays of Oriental ceramics, the overriding effect was one of exuberant and grandiose theatricality.

GEORGIAN

Historically, the Georgian period began with the accession of George I to the English throne and ended with the death of George IV. However, the description "Georgian style" is more usually applied to the architecture and interior decoration that was fashionable during the reigns of George I and II (1714–60)–the reigns of George III and IV (1760–1830) being dominated by the neoclassical Adam and Regency styles (*see* pp. 16–7 and 20–1).

Chiefly promoted by the influential Scottish architect, Colen Campbell, and the leading patron of the arts, Lord Burlington, Georgian style emerged as a reaction to the grandiose excesses of the seventeenth-century Baroque style (*see* p. 11), and was based primarily on the buildings and republished observations of the sixteenth-century Italian architect, Andrea Palladio (*see* pp. 10–1). Essentially classical Roman, rather than Greek, in origin, Palladianism in its purest form, and particularly when applied to the grandest exteriors, was characterized by bold, austere, and massive architectural elements, such as temple-front porticoes; giant Roman columns; rusticated masonry; tripartite, arch-topped Venetian windows; and coffered (compartmented) ceilings. In the finest interiors, it manifested itself in heavily sculpted Roman motifs, such as herms, eagles, dolphins, and masks that were applied to both architectural fixtures and fittings and furniture.

Ultimately, however, Georgian style–which was widely adopted in Russia, Prussia, and America (*see* pp. 14–5 and 18–9)–relied for effect not upon sheer scale, but instead on harmony of proportion and detail, and it was these fundamental characteristics which underpinned the more understated modeling and ornamentation of most Georgian houses. The Georgian drawing room (*see* left) exemplifies a style in which architectural columns, fire surrounds, linear moldings, and built-in display cabinets are positioned, scaled, and painted to establish an esthetically pleasing symmetry–a quality that also extends to the construction and arrangement of the fine Georgian furniture.

1 The ornamentation of Georgian ceilings usually reflected the status of the house. The most elaborate were divided into geometrical compartments by plaster moldings. Further embellishment–either trompe l'oeil painted or plastered–typically took the form of scrolling foliage, husks, and other classical motifs. However, many ceilings consisted of an expanse of flat plaster, painted white or in "sky" tones (such as gray, yellow, or pink) and bordered with a plaster cornice bearing bands of foliate, coin, wavescroll, or dentil motifs.

2 Full-height wooden wall paneling was used in many Georgian reception rooms up until ca. 1740, and usually flat-painted–the most fashionable color being "drab" (a mixture of gray, blue, and green)–or, in some cases, painted faux marble. However, flat-plastered walls topped with a cornice (see 1), divided by a dado rail (see 8), and bottomed with a base-board, were more prevalent, especially from the 1740s onward. Favored finishes for the field above the dado included flat paint, as here, silk damask or brocade (stretched over a series of thin wooden battens nailed to the plaster), or wallpaper. Fashionable wallpaper patterns were mostly based on stylized or naturalistic depictions of flowers and foliage.

3 Columns derived from the classical Roman Orders of architecture–Doric, Ionic, Corinthian, Composite, and Tuscan–were often installed in larger Georgian houses, either to provide structural support or, when that was not required as here, for architectural effect. This fluted column–one of a pair used to define the division between two reception rooms–is carved and turned from wood.

4 The best Georgian fire surrounds were made from white statuary marble, while the most exotic featured inlays of multicolored marbles or porphyries. Cheaper scagliola or wooden surrounds were also installed–the latter flat-painted, or painted faux marble. All surrounds had a narrow mantelshelf supported by simple brackets, architectural jambs, or pairs of carved caryatid figures. The "earred"

egg-and-dart molding that borders the jambs and divides the frieze of this surround is a typical embellishment, as are the blue and white delftware tiles lining the hearth.

5 The cast-iron dog grate, incorporating a raised basket well-suited to burning coals, became increasingly popular during the first half of the eighteenth century as coal gradually superseded logs as the primary source of fuel in Europe. Fenders, which defined the perimeter of the hearth and protected adjacent floor coverings from hot coals, were mainly brass, and often ornamented with classical details, such as urn-shaped finials.

6 Many fire surrounds had an architectural overmantel which echoed the form and ornamentation of the surround itself, and often incorporated a picture panel or a mirror-glass. The alternative was to hang a picture above the surround, or stand a gilt-framed mirror on the mantelshelf–the latter was an increasingly fashionable option in later Georgian interiors.

7 Built-in bookcases and cupboards were installed in most Georgian houses, usually flanking fireplaces. Their frames and doors were often defined by moldings that matched those employed elsewhere in the room. The best were oak or mahogany, but most were painted pine. Where glazed doors were used, the configuration of the glass panels invariably corresponded to that of the windows.

8 The profiles of wooden and plaster dado rails, like the tops of baseboards, were derived from the moldings used in the Classical Orders of architecture. Favored profiles included torus, scotia, ovolo, astragal, ogee, cyma reversa, and cyma recta.

9 While the Oriental rug in front of the fireplace is an authentic Georgian floor covering, the fitted ivory-colored carpet is a much later addition. Most rooms had oak, elm, fir, or pine floorboards, either left untreated or stained and polished at the edges to provide a border for a centrally placed rug.

AMERICAN COLONIAL

The term "American Colonial" is applied to all permanent buildings constructed in the American Colonies, from their initial settlement in 1607, to their gaining independence from Britain in 1783. Covering virtually a 200-year span, the description is thus very broad, and really embraces two distinct architectural phases: the settlement period, up to the 1720s, and the Georgian (or Palladian, or classical) period thereafter.

Except in the southern Colonies, where some of the finest houses were constructed of brick, the majority of dwellings during the settlement period were of timber-frame construction and modeled on late-medieval post-and-beam houses (see pp. 8–9)–although toward the end of the seventeenth century many had developed the symmetry of plan and fenestration, and architectural features, notably jettied overhangs, of provincial Renaissance town houses (see pp. 10–1). However, a fundamental difference between these American houses and their European counterparts lay in the treatment of the structural wall system: in Europe, the vertical studs and the wattle-and-daub panels in between were usually left exposed–an effect known as half-timbering–whereas in most Colonial houses they were sheathed in clapboards (outside) and wooden paneling (inside). The interior (see left) of an early-eighteenth-century house in New Hampshire, is typical of the American approach, which provided better insulation against the rigors of the climate, and was made possible by the considerable resources of locally available lumber.

Introduced by wealthy merchants and planters, and largely inspired by English architectural pattern books, the Georgian period witnessed the gradual establishment of Palladian-inspired housing in the Colonies–a classical style of architecture and ornament described on pages 12–3. Again, however, there was a basic difference between the English and Colonial models: while the former were constructed of brick and stone, the latter were mostly made of wood.

1 The earliest American Colonial houses had low ceilings with exposed joists and beams, between which the wooden floorboards of the floor above were left clearly visible. In the simplest dwellings the joists and beams were sometimes left with the bark intact, while in grander houses they were smoothly planed and squared and sometimes embellished with chamfering and decorative stops. However, by the late seventeenth century, plain lath-and-plaster ceilings, as here, began to be installed in new houses; sometimes these displayed slightly undulating surfaces owing to the unevenness of the joists to which the laths were attached. The favored finish was flat-painted limewash–usually white or pale off-white colors. Toward the end of the Colonial period, more flamboyant plaster ceilings appeared in grander houses. The configuration of their elaborate plaster moldings was mainly based on either English Georgian (see pp. 12–3) or German Baroque (see p. 11) precedents. It is interesting to note that as the Colonies moved closer to establishing independence, native North American motifs, such as the tobacco leaf, were increasingly incorporated into designs.

2 A variety of wall treatments were employed in Colonial houses. Plain plaster, and lath-and-plaster infills with the studs left exposed, appeared early on in the Colonial period, while in the eighteenth century, plaster fields were sometimes combined with dado wainscoting. However, given the abundance of lumber in the Colonies, full-height wall paneling was particularly prevalent in larger and smaller houses alike–although the grander the house, the more elaborate the paneling. Here, unpretentious, chamfered, tongue-and-groove planks are used, bordered at the ceiling with a simple cornice molding. Made of softwood, they are characteristically flat-painted in green–a favorite color from the Colonial palette that also included earth tones of red, brown, almond, and yellow, and slightly brighter blues. Fashionable and more decorative paint finishes included marbling and grained simulations of expensive hardwoods.

3 Paneled doors, typically with two panels in low relief, began to appear in better Colonial houses in the late seventeenth century, and more elaborate Georgian-style raised-panel doors with classical surrounds (see pp. 12–3) became increasingly common from the 1730s onward. However, most seventeenth- and many early-eighteenth-century houses had simpler battened doors, constructed of vertical boards nailed together with two or more horizontal boards at the rear. Most were made of softwood, and painted in one of the darker colors from the Colonial palette, notably earthy browns, reds, or greens. Where better-quality hardwoods were used, these were usually stained a natural wood color.

4 Chandeliers and pendant lamps were very rare in Colonial houses prior to the 1750s, and were mainly made of wood, iron, or tinned sheet iron, rather than glass or crystal. Thus the primary sources of lighting for most of the Colonial period were the glow from the fireplace, oil lamps, Betty lamps (boat- or saucer-shaped lamps filled with grease or oil) and, as here, candle lights. The simplest were made of tinned sheet iron; more elaborate versions incorporated small, concave mirrors to enhance the illumination.

5 Although the earliest Colonial houses had compacted earth floors, this butt-jointed pine floorboard, unstained and unvarnished, is typical of most houses. Marginally more sophisticated variations included tongue-and-groove and spline-jointed boards–the latter consisting of grooved boards joined by thin strips of wood. In the late eighteenth century, some wooden floors were painted in imitation of stone. Real stone floors were rare, and were usually confined to halls and porches.

6 While European or Oriental carpets were laid in the finest houses from the early eighteenth century onward, rush matting, rag rugs or, as here, painted canvas floorcloths were the staple floor covering of Colonial houses. The diagonal check pattern, which was sometimes marbled, was very popular.

ADAM

The interior (*see* left) is in Home House, in London, England, and was designed ca. 1775 by the Scottish architect Robert Adam (1728–92). It is one of the grander examples of the neoclassical style of architecture, decoration, and ornament known as Adam style, which was established by Robert Adam, and his brothers James and John, during the second half of the eighteenth century. The inspiration lay in the buildings and artifacts of Roman antiquity, the Italian Renaissance (*see* pp. 10–1), and Ancient Greek and Etruscan civilizations, and was fueled by new information on the Greco-Roman vocabulary of architecture and ornament that had come to light as a result of the archaeological excavations of classical Greek and Roman cities and towns—notably Herculaneum (beginning in 1738) and Pompeii (starting in 1755), in southern Italy. The reference material unearthed at these sites was widely disseminated throughout Europe and America by architects, designers, craftsmen, and patrons of the arts, who either personally visited them on the Grand Tour, or studied the writings and pattern books of architects such as Giovanni Battista Piranesi (1720–78), who promoted the richness and diversity of Greek, Roman, Etruscan, and also Ancient Egyptian architecture and ornament.

Robert Adam—who undertook the Grand Tour and was influenced by the works of Piranesi—drew on this wealth of information to create the eclectic and distinctive Adam style that became widely admired for its grandeur and elegance, the subtlety of its deployment of classical motifs and imagery, and its integration of the architectural structure and interior design of buildings. First fashionable in Britain, Adam style provided the inspiration for the emergence of neoclassicism in France during the reign of Louis XVI, which, in turn, influenced English Regency style (*see* pp. 20–1). Adam style also made a significant impact in Italy, Germany, and Russia and, toward the late eighteenth century, formed the basis of early-Federal style in America (*see* pp. 18–9).

1 *During the second half of the eighteenth century, most ordinary houses had plain plaster ceilings augmented with relatively simple dentil or egg-and-dart plaster cornices. However, in grander Adam-style houses, and especially in their reception rooms, plaster-work ceilings were divided by decorative panels or bands of stylized flower or leaf motifs derived from the classical vocabulary of ornament. The panels or bands were usually arranged around a central medallion or roundel, and were either painted or gilded plaster moldings, painted onto flat plaster, or painted on canvas or paper, and then fixed to the ceiling. In grand reception rooms, Adam often employed artists such as Biagio Rebecca and Angelica Kaufmann to paint some of the panels or roundels with figures or scenes from classical Greek or Roman mythology.*

2 *The ornamentation of the deep frieze below the cornice is typical of Adam style. Here, radiating bands of anthemia–stylized representations of the acanthus flower and one of the most regularly employed motifs in classical ornament–are flanked by figurative plaster roundels. The latter are encompassed by strings of stylized budlike motifs known as husks. As on the ceiling above and the walls below, the use of gilded ornament set against various shades of green is typically Adam.*

3 *On the entablature that runs along the top of the lower section of the walls, Adam has applied painted and gilded plaster urns above the pilasters (see 5). Urns, which were usually distinguished from vases by their lids, were originally employed in Greek and Roman architecture as a symbol of death, loss, or mourning. However, in late-eighteenth-century neoclassical interiors this funerary connection was rarely intended, and urns were used interchangeably with vases–the latter being probably the most enduringly popular of all classical architectural motifs.*

4 *Husks also feature on the entablature, and here they are hung from ribbons and strung as gilded-plaster festoons–the latter inspired by the fruit-and-floral garlands that were hung in Greek and Roman temples. Positioned within the swags of the festoons are plaster pateras. Based on the fluted dishes or wine holders used in classical Greek religious ceremonies, these circular (and sometimes oval) forms have the appearance of stylized flowers, and thus, from the eighteenth century onward, were also known as rosettes.*

5 *Adam has flanked the pair of double-doors with ornate pilasters. These flat, rectangular, columnlike forms are linked by the entablature (see 3 and 4) and are derived from classical architecture. As well as being decorated with acanthus-leaf capitals, figurative roundels, and bucrania (the skulls of rams or goats originally hung within festoons in Greek and Roman temples), the pilasters also frame mirrored panels. The purpose of the mirrors is to increase the sense of space and to enhance the candlelight from wall-mounted girandoles (see 6).*

6 *Gilded or painted girandoles (branched, wall-mounted candleholders) were a popular source of lighting in neoclassical interiors. Here they are mounted above candelabralike tiers of gilded wreaths–a form of decoration inspired by Roman wall paintings.*

7 *Six-paneled doors, either singles or pairs, were almost standard in neoclassical houses of the late eighteenth century. The grandest were made from polished hardwood, such as mahogany, and the most exotic were inlaid with finely figured woods such as ebony, holly, or cherry. However, softwood doors, wood-grained in imitation of expensive hardwoods, as here, or painted with motifs and imagery from the classical vocabulary of ornament, were perfectly acceptable alternatives.*

8 *Butt-jointed boards of oak, fir, or pine were the most common type of flooring during the late eighteenth century. However, in many Adam-style reception rooms, rugs–either geometrically patterned or with floral designs of Oriental origin–were laid on top.*

AMERICAN FEDERAL AND EMPIRE

Neoclassical styles of architecture and decoration began to cross the Atlantic from Britain and mainland Europe through émigré architects and pattern books just prior to the Declaration of Independence in 1776. Generally referred to as Federal style, American neoclassicism was initially based on Adam style (*see* pp. 16–7), with exteriors characterized by delicate columns, arch-top windows, and transom lights, and interiors richly decorated with classical motifs such as festoons, *pateras*, rosettes, urns, and scrolling foliage. However, early-Federal style also embraced a purer, sterner, Roman-based neoclassicism which, by the end of the eighteenth century, had largely superseded Adam style. Promoted by Thomas Jefferson, third President of the United States, as an appropriate architectural language for the new republic, this "Roman Revival" was partly inspired by English Palladian models (*see* Georgian style, pp. 12–3), partly by French neoclassicism during the reign of Louis XVI (*see* Regency style, pp. 20–1), and partly by original Roman buildings recently discovered in southern France.

During the first three decades of the nineteenth century, until the emergence of the Greek Revival style (*see* pp. 22–3), French neoclassical taste continued to exert a considerable influence, especially in the adoption of Empire style for the interior decoration and ornament of finer American houses–represented by the dining room (*see* left) of Richard Jenrette's early-nineteenth-century American Empire-style house on the Hudson River, in New York State. Empire style originated in France in the late 1790s under the patronage of Napoleon Bonaparte and his Empress Josephine, and through designers Charles Percier and Pierre Fontaine's postrevolutionary restorations of French palaces. Inherently opulent, the style was characterized by the use of Imperial Roman ornament and decoration, augmented with Etruscan, Ancient Egyptian, and military motifs, and applied not only to architectural fixtures and fittings, but also to furniture, wallpapers, carpets, curtains, lighting fixtures, and decorative artifacts.

1 Federal ceilings ranged from wooden boards (usually whitewashed) in the simplest houses, through flat plaster in larger dwellings, to flat plaster embellished with decorative moldings in the grandest houses. This dining room has a flat-plaster field and a central medallion featuring rings of acanthus leaves. More flamboyant ceilings were also bordered or segmented with bands of neo-classical motifs, such as guilloche or scrolling foliage, sometimes highlighted with gilding.

2 This relatively plain cornice is derived from the concave cyma recta *moldings used in the Classical Orders of architecture. Deeper and more elaborate cornices featured rows of other classical motifs, such as anthemia, swags-and-tails, vases, and beading.

3 The most notable development in wall treatments during the Federal period was the gradual elimination of the full-height wainscoting favored during the Colonial era. Instead, many walls were divided horizontally into a dado, field, and frieze. Some typical configurations included a wainscot or papered dado (above a wooden baseboard), a flat-painted or wallpapered field, and a plaster or papered frieze. Whatever the material, in the finer houses the dado and frieze were usually embellished with neoclassical motifs; popular wallpaper patterns for the field were florals, stripes, and pictorials of either classical or contemporary scenes. The alternative, and more austerely classical arrangement, as here, was to divide the walls vertically into panels–the divisions marked by paper cutout or paint moldings. Flat paint or painted faux marble, were usual finishes for the areas between the divisions.

4 Federal windows were distinguished from their Colonial counterparts by thinner glazing bars and larger panes of glass. As here, the windows in grander houses often extended from near the ceiling to the floor, and featured architrave embellished with neoclassical detailing, such as fluting and corner pateras; some were also set in recessed arches.

5 While most Federal houses were lit by oil-burning lamps or candles, fine glass or bronze chandeliers (mainly from England and France) were often employed in the reception rooms of more opulent houses from the early 1800s. As here, these were often supplemented with brass, bronze, or crystal candle sconces.

6 Although pictures were often hung above the fireplace in Federal houses, overmantel mirrors became increasingly popular from the early nineteenth century onward. As in Regency interiors, oval mirrors (either with flat or convex glass) were very fashionable, the most elaborate bordered with bead or dentil moldings, flanked by candles sconces, and crested with fishes or birds, notably eagles.

7 The best Federal fire surrounds were made of marble, although painted wooden ones (with marble slips) were also in widespread use. This example is relatively plain; more decorative surrounds featured neoclassical motifs such as vases, swags, garlands, pateras, and mythological scenes.

8 While stoves and imported hob grates were in widespread use by the 1780s, most Federal hearths burned logs on firedogs. Iron firedogs were most common, but in grander houses brass firedogs embellished with neoclassical urns or spherical finials were more usual.

9 The six-paneled door featured in most Federal houses, although four- and eight-paneled versions were also used. Most were made of pine, maple, poplar, or cypress, and often grained in imitation of mahogany–real mahogany doors were confined to the wealthiest households. Door surrounds invariably echoed their counterparts around windows.

10 Pine boards were the standard flooring in Federal houses, and often stenciled with neoclassical motifs or diamond patterns. Floor coverings included straw matting, stenciled or marbled floorcloths and, in the grandest houses, carpets with floral or neoclassical motifs set in geometric patterns.

REGENCY

The English Regency was the period from 1811 to 1820 when George, Prince of Wales, ruled England as Prince Regent during the illness of his father, George III. However, what became known as Regency style emerged through Prince George's patronage as early as the late 1780s, and remained in vogue until the end of his reign as George IV in 1830. The style was inspired by his admiration for French architecture and interior decoration during the reign of Louis XVI (1774–92)– a style characterized by rectilinear neoclassical fixtures and fittings, such as columns, pilasters, friezes, and architraves, providing a perfect foil for precise arrangements of mirror glass, crystal chandeliers, and fine furniture. The resulting elegance, space, symmetry, and proportion–evident in the South Drawing Room (*see left*) of the house built 1792–1824, in London, by the architect Sir John Soane–remained essential characteristics of Regency interiors. Regency style did not remain static, and around the turn of the nineteenth century began to evolve in response to the emergence of French Empire style which, under the patronage of Napoleon Bonaparte, swept first across Europe and later America. English archi-tects and designers did not simply copy Empire style, and so while French interiors were dominated by replications and adaptations of the architectural ornament of Ancient Rome, many Regency interiors combined these with classical Greek equivalents and elements of *Le Style Etrusque* (*see* pp. 16–7).

Further differences between English Regency and French Empire lay in the former's adoption of architectural features, such as pointed arches, window tracery, castellated parapets, and fan vaulting, derived from the medieval vocabu-lary of ornament. Also, exotic chinoiserie-based schemes, absent from French interiors, appeared in some grander Regency buildings, although they were often confined to one room. Common, however, to French Empire and English Regency was the use of Ancient Egyptian motifs, such as palm trees and sphinxes–their popularity fueled by the military campaigns in Egypt during the Napoleonic wars.

1 *In comparison with the highly elaborate decoration of late-eighteenth-century Adam-style ceilings (see pp.16–7), the ceiling in Sir John Soane's South Drawing Room displays the more austere ornamentation favored by nineteenth-century Regency architects. Here, a series of recessed, slightly concave compartments, or coffers (only one shown), is linked by pairs of relatively plain linear plaster moldings. Each compartment features a central pendant medallion encompassed by bead molding and, in the four corners, by classical Greek anthemia. Bead moldings also help define the perimeters of compartments.*

2 *Relatively restrained ornamentation of the cornice is also characteristic of most nineteenth-century Regency interiors. Here, the plaster molding is a simple string of plaster husks–a favorite neoclassical motif.*

3 *Most Regency architects maintained the classical tripartite division of walls. However, in the South Drawing Room, Soane has dispensed with the usual demarcation between the three sections by applying the same decorative treatment–flat-paint over plaster–to all of them. The sulphurous yellow finish is typical Regency; other fashionable colors include lilac, emerald green, crimson, deep shades of pink, strong blues, and gold. Note how the yellow paint on the walls matches both the yellow silk pelmets and tied-back curtains framing the doorways, and the top cover and bolster on the classic Regency settee. En suite wall finishes and soft furnishings were the height of fashion in grander Regency interiors.*

4 *In Soane's initial modeling of the room, full-length windows opened out onto a loggia (a pillared gallery open to the outside). In 1832, however, he enclosed the loggia with glass, removed the windows, replaced the latter with pelmeted and draped doorways, but retained the original arch-topped pier glass–its purpose, as before, being to enhance the level of lighting in the room and to increase the sense of space.*

5 *Built-in bookcases were commonly installed in Regency houses, often in reception rooms as well as libraries. Usually made of hardwood, notably mahogany, or rosewood veneer, and sometimes fitted with glass-paneled doors, they were frequently employed to display artifacts from classical antiquity, as well as books.*

6 *The candlelit, glass, metal or, as here, crystal chandelier was the primary source of artificial lighting in Regency reception rooms, with oil-burning pendant lamps favored in halls. Oil-burning table lamps also came into general use. However, gas-fueled equivalents (available toward the end of the period) were considered something of a dangerous novelty.*

7 *Overmantel mirrors were standard in Regency drawing rooms. This one has a very plain frame, although ornamentation rarely extended beyond reeding, corner roundels, or repeats of Ancient Greek or Egyptian motifs.*

8 *In its simplicity of outline and profile, this fireplace is quintessentially Regency. Characteristic elements include reeded flat jambs, a plain lintel, and a narrow mantelshelf– the latter growing deeper toward the end of the Regency as changing fashions dictated the display of an ever-greater number of decorative artifacts. This example is made of lightly veined gray-white marble, but white statuary marble, exotic colored marbles, and porphyry were also popular, while wooden surrounds, painted in imitation of marble, were acceptable for lesser rooms. The copper and iron firedogs were old-fashioned for the period–coal-burning hob grates and, by the late 1820s, register grates, were more usual.*

9 *The butt-jointed floorboards of the most fashionable Regency interiors were laid with wall-to-wall carpets stitched together from narrow widths cut around the perimeter to fit the shape of the room. Favored all-over patterns included naturalistic floral designs and verdure patterns of ferns, foliage, and palms.*

AMERICAN GREEK REVIVAL

The Greek Revival was a strand of neoclassicism that had made a major impact on European architecture and interior design from the 1780s onward, and was then enthusiastically taken up in America during the late 1820s, notably by influential architects William Strickland, Ithiel Town, and Thomas Walter. There is no doubt that the widespread commitment to the Greek Revival style in the country, which endured until the 1850s, lay in the often-expressed sentiment that America, with its democratic ideals, was the spiritual successor to the birthplace of democracy: Ancient Greece.

The primary sources of inspiration for the revival were the temple buildings and artifacts of Ancient Greece, many of which had been unearthed from the mid-eighteenth century in archaeological digs on mainland Greece and in southern Italy. During the earlier Adam-inspired Federal period (*see* pp. 18–9), the Greek vocabulary of architecture and ornament had been combined eclectically with classical Roman forms and motifs. However, in the "full-blown" Greek Revival, the vast majority of Roman elements, such as arched entrances and transom lights, were abandoned and replaced by purer Greek forms from the Greek Doric and Ionic Orders of architecture.

Characteristic features of the American Greek Revival houses included temple-front facades, rectangular windows, columnar door frames, and the embellishment of architectural fixtures and fittings, as well as furniture and soft furnishings, with Greek motifs such as anthemia, key frets, lyres, and bands of egg-and-dart. Above all, however, as the front parlor (*see* left) of Andrew Low House (built in Savannah, Georgia, in 1848) demonstrates, Greek Revival houses were also distinguished from their earlier Federal counterparts by a greater austerity of ornament and decoration. Nevertheless, as the upholstered furniture (attributed to American cabinet-maker, Duncan Phyfe) reveals, this was a purist esthetic rarely allowed to undermine domestic comfort.

1 In many Greek Revival houses, the classic tripartite division of walls into frieze, field, and dado was abandoned. Instead, walls were either vertically paneled in a manner similar to earlier Federal and Empire houses (see pp. 18–9), or, more usually, bordered at floor level with a baseboard (see 8) and topped with a deep cornice-frieze of either plain molding or decorated with Greek anthemia or key patterns. The prevalent treatment for the large field in between was either flat paint or wallpaper in terra cotta, deep pink or, as here, stone colors.

2 Window surrounds are characterized by the simplicity of their moldings, with interior ornamentation rarely exceeding reeding or fluting–although squared corner blocks were sometimes incorporated. In contrast to many earlier Federal and Empire houses, Greek Revival windows were not set in arches– these were never employed in classical Greek architecture. However, thin glazing bars, large panes of glass, and floor-to-ceiling casement windows (sometimes in the form of French doors) remained in vogue–the latter often fitted with internal wooden shutters. On upper floors, sliding six-over-six pane sash windows were also prevalent.

3 As in many Federal and Empire interiors, window hangings were often elaborate and, with the exception of light-diffusing lace sheers, purely ornamental. These red and gold, geometric-pattern lampas pelmets are swagged-and-tailed from concealed rods and, at the centers, prominent gilt-metal rosettes. Also employed here on the sides of the window surrounds (as tiebacks for the lace sheers), rosettes were very fashionable in Greek Revival interiors, and were derived from the circular, formalized floral ornaments much used in classical Greek architecture.

4 Elaborate crystal chandeliers, which first appeared in America in the reception rooms of earlier nineteenth-century Federal and Empire houses, became more commonplace during the Greek Revival period, although they remained the preserve of the wealthy. Most were still imported from England or France. However, by the 1840s they were also being produced by American craftsmen.

5 As in many grander late-eighteenth- and early-nineteenth-century interiors, pier glasses were often installed between the windows of Greek Revival reception rooms. This example has a particularly ornate architectural frame, consisting of pilasters and an entablature gilded and decorated with Greek fluting, tiers of wreaths, and theatrical masks.

6 Brass or silver Argand lamps were often used in Greek Revival houses in lieu of candles. Generally fueled by whale or lard oil, they incorporated a hollow wick which fed substantial levels of oxygen to the flames. The flames, burning within glass "chimneys," thus gave off a light brighter and cleaner than that produced by candles or Betty lamps (see p. 15).

7 Marble and painted wooden fire surrounds were generally more austere in appearance than their earlier Federal counterparts, especially those made of black and white marbles. Decoration was often confined to the figuring of the marble. However, it sometimes also took the form of fluting on pilaster jambs and Greek key patterns along the frieze.

8 Heavily molded baseboards replaced dado panels in most Greek Revival houses. Some were made of marble. Most, however, were wooden and either flat-painted (usually white or black), or painted faux marble.

9 Except in entrance halls, where stone or marble was often used, pine floorboards remained the standard flooring. If uncovered, they were usually bordered with stenciled Greek motifs, such as rows of anthemia or Greek keys. Favored floor coverings included similarly stenciled, or faux marbled, floor-cloths. However, fitted carpets–displaying Greek (rather than Roman) motifs set in geometric patterns–remained the preferred choice in the reception rooms of the wealthy.

GOTHIC REVIVAL

A revival of interest in Gothic architecture and ornament gradually emerged in Europe during the second half of the eighteenth century, and was partly fueled by a reaction to the prevailing preoccupation with classicism (see pp. 12–23). Initially, this gave rise to a style of architectural detailing and interior decoration known as "Gothick," which was based on a rather romanticized view of medieval precedents (see pp. 8–9). However, during the early years of the nineteenth century, the publication of diligent archaeological research into medieval ruins resulted in a far more historically accurate Gothic Revival–a movement that was given additional impetus and prestige by the decision in Britain in 1836 to rebuild the Houses of Parliament in the Gothic style.

Led by influential architects and designers such as A. W. N. Pugin, George Gilbert Scott, and William Burges, the British Gothic Revival lasted until the 1870s and left its mark not only on civic, ecclesiastical, and college buildings, but also on many country houses, villas, and entire suburbs. In the United States the Gothic Revival was similarly influential, but lasted longer–the fundamental perpendicularity of the architectural style proved well-suited to the modeling and ornamentation of some of the twentieth-century skyscrapers.

The drawing room (see left) is in a five-story house in Greenwich Village, New York, and displays many of the hallmarks of a mid-nineteenth-century Gothic Revival interior. The stone fire surround, the patterns of the wallpaper and the floor covering, the overall color scheme, and the subdued lighting are all highly characteristic (see right). However, as was often the case, it is the ecclesiastical-style, dark-brown mahogany furniture, more than the decorations and the architectural fixtures and fittings, which best encapsulate and instantly confirm the style–the distinctive ogee-arched and pinnacled backs of the sturdy upholstered chairs (echoed in the carved tabletop cornice) having been derived from the authentic medieval Gothic vocabulary of ornament.

1 *The walls in residential Gothic Revival rooms were invariably defined with a baseboard along the bottom and a cornice along the top. The latter, made of wood, plaster, or sometimes stone, was often highly elaborate, and usually in the style of rows of Gothic ogee arches or openwork pendant forms. The large field in between the baseboard and cornice was usually undivided, although chair rails or dado-height carved wooden paneling were occasionally installed, notably from the 1860s onward. Favored finishes on the field include flat paint (stone colors were very popular) and, especially, wallpaper. This wallpaper pattern, displaying a profusion of naturalistically depicted flowers and foliage, is typically Gothic. Even more popular, however, were the Gothic Revival papers with stenciled lattice- or trelliswork, or chevron, ground patterns embellished with heraldic emblems, such as coats-of-arms and fleurs-de-lis, or stylized fruit and foliage inspired by medieval manuscripts and textiles.*

2 *Arched recesses (or "niches") were a popular architectural motif in both classical and Gothic architecture, and were traditionally used to display sculptures or decorative artifacts, such as vases and urns. This wall niche is defined by a simple, painted wooden molding which, in the Gothic tradition, rises to a point at the apex of the arch. In an original twist to its traditional purpose, it has been filled with a large mirror-glass which serves as a light- and space-enhancing background for a display of gilt-framed fine art.*

3 *While some Gothic Revival interiors were illuminated almost exclusively with candles (like their medieval prototypes), most were lit with contemporary oil- or gas-fueled fixtures. In reception rooms, centrally hung chandeliers were often employed, and were usually made of carved wood or wrought iron, with glass "chimneys." This chandelier is particularly flamboyant–its S-shape scrolled branches inspired more by the often-exaggerated forms of eighteenth-century "Gothick" style than by the more restrained medieval Gothic originals.*

4 *Overmantel mirrors, rather than pictures, were invariably hung above Gothic Revival fire surrounds. As with this gilt-wood example, their frames were usually fashioned in the shape of ogee-arched Gothic windows–the upper sections embellished with elaborate tracery (a series of C- and S-shaped curved ribs). Additional ornament often took the form of fleur-de-lis or cross-shaped finials, and crockets (small, hook-shaped ornaments, carved or molded in the form of buds, curled leaves, or animals.)*

5 *The best Gothic Revival fire surrounds were made of stone (especially limestone), although softwood surrounds painted in imitation of stone were an acceptable alternative. Many had a pointed (four-centered) arch around the hearth, although this example is curved. Most had clearly defined spandrels (the two triangular-shaped sections flanking the apex of the arch) and the jambs (the uprights that form the sides of the surround). In terms of decoration, this surround is rather plain. The spandrels and friezes of more elaborate versions featured Gothic motifs, such as rosettes, fleurs-de-lis, coats-of-arms, and quatrefoils (four-lobed motifs similar in appearance to four-leaf clovers).*

6 *Candelabra and, as here, oil-burning lamps provided supplementary illumination for centrally hung chandeliers (see 3) in Gothic Revival houses. Free-standing or wall-mounted, most lamps were forged iron or brass (with glass "chimneys"), and bore Gothic motifs, such as pendants and crockets.*

7 *Apart from encaustic tiles or stone slabs in hallways, most Gothic Revival rooms were floored with dark-stained oak parquet or, more commonly, butt-jointed pine boards. The latter were usually dark stained, but sometimes painted faux stone, and bordered with stencil-painted decoration, or covered with pile rugs, canvas floorcloths, or, from ca. 1860, linoleum–each displaying geometric, foliate, or heraldic patterns and motifs derived from the Gothic vocabulary of ornament.*

VICTORIAN

The period from ca. 1850 to ca. 1870 was marked by the adoption of an eclectic mixture of architectural and decorative styles on both sides of the Atlantic. For instance, while a Gothic Revival (*see* pp. 24–5) captured the imagination of many, it faced strong competition from various classical revivals. Notable examples of the latter included the last stages of the Greek Revival (*see* pp. 22–3); Renaissance and Baroque Revivals (*see* pp. 10–1)–the latter known as Second Empire style in the United States; and often rather heavy-handed reworkings of late-eighteenth- and early-nineteenth-century neoclassical styles (*see* Adam, Federal, and Regency, pp. 16–21). In addition to these various historical revivals, the styles that were derived from the Chinese, Persian, Indian, Arabian, and African vocabularies of architecture and ornament were also assimilated following increased trade with, and travel to, these regions.

In some Victorian houses, one particular decorative style prevailed. However, in other houses it was not unusual to find, for example, a neoclassical hallway, a Gothic Revival dining room and library, a Moorish-style boudoir, and a Baroque Revival drawing room. But such stylistic eclecticism often went further than that, as many architects, designers, and builders pilfered and adapted forms, motifs, and imagery from numerous and diverse historical sources, and creatively combined them in a single room.

While the architectural fixtures and fittings and furnishings of such rooms may have been eclectic, the overall style invariably had a coherence that became instantly recognizable as "Victorian." However, the distinctiveness of the style–as Jonathan Hudson's re-creation of a typical Victorian drawing room (*see* left) illustrates–resides not only in the eclecticism of its component parts, but also in the combination of rich colors, intricate patterns, multilayered drapery, heavy furniture, overstuffed and deep-buttoned upholstery, and displays of numerous decorative artifacts, all of which are uniquely Victorian.

1 *A plaster ceiling medallion was a fairly standard fixture in Victorian rooms, the intricacy of its ornamentation reflecting both the status of the room and the house. This one features boldly carved acanthus leaves radiating from a gilded rosette and bordered by a ring of small palmettes–all foliate motifs derived from the classical vocabulary of ornament. In the finest reception rooms, the flat plaster around the medallion could be embellished with Baroque- or eighteenth-century-style plaster ribs, swags, and festoons (or embossed paper simulations in lesser houses). Here the flat plaster is papered with a realistically colored willow pattern. Equally fashionable mid-nineteenth-century alternatives included oak leaf, ivy, and grapevine patterns.*

2 *Regardless of the type of decoration on the field of the Victorian ceiling, the border with the walls was always defined by a cornice. This example is characteristic of the period, its bands of rosettes, scrolling foliage, and other foliate motifs typically echoing the classically inspired motifs on the central medallion.*

3 *Most Victorian walls were papered, rather than paneled, although some were flat-painted and then stenciled at dado and frieze level. A wide and diverse range of patterns was popular. These included the geometric designs favored in Gothic Revival houses (see pp. 24–5), naturalistic willow and acanthus leaves, and stylized fruits and lotus and bamboo leaves. Most popular, however–as here–were intricate patterns of realistically represented large coarse flowers, such as dahlias, hollyhocks, and hydrangeas.*

4 *This window treatment is typically Victorian. Lace sheers are employed to diffuse incoming sunlight (they also serve as an insect barrier in hotter climates). Over these, multilayered, heavy, tassel-edged drapes, which hang from a substantial brass pole, provide insulation and establish a sense of comfort and opulence. The valance and the outer, tied-back drapes are swagged-and-tailed–a configuration inspired by neoclassical drapery.*

5 *Enclosed glass or crystal pendant lights vied for popularity with chandeliers in Victorian reception rooms. In dining rooms, pendant lights sited over tables were often attached to pulleys, so that they could be raised and lowered, depending on whether the table was out of, or in, use.*

6 *Overmantel mirrors were sited above most Victorian fire surrounds, and in some cases were built into an overmantel unit which sat on the mantelshelf and incorporated shelving for the display of decorative artifacts. This wall-hung oval mirror has an ornate, gilded wooden frame, like many of the chain-hung pictures that proliferated on Victorian walls. However, polished hardwood frames, usually of mahogany, were also popular.*

7 *Fire surrounds in Victorian rooms were modeled on a wide range of historical precedents, notably Gothic, Renaissance, Baroque, and Georgian. Favored materials included intricately veined and colorful marbles; black and gray slate; finely figured hardwoods (often mahogany and rosewood); flat-painted, faux marble, or wood-grained pine; and cast iron–the latter mass-produced in large quantities from the mid-century onward. Characteristic of most types were patterned tile slips, and a deep mantelshelf often covered, as here, with a tour de cheminée– a fabric mantel frill or pelmet.*

8 *In keeping with the extensive use of fabrics for windows and as floor coverings, Victorian table lamps were, as here, often dressed with fabric shades, although glass "chimneys" were also employed, as in previous eras.*

9 *Apart from in hallways and kitchens, where patterned encaustic or plain quarry tiles, or patterned linoleum, were usually laid, most Victorian rooms had a central carpet or floorcloth, displaying patterns of Oriental or European origin. These were bordered with either dark-stained or stenciled pine boards or, in grander interiors, more expensive hardwood parquet laid in geometric patterns.*

AMERICAN VICTORIAN

In terms of architecture and design, the second half of the nineteenth century witnessed a significant movement away from the Greco-Roman classicism that had previously dominated (*see* Federal style, pp. 18–9, and American Greek Revival, pp. 22–3). Diverse styles were adopted and developed, mainly from historical and contemporary European models, all usually categorized under the broad heading American Victorian. Examples included a Gothic Revival, similar to the British version (*see* pp. 24–5); Italianate, loosely based on English Regency (*see* pp. 20–1); Second Empire style, inspired by a French revival of Renaissance and Baroque ornamentation (*see* pp. 10–1); a Colonial Revival (*see* pp. 14–5); and an eclectic style similar to British High Victorian (*see* pp. 26–7). However, one of the most distinctive styles–Eastlake–was inspired by the English architect and designer Charles Eastlake (1836–1906), and was to provide an important link between the Gothic Revival and the emerging Arts and Crafts movement (*see* pp. 30–1).

The interior (*see* left) is in Durfee House, built ca. 1880 in Los Angeles, California. It is typical Eastlake style, which became fashionable following the publication of Eastlake's *Hints on Household Taste in Furniture, Upholstery and other Details* (1872), and after Clarence Cook's book *The House Beautiful* (1877) and the Philadelphia Centennial Exhibition (1876) promoted Eastlake's work and ideas. Underpinning the style was a rejection of the overelaborate eclecticism of many Victorian interiors, and a return to the clarity and simplicity of design typical of medieval-Gothic and early-English Renaissance architecture, decoration, and furniture. This approach was also evident in the work of Arts and Crafts designers. Unlike many of them, however, Eastlake preferred less expensive machine-made equivalents to hand-crafted fixtures and furnishings, believing them acceptable in an age of industrial mass-production–provided attention was paid to quality control. This not only endeared Eastlake to the manufacturers, but it also meant that most Eastlake-style products were affordable to the public.

1 While tongue-and-groove wooden boards or tin sheeting were often used for ceilings in the less important rooms of American Victorian houses, reception-room ceilings were usually made of plaster and tended to be highly decorative. Flat plaster was embellished with elaborate cornices and central medallions, and plaster paneling, were very much in evidence, and were painted either plain white or polychrome. Colorful paper-paneled and stenciled ceilings were also fashionable. However, in many houses–especially those designed in Eastlake style–coffered (compartmented) ceilings similar to those found in late-medieval and early-Renaissance European dwellings enjoyed a revival. Some of the grandest examples boasted molded wooden bosses or pendants sited on the intersections between the wooden straps, while others carried repeat motifs–either inlaid or painted on the straps. In most cases the sections of flat plaster between the straps were finished with patterned papers.

2 The division between adjoining reception rooms in larger Eastlake-style houses was sometimes marked by arcading–a series of linked arches supported by piers, columns, or colonettes. Stone or wooden arcading had featured in many medieval-Gothic and early-Renaissance buildings. In Victorian houses, the arcading was invariably hardwood, such as oak or mahogany, or softwood, such as pine or fir, grained with paint in imitation of hardwood. The best examples boasted highly intricate pierced and carved arches.

3 On walls (usually above the dado), as on ceilings, paper patterns tended to be either geometrical or based on plant forms. The latter were either naturalistically depicted, like the medieval-style millefleurs pattern to the left of the arcading, or botanically correct but highly stylized, as on the right of the arcading.

4 Complementary colored but contrastingly patterned border papers were also often applied above the dado or, as in the entrance hall beyond, above the picture rail.

5 From the early 1880s, the walls below the dado rail in hallways and many reception rooms were often covered with Lincrusta– a type of wallpaper made from linseed oil, gum, resins, and wood pulp spread over a canvas backing. Deeply embossed with patterns (often stylized fruit and flowers) in imitation of traditional and more expensive relief moldings made of wood or plaster, Lincrusta could be painted, stained, or gilded, and provided a durable finish well-suited to these busy areas of the house.

6 In many Victorian houses, the staircase was often sited asymmetrically, rather than centrally, in the hallway, and usually ran in single flights from floor to floor. Made from hardwood, or sometimes painted softwood, most staircases had elaborate, rounded balusters and turned, faceted, and chamfered newel posts.

7 Most interior doors in American Victorian houses were paneled. Four or six panels were usual, in various configurations, and sometimes the panels were raised and fielded. Some doors were also embellished with decorative carvings which, in Eastlake-style houses, often took the form of linenfold paneling derived from fifteenth- and sixteenth-century models. The best doors were made of hardwood, notably mahogany and rosewood. However, pine doors grained in imitation of finely figured hardwoods were acceptable.

8 In urban areas, gas lighting had been in use since the 1850s, although it was usually augmented with oil-burning lamps. However, during the 1890s, cleaner and brighter electric lighting became available. Brass fixtures with glass shades were especially popular during this period.

9 Although wall-to-wall carpets were laid in many reception rooms, there was a notable revival in the use of stained and polished, butt-jointed wooden boards and parquet flooring in many houses–the flooring embellished with Oriental-style rugs.

Arts and Crafts

The Arts and Crafts movement emerged in Britain in the late 1860s, and soon after in the United States, as a reaction to the stylistic eclecticism, the clutter of ornament, and the often poorly-made, mass-produced furnishings prevalent in Victorian houses during the third quarter of the nineteenth century (*see* pp. 26–7). Initiated by English commentators, architects, designers, and craftsman, such as John Ruskin, William Morris, and Philip Webb, and taken up in America by, notably, William Eyre, Elbert Hubbard, Gustav Stickley, and Charles and Henry Greene, the movement's members advocated not only a simpler, more coherent style, but also the re-establishment of traditional materials and pre-industrial standards of craftsmanship for the manufacture of furniture, textiles, wallpapers, and architectural fixtures and fittings.

The primary sources of inspiration to the movement were the medieval vocabulary of architecture and ornament (*see* pp. 8–9), and the related, but simpler, vernacular architecture of old English cottages and farmhouses. However, Renaissance, Middle Eastern, Oriental, and Art Nouveau (*see* p. 33) forms and imagery were also, to varying degrees, accommodated to enrich the style. The early-twentieth-century American interior (*see* left) embraces most of these essential ingredients, and displays throughout the qualities of craftsmanship and design that characterize Arts and Crafts houses. The latter are evident in the medieval-style pictorial wallpaper frieze, the Art Nouveau-style lights, and the Oriental-style rugs. However, they are most clearly represented by the carpentry and the wooden furniture. The door, the window, the wall paneling, the floor, and the table and chairs are all exceptionally well made. They are also "honest" in the manner in which they emphasize, rather than disguise, the traditional methods of construction (with pegging, and dove-tail and mortise-and-tenon joints), and also enhance the inherent esthetic qualities of the material (in this case oak) from which they are assembled.

1 *Most ceilings in Arts and Crafts houses were modeled on late-medieval architectural forms. The simplest had exposed wooden beams and ribs infilled with lath-and-plaster or, as here, plain wooden boards. In larger houses, the beams and ribs were invariably embellished with chamfering, pendants, and bosses, and in many cases the ceiling was barrel-vaulted (curved). Flat or barrel-vaulted plaster ceilings were also employed in some houses, the grandest compartmented with low-relief plaster moldings. Favored finishes for plaster surfaces included flat-painting (often white or beige), and stenciled, or hand-painted, or papered patterns (mostly depicting medieval or Oriental motifs and imagery).*

2 *Most Arts and Crafts architects retained the classic tripartite division of walls into frieze, field, and dado, although the field and dado were often effectively combined where wall-paneling was used (see 4). While stencil-painted decoration was commonly used on the frieze, wallpapers were equally popular. Fashionable designs included simple flowers, such a poppies, daisies, marigolds, and jasmine, set within formal pattern structures and, as here, pictorials. Medieval imagery was often favored for the latter, notably beasts and birds among stylized or naturalistic plant forms, and heraldic motifs such as emblems and coats-of-arms. (This paper frieze,* The Lion and the Dove, *is by Bradbury & Bradbury–see Directory of Suppliers, pp. 174–87).*

3 *English medieval, Georgian, and Victorian precedents provided the inspiration for Arts and Crafts doors. This door, with elongated wooden panels set beneath two rows of small, glazed panels, is based on a design in the English vernacular tradition by C. F. A. Voysey. Much imitated, it became the standard American early-twentieth-century Arts and Crafts door. Alternatives included the Georgian six-paneled door, often modified by widening the panels to create a sense of horizontality, and Victorian four-paneled doors, painted or papered with plant-form motifs.*

4 *Three-quarter-height wainscoting was very common in Arts and Crafts rooms, with full-height paneling sometimes used in halls and dining rooms. Stained, indigenous hardwoods, notably oak, as here, were preferred. However, cheaper pine or fir was also used, and often flat-painted–ivory white and sage and olive green being fashionable colors. The alternative to wainscoting was wallpaper, depicting floral, medieval, or Oriental imagery.*

5 *Wooden casement windows were also common to Arts and Crafts houses, and either uniformly divided by rows of leaded lights, or, as here, made up of a large single pane topped by smaller panes. Bay windows, consisting of a series of casements, were also widely employed (see pp. 32–3). However, sliding sash windows were also used, usually an upper sash of small rectangular lights over a single-paned lower sash, as were stone mullions in the grandest houses.*

6 *Fitted furniture played a crucial role in Arts and Crafts houses. Window seats and settles built into inglenooks (both with integral storage space), and fitted sideboards, bookcases, and kitchen cabinets, symbolized the craftsmanship inherent in Arts and Crafts interiors, and helped minimize unnecessary clutter.*

7 *While candlelight and gas lamps remained the common sources of lighting during the late nineteenth century, electric lights did appear in Arts and Crafts houses as early as the 1880s. Art Nouveau-style, electric table lamps by makers such as Tiffany found favor around the turn of the century, although copper, brass and, as to the right of the window, wrought-iron wall lamps (oil or electric) were more in keeping with the Arts and Crafts look.*

8 *Apart from in halls, where stone flags were favored, wooden flooring was almost universal in Arts and Crafts houses and, as here, was invariably chosen to match the wall paneling. Favored floor coverings included Turkish, Indian, and Persian rugs, and European carpets with floral or simple geometric patterns.*

EDWARDIAN

The era that began with the death of Queen Victoria and the coronation of Edward VII in 1901, and endured until the outbreak of the First World War in 1914, was characterized by a widespread acceptance of eclecticism in architecture and interior design. Thus, an early-Renaissance (Tudor) Revival (*see* pp. 10–1), late-eighteenth- and early-nineteenth-century French and English neoclassicism (*see* pp. 16–7 and 20–1), Arts and Crafts (*see* pp. 30–1), and Art Nouveau (*see* right) all proved fashionable during this period. As in the Victorian era, these historical-revival styles were rarely fastidious replications of the originals. Indeed, elements of more than one style were still sometimes incorporated in the same interior. However, such styles were distinguished from their Victorian counterparts by a greater clarity of line and a notable reduction of clutter in the architectural fixtures and fittings and in the furnishings.

The Arts and Crafts-influenced drawing room of a large house in Yorkshire, England (*see* left) is a good example of this Edwardian "thinning out" or "watering down" of the late-Victorian look. For example, the ceiling, although still ornate, is painted a subtle monochrome (a fashionable cream color), rather than a more intense and busy polychrome, and there is a characteristic absence of "distracting" pattern in the pine-paneled walls (equally restrained but popular painted paneling, woodwork, and wallpapers included off white, oyster, lilac, stone gray, pale blue or green, and dusty pink). Also significant is the disappearance of overstuffed late-Victorian upholstery, the employment of a relatively simple pelmet and drapes in the bay window, and the installation of a built-in window seat. The plain wooden floorboards (augmented with rugs) and the reduction in the quantity of decorative bric-a-brac contributed to the creation of a lighter and more spacious look. However, despite these embryonic moves toward later twentieth-century minimalism, the emphasis remained firmly rooted in practicality of use and, above all, comfort.

1 While Edwardian ceilings were generally plainer than their Victorian counterparts, a variety of ornate historical styles was adopted in many grander houses. Typical examples included Renaissance ceilings with exposed oak beams, and Baroque, Georgian, and Adam styles with elaborate applied moldings made of either plaster, composition, embossed paper, or stamped tin or steel. This plaster ceiling is a mix of sixteenth-century Renaissance and seventeenth-century Baroque.

2 Few Edwardian houses had an electricity supply, so gas lights, oil lamps, and candles remained in widespread use. In reception rooms, chandeliers were augmented by wall sconces and table and standard lamps, while in corridors and bedrooms small pendant lights with cut-glass shades were preferred.

3 While sliding sash windows were installed in many houses, this wooden-framed window bay, with its leaded casement windows and tinted glass, is typical of row houses and larger Edwardian houses. (Gunmetal or bronze frames provided maintenance-free alternatives.) The built-in seat reveals the enduring influence of the Arts and Crafts movement.

4 Oak, walnut or, as here, pine wainscoting was often installed in Edwardian houses. However, papered or stenciled friezes, papered fields, and painted Anaglypta or Lincrusta dados–divided by linear wooden moldings–were also popular, with patterns and motifs mostly derived from Georgian, Adam, or Regency prototypes.

5 Renaissance-, Georgian-, Arts and Crafts-, and Art Nouveau-style fireplaces were all fashionable during the Edwardian era. Many surrounds were wood, either stained and polished or painted–gloss white and matte green being popular colors. However, cast-iron, slate, brick, and fully tiled surrounds were also much in evidence, as were briquette and plain or patterned tile slips. Framed by matching wainscoting, this pine surround is inspired by English Renaissance models, and features a dog grate suitable for burning large logs.

6 Oriental-style rugs were laid in many Edwardian reception rooms, and were bordered with either butt-jointed boards or herringbone-pattern parquet. However, quarry tiles, mosaics, linoleum, and even marble were favored in hallways and kitchens.

ART NOUVEAU

From ca. 1890 to ca. 1910, Art Nouveau–a distinctive style of architectural detail and decoration–became fashionable in Europe and, to a lesser degree, Britain and the United States. In Scotland, Germany, and Austria it was characterized by the use of austere, elongated rectilinear forms; in France and Belgium by flowing curvilinear elements; and in England and the United States by a combination of the two (as in the copper fire surround embellished with stylized plant-form motifs shown left). Other keynote elements of Art Nouveau included the abandonment of the tripartite division of walls and the use of "greenery-yallery" colors, such as lilac, violet, sage green, olive, and mustard.

THE DETAILS

Having outlined the predominant styles of architecture and decoration from the late Middle Ages to the end of the First World War (*see* pp. 8–33), the focus shifts to specific architectural fixtures and fittings–in other words, the basic components of each of the historical styles. Over the following pages you will therefore find sections devoted to various exterior details (including external doors, transom lights, porches, verandas, shutters, railings, and gates); internal doors; windows; stairs; floors; ceilings; walls; fireplaces, and lighting. In each of these sections, representative examples of these different elements are illustrated either in their original or restored form, or as modern reproductions, or both.

You will also find two sections dedicated specifically to bathrooms and to kitchens. These two areas are treated in a slightly different way to others in the book, as they were really only incorporated into most houses from the nineteenth century onward. Consequently, unlike other rooms, they have not been subject to the full range of period styles of decoration and ornament. Moreover, given the major advances made in bathroom and kitchen technology during the course of the twentieth century, it was inappropriate to illustrate many pre-nineteenth-century appliances that are now either inefficient and impractical (such as prototype water closets), or are simply unreliable and dangerous (notably some of the early enclosed cooking ranges).

Of course, such restrictions are not applicable to the other principal rooms of a house, where the primary considerations are esthetic, and the onus is on an attention to authentic detail. However, successful results are also dependent upon keeping an eye on the bigger picture–on marrying the micro to the macro, matching the right doorknob to the right door, wall, floor, and ceiling treatment. For this reason the majority of individual fixture and fittings, and different decorative treatments, are displayed within the context of their period settings, rather than in isolation.

FRONT DOORS

The style and fashion of door design evolved from practical requirements–access, materials, strength, and weather. In Tudor doors, nail studs, sealing strips, and decorative chamfered moldings protected the frames. Baroque doors were often glazed, inscribed, and ornamented, and framed by ornate columns and hoods. The Georgian door's facade–its principal decorative feature–followed the classical form and detail of the pattern books. Doors had six field panels, were made from oak–later from fir or pine–and were often painted black. Regency doors had reeded moldings, and geometric paneling or studs in the Greco-Roman style, and were set within a brick or stucco arch or shallow porch with pilasters or console brackets. Victorian door style could be Gothic, Greek, French, or Italianate Revival. The Edwardian door's simplified style was influenced by the Arts and Crafts movement.

1 This typical fifteenth-century English Tudor door is made of broad oak planks, which have been strengthened with extended iron hinges and nails driven into the interior ledges or battens. Oak pegs were used as an alternative to iron nails. Here, quatrefoils decorate the spandrels within the simple carved frame, whose shallow arched (four-centered) heading is characteristic of the period.

2 Gaps between vertical planks were often protected by strips of oak, and cross-boarded on the interior for strength. Doors had either strap hinges secured by a pintle (hook) let into the door-jamb, or were hung on a pivot and a plate nailed into the jamb. The window and the later addition of over-door lights maximized the available daylight.

3 Copied from a period example, this door is a fine reproduction only distinguishable from the original by its pale color, as yet unpatinated by age. As in door 2, the vertical lapped planks have covered laths to exclude drafts, and the interior is cross-boarded. This version, however, has disguised integrated door locks.

4 Most door designs during the eighteenth century were taken from pattern books. This ca. 1725 entrance has Doric columns flanking a deep-set paneled door. The door was reduced in height during the mid-seventeenth century to accommodate the period rectangular transom light–a common alteration that did not disrupt the architectural equilibrium.

5 American architects of the late eighteenth and early nineteenth centuries favored the use of columns–particularly Ionic–to support their porches, porticoes, and balustrades. Here, elegantly tapered reproduction columns are incorporated into a restored facade that brings together English Regency, Gothic, and American Classical Revival influences.

6 Dating from the mid-eighteenth century, this handsome door has raised panels and reeded moldings, and is set between classical fluted pilasters. In accordance with contemporary style, it may have been finished in white lead paint, but in this case is painted black, also a popular color of the time. Unlike many doors, this one has retained its original proportions without the addition of a transom light.

4

5

7

8

7 This grand mid-eighteenth-century entrance is of aedicular (literally "little house") design, displaying the fashion for neoclassical elements. (Aedicules reappeared during the Victorian Neoclassical Revival.) The columns are embellished with classical motifs and support a pedimented hood, giving protection from the elements and adding architectural elegance to the typical four panels. The door has been shortened to include a transom light.

8 From the mid-eighteenth century, chinoiserie decoration in metal was used as an architectural device. Here, it embellishes a late-Regency porch beneath a pagoda-shaped leaded hood. The design's lightness is complemented by the white paint and the elegance of its panels.

9 This late-nineteenth-century four-paneled door in Philadelphia is simply decorated and detailed. Made of hardwood, the door is plain; the surround is unembellished; and the transom light has only the house number for decoration– all typical features. Other designs of this period were more flamboyant, with Gothic, Renaissance, neoclassical, and Italianate influences.

6

9

1 The double-doors to Cliveden, in Philadelphia, Pennsylvania, dating to ca. 1763, have an aedicular arrangement of Doric half-columns and bracketed pediment. It exemplifies the period's style and fashion for focusing on the Georgian facade's doorway as the main architectural embellishment. In America, however, this example is uncharacteristic, as the surround is carved from stone rather than wood.

2 Architectural symmetry and harmony were all-important throughout the eighteenth century. This ca. 1793 doorway in Fitzroy Square, London, England, is typical of late-Georgian urban development. A solidly constructed six-paneled door, it is made from oak, painted black, and set within a classical surround. This type of door would have been employed throughout the entire square.

3 Of similar style and date to door 2, this entrance is in Bedford Square, London. Wooden door frames were banned by the London Building Act of 1774 to reduce the effects of fire. Stone and Coade stone (artificial stone invented in the late eighteenth century), was used as replacements, allowing greater architectural versatility.

4 Although many doorway designs were taken directly from pattern books, designers such as the architect Sir John Soane still created ingenious innovations. Here, he rethought the contemporary Regency doorway for a London house ca. 1812 by adapting Greek or Roman studding in symmetrical rectangles instead of panels. Double-doors permitted generous proportions without jeopardizing the overall scale. The lantern and transom light illuminate the interior and exterior.

5 This Regency doorway (ca. 1815) is located in King's Cross, London. Typical doors of this period were heavily paneled, had applied lozenges or circles, and an arch containing a transom light. Painted black or bronze-green, the doors had a knocker and handle.

6 This reproduction of a typical Edwardian suburban front door (ca. 1912) was copied from a contemporary London builders' merchant who mass-produced popular patterns of the period. The glazed panels maximize light filtered into the hallway, which is shadowed by the porch. Extra light is afforded by the side lights and by the plain, rectangular twentieth-century over-door glazing.

7 *This late-nineteenth-century doorway is a combination of different influences: early-Georgian classicism in its architectural surround and transom light frame; the esthetic craftsmanship of the Arts and Crafts movement of the door itself; and a hint of Queen Anne Revival in the upper glazing bars, brought up-to-date with colored glass.*

8 *Characteristic of a late-Victorian middle-class suburban dwelling, this doorway has a Gothic hood supported on composite columns, rectangular panels of colored glass, and a pair of decorative door panels. Incorporating the house number in the transom light is typical of this period.*

9 *This modest but stylish door is a reproduction of an Arts and Crafts door of the type favored by the influential architect C. F. A. Voysey, who admired the vernacular form and abbreviated decoration. Plain glazed lights and flat vertical lower panels exemplify this style.*

10 *A pair of simple Victorian doors in a line of row houses is united and embellished by a purely ornamental machine-tooled hood. Typically this would be matched by verge-boards beneath the gables. The Victorians used a variety of paint colors, but external doors were mainly painted green or they were wood-grained.*

7

8

9

ARTS AND CRAFTS DOORS

The Arts and Crafts movement shunned mass industrial production and promoted the artisan craftsman. Proponents sought to create an esthetic environment that was based on historical and vernacular precedents, using fine craftsmanship and high-quality materials. The door on the left characterizes this ideology. It shows the interior of the front door of the Red House, in Bexleyheath, near London, England, designed by Philip Webb in 1859 for William Morris, a founder of the Arts and Crafts movement. It is obviously medieval in influence in its use of planks and battens for the door, and iron hinges and latch in place of a knob or handle. However, the door is beautifully crafted and also highly contemporary in the way that it employs the chevron decoration and stained-glass inserts.

10

TRANSOM LIGHTS

Transom lights allowed natural light into hallways and passages. Those of the 1720s were often rectangular, and were created by cannibalizing the upper register of a tall door's panels. Early styles had semicircular dimensions, and were made of wood in modest houses and of wrought metal in grander dwellings. As door frames became plainer, transom lights became more fanciful. Mid-eighteenth-century examples featured an inner tracery arch divided into segments using a thin iron frame with cast-lead details. In 1774, Francis Underwood patented a composite glazing bar made by soldering a lead molding to a strip of metal–this became standard methodology. The 1760s and 1770s were the great age of transom lights. Influenced by the Adam brothers, transom lights had delicate radiating iron tracery overlaid with cast-lead ornamentation of fans, scallops, and lacy motifs. The early nineteenth century saw simplified geometric circles and curves, teardrop and bat's wing, loops and spider's web to match more adventurous door design. Cast iron allowed for mass production and the introduction of gas lighting meant lanterns could be incorporated. From 1832, sheet glass negated the need for segmentation and glass was often inserted into the door's body and surround. Many Victorian transom lights were simple rectangles with geometric glazing bars or colored glass inserts.

1 The entrance door to the Morris-Jumel Mansion, which was built ca. 1765, in New York, is embellished with an elliptical transom light and side lights that previously were much plainer in style. They are part of the extensive alterations that were made to the original building during the early nineteenth century, and were influenced by the owner's travels to Europe. The colored glass inserts are a variation of the classic tracery that is more usually seen during this period. This style of door, with its substantial side lights, is typically American in design.

2 This elliptical transom light is contained within the top storey of the ca. 1800 Gaillard-Bennett House, in Charleston, South Carolina. The elegant semicircle and the unfussy glazing pattern are a perfect foil for the dentilated pediment above. Such an arrangement shows how well this device could be incorporated as an architectural feature in its own right, and not merely as a light source over a door.

3 Here, a classic transom light of the mid-eighteenth century is identified by its semi-circular shape and "fan" design. This form is well-suited to the geometry of the door frame, whose key stones echo the shape of the tracery. The generous shape of the transom light maximizes the filtration of available light more effectively than later lights of elliptical design.

4 *Transom lights became more delicate and complex in design as the eighteenth century progressed and cast-iron manufacturing techniques became more sophisticated. Robert Adam's designs of intricate tracery epitomize the zenith of this fashion between 1770 and 1790.*

5 *The classic transom light form, such as this example from ca. 1793, has an inner semicircle and "fan" spokes that radiate from the center base. This is typical of the designs in* A Book of Designs, *by Joseph Bottomley, the influential transom-light maker, published in 1793.*

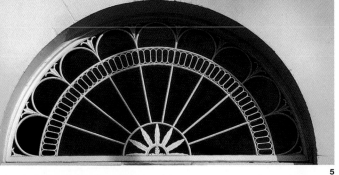

6 *Early-Georgian doors were often reduced in height in order to accommodate a transom light, which would therefore have been rectangular in shape. Here, the glazing is in simpler form than in transom lights 4 and 5, and the bars are slightly thicker.*

7 *This simple transom light is in the Morris-Jumel Mansion, in New York. The ca. 1765 door escaped the extensive nineteenth-century alterations elsewhere in the building. The light exhibits sturdy wood glazing bars, precursors of later wrought- and cast-iron tracery.*

8 *The interior of the entrance to the Morris-Jumel Mansion illustrates the contrast in style after the owner's European travels influenced the alterations. Colored-glass insets add a purely decorative dimension to the large transom light and side lights.*

9 *This characteristically American doorway has a black-painted, classically paneled door that is framed by side lights and has a broad-arched transom light. The delicate spider's-web glazing in the transom light was a popular decorative detail on both sides of the Atlantic.*

HOODS AND PORCHES

Tudor doorheads often had hoodmolds and projecting cornices or drip moldings, but in the sixteenth century robust porches became popular. Mid-seventeenth-century hoods and porches were intrinsic to the doorway's design, adding canopies decorated with shells, acanthus leaves, fruit, flowers, and cherubs to an otherwise flat-fronted house. From 1720, doorways often had a plain, flat shelf supported by carved brackets. The overdoor of the Palladian house was superseded by the neoclassical surround, although, in America, porches were fashionable and were often added to the facades of older houses. The Regency period saw a porch revival, using delicate filigree ironwork, while in America, balconies and verandas were favored. The Victorian porch conveyed social standing—a projecting porch denoted a higher status than a recessed one. The Arts and Crafts movement adapted past styles such as Queen Anne shell and double-ogee canopy shapes. The Edwardian period also featured timbered porches and mass-produced cast-iron porches with glazed roofs.

2

3

1 Tudor houses often had a jettied upper floor which gave some protection to the entrance below. Here, a beam has been added to the length of the overhang, shaped to sluice off the rain, and protect the fabric of the lower story. At this time, many streets were so narrow that there was no room for a more substantial frontage.

2 Uniquely American in character, this elaborate ca. 1758 entrance features pilasters and a segmented arch with extravagant pineapple carving, reminiscent of a Chippendale-style high chest. Hoods were popular in town and country houses alike as they provided a stylish accent without the expense of porch construction.

3 A typical Edwardian practice was to borrow a Queen Anne motif of a shell design on carved brackets, adding iron and glass details. The glazed door—again echoing Queen Anne style—and original green paint are very much of this period.

4 Large town houses of the last quarter of the eighteenth century were often fronted by a classical porch, which was typical of those favored by the architect John Nash for his grand London squares and row houses. Severe and noble, and without any unnecessary ornamentation, such a porch gives the entrance stature and interest.

1

4

5 *This Victorian middle-class house is fronted by a Gothic Revival porch, whose pointed roof apex over double inner arches is raised on steps leading to wood-grained double-doors. The porch was a good way to dress a facade to exhibit social standing.*

6 *Heavily influenced by the Renaissance architecture of rural northern Italy, this ca. 1860 American house has the addition of an open, balustraded porch balancing the bracketed deep eaves. American Victorians were very enthusiastic borrowers of international and historical styles.*

7 *This is an Edwardian interpretation of a Queen Anne canopy on brackets with an integral glazed porch. Its dimensions echo that of an eighteenth-century door with a transom light and side lights. The squared glazing bars, white woodwork, and checked paving are typical of this period.*

8 *Imaginative American architecture created this ca. 1889 mansion in Port Townsend, in Washington State. Although Craftsman style, the porch is influenced by a mixture of French château style and Colonial detail in its raised, pedimented porch with a transom light.*

9 *Characteristic of the American fashion for mixing simple and ornate elements, the main entrance of the ca. 1888 Hale House, Los Angeles, has an ornate pediment, turned supports, and broad steps leading to relatively plain double-doors.*

10 *David Whitcomb built this magnificent edifice on the Hudson River in New York in 1983. The temple-front portico, plain triangular pediment, and unfluted columns are all classical features.*

5

7

9

6

8

10

BALCONIES AND VERANDAS

The balconet, the mid-eighteenth century precursor to the balcony, had diagonal railings, with rosettes, anthemia, crossed spears, and Gothic tracery. By 1770, balconies were more fashionable–running the width of three drawing-room windows on the *piano nobile*, and often painted green. Some late-eighteenth- and early-nineteenth-century cast-iron balconies were partly glazed and roofed in copper or zinc, and usually in the typical Regency pagoda style. These developed into elaborate double-story verandas, with chinoiserie or Greek key motifs, or rectangular balconies in geometric trellis and floral designs. By 1820, cast iron had superseded wrought iron, and verandas were manufactured in pieces and sold by catalog. Balconettes in wrought-iron "bellied" form were favored after 1830. In America, neoclassical, Chinese, and Greek key designs in ironwork were used in the late-eighteenth-century Federal period, while European craftsmen popularized old continental and neoclassical styles. Cast-iron carvings were used in the two-story verandas of the 1850s, while turn-of-the-century balconies and verandas had decorative woodwork.

3 *The abolition of the Window Tax in England in 1851 encouraged a more generous use of glass. Consequently, the bay window became almost a required feature for the modest Victorian house, allowing good light and viewing. It also provided a broad balcony on the second floor, which was often echoed, as here, with a balustraded parapet to provide symmetry as well as a safety route in case of fire.*

1 *This elegant wrought-iron balcony (ca. 1810) fronts the width of the second story, or piano nobile, of a stucco-faced residence. Balconies of this period were usually fashioned in geometric or key shapes, with running floral top and bottom rails. This style of narrow rectangular balcony was more decorative than practical.*

4 *This interior recessed balcony of an early-nineteenth-century American mansion overlooks a double-story hallway embellished with neoclassical pillars and cornice. Interior double-doors open onto a semi-circular balcony, guarded with a dignified railing of geometric design, with a delicate filigree "apron" centerpiece.*

2 *By the early-Victorian period, manufacturing cast iron had become a highly skilled operation, and foundry catalogs began to sell ready-to-assemble panels for verandas, balconies, and conservatories. During this period, windows became larger and balconies sturdier, as seen in this example on a London town house.*

5 *Drayton Hall in South Carolina, ca. 1738–42, is America's finest Palladian mansion. Its noble proportions are graced by a two-story pedimented portico. This classic feature, often seen in the grandest American architecture, displays minimal decoration in its balcony railing below a dentilated pediment with lozenge-shaped relief.*

6 *The ca. 1800 Gaillard-Bennett House, in Charleston, South Carolina, underwent alterations in 1819 and 1850, at which time the portico and balconies were added. American architects were very enthusiastic about giving their buildings an updated look, although it took time for English fashions to become popular. Classical Revivalists rejected the neoclassical idiom of the Adam brothers, and instead embraced a uniquely American robustness that relied more on structure than on applied decoration. This portico is a good example. Its Doric columns on the first tier and Corinthian columns with cast-iron capitals on the second are topped by an imposing dentilated pediment and transom lights.*

7 *The Inn at Antietam, in Sharpsburg, Maryland, was built before the start of the Revolutionary War in 1775, and although some of the architectural elements are similar to the later Gaillard-Bennett House, it has a more accessible, domestic aspect. This homeliness is characterized by the combination of clap-boarding, shutters, vergeboard detail, and typical wrap-around veranda. In later years, these verandas and porches became highly decorative features.*

8 *The veranda gave great scope for inventive architecture, either as an integral part of the original design, or as an addition to an older property to update the look, provide an outdoor "room," or simply to create a place to shelter from the elements. Here a round-ended loggia fits neatly into an angle of this 1880s New York house.*

9 *Hale House, in Los Angeles, California, is late nineteenth century in style, and mixes both simple and complex architectural devices in a harmonious manner. The turned wooden columns that support the elaborate painted entrance porch are continued around the house, providing a shady veranda.*

10 *American houses have adopted every style of veranda and balcony to suit their architectural and domestic requirements. These ranged from the wonderful ironwork confections of Spanish and French inspiration in New Orleans, to the chinoiserie and classic Greek motifs gracing the facades of Boston mansions, to the highly decorative woodwork of the Victorian crafts-men, to this simplest of glazed porches, provid-ing space and shelter.*

SHUTTERS

Exterior shutters protect the interior of houses from the elements–whether it is winter snow or summer heat. They also allow the control of light and the passage of air, provide security, privacy, and decoration, and can dramatically change a window's proportions, and indeed the character, of a building's face. Shutters seem more suited to these uses and to the architecture of the continent and of the hotter states of America than they do to Britain, as they blend well with different styles of window and building materials. Also, Britain doesn't have such extremes of temperature, nor the intensity of light, nor (usually) the need to protect glass against hurricanes. In Britain, shutters were nearly always added to the inside of buildings, not to the exterior. The Building Act of 1709 in Britain dictated that windows should be set back from the facade of a building by one brick's width and, as a result, windows from this date were very often furnished with interior shutters folding into the reveals. Early-American Colonial shutters were sometimes louvered with simple cutouts as a decorative detail. As a rule, internal shutters were used in brick houses, but external paneled and louvered shutters were common on wooden buildings in the early eighteenth century. In the second half of the nineteenth century, louvered and Venetian shutters continued to be standard, although canvas awnings were sometimes used as a substitute. In Britain during the Edwardian period, continental travel on a large scale brought back a taste for wooden louvered shutters, called *jalousies*, and these worked quite happily on the villa-style houses that were popular at the time.

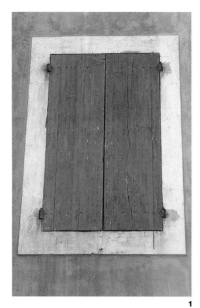

1 The simplest type of unpainted plank shutters on a Provençal farm-house window creates a charming picture bordered by a white surround within a pink limewashed "frame." The shutters keep the interior cool in the summer heat, and are then opened in the evening to let in the cool air.

2 Cliveden, built in ca. 1763, in Philadelphia, Pennsylvania, is associated with grand Colonial-style houses, but surprisingly these shutters front a window in the service area of the house, unseen by the public. Such battened shutters hung on iron strap hinges were typical of modest houses, too.

3 Despite their rustic simplicity, shutters on the windows are typical of many French country houses of standing, and afford great character to the building. This batten-and-hinge style also provides good security with its heavy locking bars.

4 This sturdy, rough stone French dwelling has a practical arrangement of solid, serviceable shutters, which close out the extremes of weather, and de rigueur lace curtains behind a window screen.

5 *This sash window is located on the raised entrance level at Cliveden, in Philadelphia, Pennsylvania. The design is borrowed from the English Queen Anne style, with that period's characteristic twelve-over-twelve pane window pattern. The paneled shutters take their design from classic early-eighteenth-century door proportions, and their dimensions are a suitable complement to the key-stone arch and the lipped window-sill. Interior slatted blinds control the filtering of light into the room.*

6 *Louvered shutters have never gone out of fashion. In addition to their decorative appeal, they allow air into rooms and, at the same time, provide shade to keep out the heat. They can also be given an individual flavor, as here, with personalized embellishment. This example, painted in cool gray, which is suited to the unpretentious country style, has a sentimental horseshoe for good luck and a letterbox inserted into the structure.*

7 *Dick Dumas painted this brilliantly executed trompe l'oeil pair of shutters to amuse and embellish this stone house. These painted shutters can give the house a period feel, or disguise or soften an unappealing wall.*

8 *Sometimes mountain houses have the tiniest windows– they are more like portholes rather than windows–on the north side of the building, and they will be well protected by basic, functional shutters such as these.*

9 *This ca. 1890 American house in Middletown, Maryland, appears to have been influenced by Dutch architecture, with its steep gables, red-brick structure, and very narrow-louvered shutters.*

DOOR HARDWARE

Medieval door hardware consisted of an iron pull or drop handle. Wrought-iron and brass box locks were a luxury in the early sixteenth century, but iron latches lasted well into the twentieth. The Baroque period saw decorative hinges in L-shape, butterfly, and cock's-head form, and the rich displayed their wealth with decorative brass locks. Knockers, originally simply styled, became more ornate by 1700. Georgian door hardware was often black-painted cast iron–not brass. Knobs were usually at waist level, centered in the middle door rail. As door design was modernized in the early nineteenth century, pull handles in the form of rosettes or solid turned balls became popular. Knocker shapes were numerous–from neoclassical heads to lion masks. By 1890, brass and porcelain electric bells replaced knockers and bell pulls.

1 Only a ring handle was needed on medieval and Tudor doors, which were barred from the inside at night. Early wrought iron had a twisted ring, but here the backplate is more ornate than usual.

2 Stylistically, this simple clutch handle could belong to the fifteenth century onward. Brass, however, was a luxury until the Industrial Revolution, and only available to the rich.

3 The functional purpose of front door knockers may have remained the same over the centuries, but the material, style, and placement give clues to their correct dates. This reproduction knocker would be fitting for a late-nineteenth-century door.

4 This knocker is a reproduction of a style dating to the fifteenth century. It is made from simple forged iron with an authentic-looking hammered ring, and is suited to a rustic oak door.

5 Here is an updated version of the knocker shown in 4, but this time it is reproduced in brass. Although not genuine period material, this knocker would be appropriate if the rest of the door hardware were also brass.

6 A classic design of an urn in relief, this pattern is characteristic of the late-Georgian period, and continues to be popular. Unlike this reproduction, the original would have been made of iron and painted black.

7 This charming lion-and-wreath iron knocker is in grand classical style, and is well-suited to the weathered door it graces.

8 The Georgian period saw the arrival of many kinds of knocker design. Apart from the somewhat sad-faced lion, there were fish, classical heads, and vases. This reproduction has an unusual bronzed finish.

9 This ornate "knocker" is in fact a modern door bell. Made of solid brass, it is based on a turn-of-the-century design at a time when the Victorians were fond of "novelties."

10 A variety of letter-box styles has been utilized since 1840. This reproduction's minimalist lines make it perfect for a modern door.

11 The earliest Victorian letterboxes were small and slim. This elegant shape, with curved, chased edges, suits a late-nineteenth-century four-paneled door.

12 Of an unusual style, and with a sinuous out-line, this reproduction letterbox may have been derived from the Art Nouveau fashion of the late nineteenth century.

13 This sophisticated reproduction letter-box, with its integrated knocker handle, is finished in polished metal, and has the lean look of early-twentieth-century design.

14 A sleek design in unadorned brass would look well as a letterbox where the date of the doorway is in doubt. This example would suit doors after the 1900s.

15 Here, a reproduction mid-Victorian letterbox is combined with its own knocker. The earliest examples were inset vertically, and so were separate to the knocker.

16 This black-iron letter-box is in Arts and Crafts style, its fixing plates echoing medieval hinges.

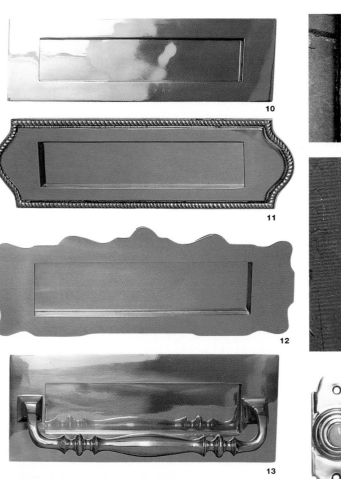

17 Before exterior locks, doors were barred on the inside for security, as here, on this American nineteenth-century house.

18 Unusually, this lock has been fashioned from wood, but it is of a timeless rustic construction.

19–21 By 1890, electric bell pushes had generally superseded manual bell pulls. These reproductions show some typical examples in brass.

22 This is a twin to the gargoyle knocker/bell ring illustrated in 9. The bronze finish lends it an element of antiquity.

23 An early-Victorian house bell would have been placed in the service passage to alert the staff to the arrival of a guest. Originally wire-and-pulley operated, today's reproduction has battery or electric power.

49

RAILINGS AND GATES

The character and prestige of a house are greatly affected by its exterior boundaries. Esthetically, much can be won or lost by the choice of barrier between private and public property. Moreover, walls, fences, and hedges all reflect the standing and impact of the building and the homeowners within. Ironwork fencing was introduced to Britain in the late seventeenth century, and its versatility has kept it in constant use ever since. It looks well combined with stone and brick; it can be painted or gilded; and it lends itself to myriad designs. The most enduring styles had plain railings with, for example, spear-head or fleur-de-lis finials, which became the uniting face of the Georgian urban development. In the American Colonial period, iron gates and fences were most often a feature of public buildings, but their grandeur appealed to the owners of pretentious domestic dwellings. Cheaper cast iron, sold by catalog, made stylish fencing readily available to all by the Victorian period. Wooden fencing maintained its popularity in America. In Britain, apart from continuous rustic usage, it made a fashionable reappearance during the Arts and Crafts period of the second half of the nineteenth century, and as a companion to the Edwardian decorative trelliswork and Tudor Revival buildings.

3 *A late-Victorian house, built ca.1897, in Middletown, Maryland, is influenced by Gothic Revival style in its churchlike spire turret and dormer windows. The street-side garden fence illustrates another shape of picket–flat-cut with spear-top Gothic spindles. The straight line is interrupted by the arch of the gateway. The picket fence is a purely decorative device to delineate the boundaries of a property.*

4 *In Italianate fashion, this Edwardian villa has been embellished with a balustraded stairway entrance that matches and balances the second-floor balcony. The Edwardians were strongly influenced by their travels to the continent, especially the romanticism of Italian architecture and gardens. This reproduction balustrade is made of reconstituted stone and is a realistic light buff color.*

1 *The open front of this classic country-style property has a pleasing visual definition. This is achieved through its whitewashed clapboard, gray paneled shutters, steeply pitched stone roof, low picket fence, and driveway with its a timeless post-and-chain borders.*

2 *The picket fence is particularly associated with the Eastern seaboard of America, where an abundance of readily available continental lumber made wooden construction a natural choice for houses and gates. This kind of fencing is as appropriate and charming today as it is in an historical setting.*

5 *This stone balustrade was designed and carved for a show stand at the 1997 Chelsea Flower Show in London. Such a classic design will never go out of fashion, and even a short length–which is sometimes to be found in reclamation yards–will make a fine architectural statement in a garden.*

6 *Suitably classic and timeless, arrow-headed, wrought-iron railings front an early-nineteenth-century London house. The uncluttered treatment of the paved frontage enhances the classical symmetry.*

7 *The same type of railings as 6 has been used in a different setting at the entrance to a newly built Dutch Colonial-style mansion. Here the spindles are finer, and finished with delicate gilded finials.*

8 *The plainest iron fencing is suitable to use as a neutral barrier between the house and the road. Durfee House, which was built ca. 1880, in Los Angeles, California, is a bright confection of painted clapboard, and is known as a "pink lady." Its fancy fretwork decoration needs no further ornamental distraction.*

9 *The scale of the entrance gate is important, especially when it partners such an imposing-looking building. This ca. 1877 house, built in early-nineteenth-century style, has tall, narrow windows on the piano nobile that accentuate its height, which is reflected in the tall sweep and decorative detail of the wrought-iron gate.*

GILDED IRON

Most wrought- and cast-iron gates and railings have been simply painted, mainly in black or green. However, as with this scrolling plant-form finial (on a neoclassical, Greek-key pattern gate), some of the most prestigious examples have also featured gold-leaf detailing–a popular decorative convention during the seventeenth and eighteenth centuries, and often replicated using less expensive gold-metallic paint during the nineteenth century.

ORNAMENTATION

Exterior ornamentation embraces many forms, from the addition of a naïve carved wooden detail on a door frame to the ornate statuary of High Victorian architecture– all of which in some way refines a building's esthetic impact. Baroque style saw a plethora of voluptuous carved-stone decoration, particularly above main doorways. The more studied classicism of the Georgian period confined exterior ornament to such elements as porch brackets, *pateras,* and carved pediment insets. The style for embellishment in the second half of the eighteenth century was influenced by Robert Adam's sinuous, elegant swags, ribbons, and arabesques. Later, Coade stone (an artificial, castable material) permitted cheap high-relief decoration. Strongly accented molding, reeded and incised patterns, and blind niches are the essence of sophisticated Regency architectural detailing. The broad use of decorative elegant metalwork heralded a Victorian passion for ornamentation in Britain and America.

2 This detail is from a ca. 1880 Queen Anne Revival-style apartment house in Cadogan Square, London. The ornamental brickwork shows Flemish, Gothic, Renaissance, and Chinese influences, with the exuberant decoration combining terra cotta, red brick, and Portland stone. The Victorians loved to mix historical architectural styles and diverse materials, using both traditional and modern manufacturing methods. The Rococo-patterned frieze divides the two levels of leaded windows, and carved stone figures hold up a pagoda-shaped copper canopy.

1 The Victorians were conscious of creating a good first impression, and an elaborate entrance was therefore desirable. Holly Village, in Highgate, London, was built in 1865 by Henry Darbishire, who conceived a pastiche of an English village green, surrounded by medieval cottages. This gateway characterizes his passion for Gothic detail, with its churchlike archways and flèches (spires), its decorative lattice fascias, small oriel window, and pious-looking statuary. The ravages of pollution have obscured much of the subtle detail, resulting in a gloomier impression than was originally intended.

3 Griswold House, home to the Newport Art Museum on Rhode Island, is a splendid example of American Tudor Revival during the Victorian period, adapted to the eccentricities of the architect. This pastiche of a Stick-style building is based on the traditional English half-timbered house. Its picturesque effect is achieved with wood that is in fact only applied decoration, and a structure that is composed of ornamental wooden cladding, rather than plaster and decorative pargeting.

4 An example of exterior embellishment favored by the Victorians, this impressive entrance facade makes use of crafted Portland stonework for the spandrels, pilasters, and statuesque finials.

5 A detail of Hale House, Los Angeles, ca. 1880, shows a delicate filigree ironwork veranda cresting on the roof, with a newel-post division that matches those on the ornate porch. From the 1870s, iron roof crestings often appeared around the square roof line of Second Empire houses.

6 A rare stone edifice in its time, Cliveden, ca. 1763, in Philadelphia, illustrates the classical idiom in the pedimented roof, where a grand urn tops the chimney.

7 Inventive architectural ornamentation is shown on this roof edge, which has been designed as a cornice; with deeply overhung eaves supported by twinned console brackets.

8 Vergeboards, as here, provide a decorative seal between tiles and wall on the gable end of a roof. Used since Tudor times, vergeboards became more decorative and widespread when machine-cutting made complex designs cheap to produce.

9 Medallions, plaques, and cartouches have been used from the Baroque period to embellish doorways and walls. This reproduction of a late-Georgian terra cotta and plasterwork piece typically portrays a woman in classical dress. Other examples have a shield of crossed arrows.

10 This modern version of a Georgian carriage lamp with its shaped storm cowl serves today's requirement for exterior lighting and security. It is made of solid cast brass and has beveled plate glass.

11 Medieval or Arts and Crafts houses would have used this type of wall lantern, which has very simple lines. This, example, however, is an electrified reproduction.

12 Copied from a traditional Georgian wall-light design, this modern lamp is made of weathered brass, but black-aluminum and verdigris finishes are also available.

13 An alternative style to 12 is this squared wall light, which would have been seen throughout the English Georgian period. American lamps were more usually made of wrought iron.

INTERNAL DOORS

From a constructional point of view, two basic types of internal door have been in widespread use since the Middle Ages: battened-plank and paneled. The former (*see* pp. 56-7) were prevalent in most houses up until the seventeenth century, and thereafter were mostly confined to those dwellings (predominantly, but not exclusively, rural) built in traditional vernacular styles–such as many late-nineteenth- and early-twentieth-century Arts and Crafts and Colonial Revival houses. Conversely, paneled doors (*see* pp. 58-61) were relatively rare from the Middle Ages through to the early seventeenth century–the high standards of craftsmanship required to hand-cut their mortised-and-tenoned frameworks rendering them more expensive and the preserve of the wealthiest households. Nevertheless, by the early eighteenth century they had supplanted battened-plank doors in most houses. This was in part due to a reduction in the skill, time, and cost of their manufacture, following the introduction of "semi-automated" cutting techniques (often fully automated by the Victorian era). However, it was also fueled by the fact that most paneled doors required less solid wood than their plank counterparts–an increasingly economical option as lumber resources (particularly hardwoods) began to diminish, especially in Britain, as early as the late seventeenth century.

The vast majority of doors since the medieval period have been made entirely from wood: either hardwood or softwood. As nowadays, hardwoods were invariably the more prestigious and most expensive. This was largely due to the attractive figurings displayed on their surface when they were cut at various angles or from different parts of the tree, and enhanced by staining, waxing, and varnishing–the preferred finishes for hardwood doors. The most popular hardwoods have included oak and elm (for battened-plank doors), and mahogany, rosewood, oak, walnut and, notably in America, cherry and maple (for paneled doors). Softwoods are blander in appearance than most hardwoods, but being faster-growing and more abundant they have provided a cheaper raw material–especially for paneled doors since the early eighteenth century. The most commonly used have been the various species of pine and fir, and to conceal their blandness, these were traditionally flat-painted or wood-grained in imitation of a hardwood, often en suite with the other woodwork in the room or house.

In addition to the display of figuring and grain, or the particular color of flat paint, the factors that have determined the overall appearance of a door are the the structure and style of the surrounding framework (*see* pp. 62-3), the type of wooden, metal, or ceramic door furniture employed (*see* pp. 64-5) and, most significantly, the configuration of the basic structural components. For example, during the Middle Ages and early Renaissance, many battened-plank doors were constructed from vertical planks of varying width. Thereafter, however, the planks gradually became more uniform and narrower. Similarly, while paneled doors have always been divided into as little as two and as many as twelve panels, specific historical periods or styles have become strongly, albeit not exclusively, associated with particular numbers–for example, between two and five for Baroque, six for Georgian, and four for Victorian.

Equally subject to changing fashions in architecture and ornament have been the shape and decoration of the panels. Thus, carved linenfold patterns were in vogue during the early Renaissance, and in the nineteenth-century Gothic and Renaissance Revivals; cartouche-shaped panels were often employed in Baroque, and Baroque and Renaissance Revival houses; and rectangular panels–sometimes fielded in the eighteenth, nineteenth, and early twentieth centuries, and usually defined by thin, rectilinear moldings–were prevalent in Classical Revival and neoclassical interiors. Other decorative conventions of note have included the use of engraved glass panels in many Victorian houses during the nineteenth century, and the application–particularly in neoclassical, Esthetic, and Art Nouveau motifs–of painted motifs and imagery, mostly based on plant forms.

BATTENED-PLANK DOORS

Internal battened-plank doors were in widespread use in all types of houses up until the seventeenth century. Thereafter, they were gradually supplanted by paneled doors (*see* pp. 58–61), although they continued to be used in houses built in the vernacular tradition, and enjoyed a revival in the Arts and Crafts houses of the late nineteenth and early twentieth centuries. The simplest examples were made up of two or more vertical, butt-jointed or tongue-and-groove, wooden planks nailed to two or more horizontal wooden battens on their reverse side–the number of cross-battens usually increased in relation to the weight of the planks. Variations have included the insertion of diagonal braces between the battens; "double-boarding," in which a set of horizontal planks, rather than spaced battens, are fastened to the reverse of the vertical planks; the use of wooden moldings to create decorative paneling on the surface of the planks; and nailhead ornament (*see* right). Traditionally, battened-plank doors are hung on surface-mounted hinges (*see* p. 64). Favored woods have included oak and elm, and softwoods such as pine–the latter often painted, rather than stained, waxed, or varnished.

1 The fifteenth-century Frog Pool Farm, in Avon, England, has retained many of its original doors. The heavy, three-plank, battened oak door on the right has a wrought-iron latch, and is hung on a pair of large strap hinges. The five-plank oak door on the left is lighter, and is hung on a pair of wrought-iron pivots and plates–both typical of the period.

2 Hung in a converted olive mill, in Andalucia, Spain, this heavy plank door is a type often used in European vernacular architecture from the Middle Ages to the twentieth century. The planks on the show side, displaying ornamental nailheads, are secured on the reverse by a set of planks laid at right angles to them. This configuration is known as "double-boarding."

3 Apart from exposed nailheads, decorative embellishments on early plank doors were non-existent or very minimal. On this reproduction oak example, they are restricted to simple moldings along the edges of the planks.

4 Before the seventeenth century, doors were often constructed from planks of varying widths (up to 26 inches). Here, in an English cob house, they are made of elm.

5 *Chamfered battens are often found on American Colonial plank doors. In this restored period house, the three-plank, cross-battened door is made of soft-wood, and is painted en suite with the wall paneling inh a rust-red milk paint.*

6 *This arch-top, English Jacobean door is of a type only employed in very grand houses. The main body of the door is constructed from butt-jointed vertical planks. However, unlike most plank doors, these are secured within a frame, and are embellished with a series of linked, geometric-shaped panels made up of applied wooden battens. The fan-molded arch top is a particularly prestigious addition.*

7 *As on door 5, this milk-painted plank door in an eighteenth-century American Amish log house has chamfered cross-battens. For extra security, its iron latch is supplemented with a sliding wooden bolt.*

8 *To prevent warping, the cross-battens on lightweight plank doors were often augmented with a pair of diagonal braces mitered at the ends to sit flush with the cross-battens. This modern reproduction is hung in an English farmhouse kitchen.*

5

6

7

8

NAILHEAD ORNAMENT

Since the Middle Ages, a fashionable decorative convention employed on battened-plank doors has been to leave the heads of the wrought-iron nails (which secure the planks to the battens) exposed, rather than sinking them under the surface of the wood. Usually, the pattern formed by the nailheads exactly corresponds to the number and position of the battens on the reverse–in other words, a series of horizontal, parallel lines. These were also sometimes interspersed with vertical rows of nailheads running up the inner and outer edges of the doors–as on this pair of limewashed Moroccan cupboard doors. However, on some plank doors, purely ornamental nailheads were employed, in addition to those that also served a constructional purpose. The former were usually configured as simple motifs or emblems. Notable examples include shields and stylized floral forms (such as fleurs-de-lis), mainly derived from the heraldic vocabulary of ornament.

PANELED DOORS

Although paneled doors were sometimes employed in grander houses prior to the seventeenth century, they gradually replaced battened-plank doors (*see* pp. 56–7) as the standard internal door that was used in most houses. The basic construction–in which the panels are secured in a wooden framework of (vertical) stiles and (horizontal) rails, mortised-and-tenoned together–has never altered. However, there have been numerous stylistic variations. For example, the number of panels has ranged from two to ten, or more–with four, five, and six panels being the most prevalent. The embellishment of the panels has also varied: they can be flat and sit below the frame, or be raised ("fielded") in the center to lie flush with it; be defined around their perimeter with decorative moldings; and be plain, or decorated with carving, or additional applied moldings, or painted motifs and imagery. Although glass panels have been used, most paneled doors have been made entirely of wood–the finest from finely figured, waxed or varnished hardwoods, such as oak, mahogany, or rosewood, but more commonly from cheaper, painted or wood-grained softwoods, such as fir or pine.

2 Characteristic of early-eighteenth-century reception rooms, this pair of full-height, three-paneled double-doors echoes the configuration of the wall paneling. They are made of fir or pine and are painted in one of the grayish green-brown colors– collectively known as "drabs"–that were very fashionable in early- and mid-Georgian houses. Also typical is the plain brass rim lock, which would have been made of iron in poorer houses, and probably engraved or chased with motifs in wealthier ones.

1 Linenfold carving was a popular method of embellishing the panels of reception-room doors in wealthy households from the early sixteenth to the mid-seventeenth centuries. (It was revived in the second half of the nineteenth century.) Inspired by the folds in the fabric wall hangings used in medieval and Renaissance interiors, the carving was often extended to adjacent wall paneling, as on this reproduction oak-paneled door and full-height wainscoting. As here, the linenfold patterns in the top panel of the door and wainscoting could be offset with other carved motifs and imagery, usually of organic origin.

3 While battened-plank doors retained their popularity in some rural areas, the six-paneled door, with the panels configured as here, became the standard choice in town and city houses, although two- and three-paneled versions (see 2) were also employed. The panels on this door are flat, and defined by simple mitered linear moldings; fielded panels became more common during the second half of the eighteenth century (see doors 4 and 6). A popular alternative to this flat-painted finish–applied over fir or pine–was wood-graining, notably simulations of expensive hardwoods such as mahogany or rosewood.

4 Bearing a painted faux-limed finish, this grand reproduction Georgian door has the same paneling configuration as door 3. In this case, however, the panels are raised and fielded, and are defined by more ornate linear moldings, carved as bands of stylized foliate motifs. Its prestigious surround is similarly ornamented with carved acanthus leaves, scrolling foliage, rosettes and, in the tympanum of its broken pediment, a shell motif. All of this decorative imagery is derived from the classical Greco-Roman vocabulary of ornament, and is typical of grander neoclassical interiors on both sides of the Atlantic during the second half of the eighteenth century.

5 Framed by a surround capped with a row of neoclassical rosettes set under a dentil molding, this pair of wall-cupboard doors are in Home House, London, designed ca. 1775 by Robert and James Adam. The lower section of each door has a raised and fielded panel; the larger upper section is fitted with a latticework metal grill, backed with pleated fabric. More expensive than glazing, latticework panels were also often fitted without the fabric to bookcase doors in the late eighteenth century.

6 Decorated with a red milk paint, this large, six-paneled door is in an Amish farmer's log house that was built in the mid-eighteenth century, and moved by its current owners from Lancaster County to Chester County, in Pennsylvania. The door's panels are raised and fielded; its latch is made of wrought iron.

7 This four-paneled, painted softwood door is hung in a restored, late-eighteenth-century Connecticut farmhouse. The panels are set flush with the frame, and their sides defined by simple moldings. The damaged lower panels have been reinforced with an extra bottom rail. The wrought-iron thumb-latch is of a type widely used in the late eighteenth and nineteenth centuries.

8 This pair of white and gilt doors are in a New York apartment, and were designed by the owner, Bernd Goeckler. The panels are made of applied moldings, and the applied motifs are derived from the neo-classical vocabulary of ornament. The winged figures in the lower panels, like the winged Pegasuses on the frieze above, are strongly associated with Empire style–the source of inspiration for the overall decorative scheme of the apartment.

59

1 Ionic columns frame this substantial pair of eight-paneled sliding doors at the Old Merchant's House, which was built in New York, in 1832, in the Greek Revival style (see pp. 22–3). Sliding doors were often hung in American Greek Revival town houses, usually to divide the principal reception rooms. These are made from flame-cut mahogany, and are known as "pocket doors" because they slide open into pockets or compartments recessed into the walls.

2 This four-paneled door is of a type commonly found in modest Victorian houses built during the second half of the nineteenth century. The stiles and rails that make up its framework are no more than 1-inch thick, and thus substantially thinner and lighter than the 3-inch framework of the sliding panel doors in 1. Consequently, the door's sound-proof qualities are far less impressive. Moreover, while sliding doors were constructed from expensive, solid mahogany, this door is made of much-cheaper deal (fir or pine), and has been wood-grained to simulate the color and attractive figuring of mahogany. Its door handle is a black china knob–again, a cheaper alternative to brass.

3 Framed by a pair of swagged portieres (door curtains), these Victorian double-doors have upper panels of "frosted" etched glass. Used to introduce more light into a room, while preserving privacy, such panels became popular in the late nineteenth century. The sophistication of the decorative motifs usually reflected the status of the household–these are particularly ornate, and are based on the stylized, interlaced foliage patterns known as arabesques, which originated in Islamic art.

4 Clear-glass door panels provided a less expensive alternative to "frosted" etched glass panels as in the doors in 3. To provide insulation and, when necessary, to shut out what the Victorians sometimes referred to as "borrowed" light, a fabric portiere was usually draped from a rod or wire fixed to the top of the door. This painted and glazed, seven-paneled door is made of softwood, and is in a mid-nineteenth-century French château. Its lower wooden panel is typically picked out in a paler shade of the gray-blue color applied to the frame and the glazing bars. The check-pattern portiere is original, and made from a cotton Carreaux du Perigord fabric.

5 *These stained and polished mahogany double-doors are in a substantial French Renaissance Revival mansion built on Rhode Island, in the late nineteenth century. Each door has five panels: plain rectilinear at the top and bottom, and three cartouche panels in between. Cartouches were widely used in Renaissance ornament, and can have concave, convex, or flat centers– either decorated with motifs or, as here, plain. (The push plates and lever handles are brass– the former stamped with a Renaissance-style tracery pattern.)*

6 *These double-doors are made of oak, and hung in an American "Tudor-style" mansion, built in Forest Hills, New York, in the late nineteenth century. Six panels are carved with a stylized, linenfold pattern, relieved with diamond motifs, while two are carved with portraits of English royalty.*

7 *Leaded, stained-glass door panels were very fashionable in the late nineteenth and early twentieth centuries, particularly in Arts and Crafts houses. These elaborate panels, set in an oak door and surround, incorporate arcading and a central roundel, and display colorful flora and fauna.*

5

6

7

PAINTED PINE

From the late Renaissance to the end of the Edwardian era, most doors made from pine–such as this late-eighteenth-century English kitchen door–were painted or wood-grained. This was because the figuring and grain of pine were usually considered too bland for the semitranslucent, stained and polished finishes favored for the more decorative hardwoods such as oak and mahogany. However, during the late twentieth century, it became fashionable to strip off the paint, and replace it with a clear wax or varnish. Decoration has always been subject to the vagaries of fashion, but such treatments do almost inevitably compromise period authenticity.

DOOR SURROUNDS

Most internal door surrounds are made of either hardwoods or softwoods–the latter usually painted. However, stone has also been used, mainly in grander houses, prior to the eighteenth and during the late nineteenth and early twentieth centuries, as has plaster–the latter generally restricted to entablatures or pediments in neoclassical and Classical Revival houses. The form and decoration of surrounds have been largely determined by changing fashions in architecture and ornament. For example, flat-headed surrounds have been consistently employed since the Middle Ages, while pointed-arch Gothic surrounds (either four-centered or ogee) were also popular in medieval, "Gothick," and Gothic Revival houses, and curved Roman-arch surrounds were often installed in Renaissance, Baroque, and Roman Revival Federal homes. Similarly, the jambs (the sides) of the surrounds have been chamfered, especially if they are stone; molded to various profiles, mostly derived from classical architecture; and carved or painted (and sometimes gilded) with motifs from the Gothic, classical, or Oriental vocabularies of ornament. In terms of visual impact and prestige, the most impressive surrounds–confined to the finest houses–have been topped with classical pediments (broken and unbroken), or with classical entablatures supported on consoles, columns, or pilasters, and encompassing friezes bearing carved, molded, painted, or gilded imagery.

1 *Stone door surrounds were in widespread use during the Middle Ages and early Renaissance. This example, framing a plank door, is at Frog Pool Farm, in Avon, England, which dates to the fifteenth century. It has chamfered jambs and a four-centered arch.*

2 *These reproduction, late-fifteenth and early-sixteenth-century door surrounds have four-centered arch inserts spanning the tops of their jambs. Like many internal door surrounds of this period, they are made of oak.*

3 *In 1912, the Edwardian library at Temple Newsam, in Leeds, England, was converted into a replica early-Georgian library. Like the room's other architectural moldings, those of the door surround are elaborately carved, and highlighted with gilding. Notable elements include the scrolled, acanthus-leaf consoles, and a frieze of scrolling foliage flanking an urn.*

4 *This painted, built-in cupboard is in Mount Pleasant, Philadelphia, and dates to 1761–2. Its arched door surround breaks into an acanthus-carved key stone– the latter invariably used to support, within the broken pediment, a classical bust, urn or, as here, a vase.*

5 This late-Georgian paneled door and surround are in Home House, London, England, designed ca. 1775 by Robert and James Adam. The painted wooden architrave that frames the door opening is in the form of simple, rectilinear moldings. Characteristically, the entablature above is more elaborately ornamented, with strings of husks swagged-and-tailed from ribbons, and a plaque depicting nymphs at play.

6 Located in Richard Jenrette's early-nineteenth-century American Empire-style house on the Hudson River, in New York State, this door surround displays the essential symmetry and proportion of neo-classical architectural fixtures and fittings. Mounted on marble blocks, and joined by corner blocks bearing gilded floral motifs, the rectilinear architrave moldings have the look of a classical temple-front opening.

7 The double-doors between the parlor and dining room of the Belle of the Bends Inn, in Vicksburg, Mississippi, are hung in a painted wooden, elliptical-arched surround–the latter typical of grander American Victorian houses designed in the Italianate style.

5

6

9

7

8

8 During the second half of the nineteenth century, it was fashionable in houses that were designed and decorated under the aegis of the Esthetic and Arts and Crafts movements to ebonize (stain and black lacquer) wood-work. This ebonized paneled door and surround is in Leighton House, built in the 1860s in Kensington, London. The carved plant-form motifs are typical Esthetic details.

9 This late-Victorian five-paneled door and surround are made of pine and wood-grained with a faux-walnut finish. The basic surround is made up of a bulbous, pilasterlike, rectilinear molding, which is stop-chamfered on either side of the bottom of the door. The arched pediment on top of the surround is inset with an elaborately carved shell motif which provides, in turn, the backdrop to an aegricane (a ram's skull).

DOOR HARDWARE

The basic categories of internal door hardware are hinges: locks and latches; knobs and handles; push plates; and keyhole escutcheons (*see* right). Before the seventeenth century, all hinges were surface-mounted, and fashioned as either long straps (simply tapered, or terminated in decorative shapes, such as arrowheads, hearts, or stylized flowers), or as smaller H, L, cock's-head, or butterfly forms. These were superseded on paneled doors by less decorative, "concealed" iron, brass, or steel hinges, which were cut into the side of the door. Until the early nineteenth century, doors were secured with wooden or iron latches or, in grander houses, expensive, surface-mounted box locks made of wood, iron, or brass–the latter largely confined to the late-seventeenth and eighteenth centuries, and often engraved with decorative motifs. While latches continued to be used in some vernacular houses, box locks were gradually replaced on paneled doors by cut-in mortise locks, which were usually faced with decorative push plates housing the lever handles or door knobs. Favored materials for the plates, handles, and knobs included wood, iron, brass, china and, in affluent households, even silver or gold. As with box locks, the plates and knobs often bore geometric patterns or decorative imagery.

1 The large strap hinge is made of wrought iron, and is of a type used to hang battened-plank doors since the Middle Ages. The strap is fixed to the face of the door, and pivots on a plate screwed or nailed to the door frame. Some strap hinges pivoted on a pintle (hook) sunk into the frame. The wrought-iron, H-shaped hinge above it came into widespread use during the seventeenth century. Popular variations included the butterfly and S-shaped cock's-head hinges.

2 This wrought-iron thumb-latch, which is on a late-American Colonial framed-plank door, were used from the Middle Ages to the early twentieth century. It is locked from the inside with a wooden wedge. The iron hook above secures the opened door to a wall or post.

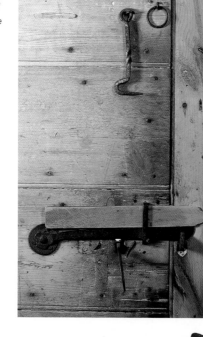

1

2

3 This combination thumb-latch and door handle is also late-American Colonial, and fitted to a door in Hunter House, on Rhode Island. While the profile of the thumb-shaped lever, which operates the latch on the reverse of the door, has remained largely unaltered over the centuries, the handle and push plate have been subject to many variations of shape and decorative detail.

3

4

4 Rim locks were luxury items prior to the eighteenth century, but came into common use after that. The example at the top is made of wood, and fitted to the front door of the Red House, built in 1859 near London, for William Morris, the leading exponent of the Arts and Crafts movement. The middle lock is on a paneled American Colonial door; it is made of brass, but painted black to simulate cast iron. The example at the bottom is polished brass, and dates to the late eighteenth century.

5 Both of these door pulls are made of brass. The top one is modeled in the Gothic Revival style; the shape of the bottom one is primarily based on classical forms. Pulls such as these are traditionally used on both room and cupboard doors.

5

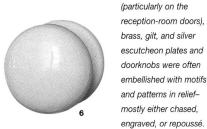

6 *These three door-knobs are made of, in descending order, polished brass, transfer-printed white china, and white china. Round doorknobs first became fashionable in the seventeenth century, and were very popular in the late eighteenth and nineteenth centuries.*

7 *In the finest houses, (particularly on the reception-room doors), brass, gilt, and silver escutcheon plates and doorknobs were often embellished with motifs and patterns in relief–mostly either chased, engraved, or repoussé. This American repro-duction knob and plate display a highly intricate Renaissance Revival pattern of stylized foliage motifs.*

Before the Victorian era, they were usually made of brass, but also gilt or silver in grander houses, and could be either plain or engraved (see 7). China knobs–porcelain or glazed earthenware, and mostly white, black or, as here, patterned– were much in favor during the Victorian era.

8 *Brass lever handles first became widely fashionable in the neoclassical interiors of the early nineteenth century, although there-after never proved quite as popular as round or oval doorknobs. As these three polished brass examples illustrate, differences of style center on the profile of the handle, and on the*

shape and decoration of the push plate. In contrast to the plain, rectangular example on the right, the one in the center, like the one on the left, is arched at either end. The perimeter of the latter is ornamented with bead molding, which was a popular definitional device derived from classical architecture.

9 *Separate push plates were fashionable from the late eighteenth century onward. The Victorian blue china plate has ogee-arch-style ends and black banding around its perimeters. The perimeter of both the Georgian brass plates are defined with rope molding.*

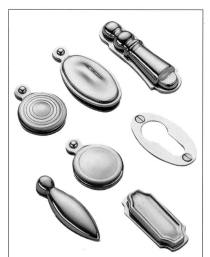

KEYHOLES

Small metal escutcheons, designed to protect the door surface around the rim of a keyhole, became widespread during the early nineteenth century. Used with the newly developed mortise locks which, unlike surface-mounted rim locks, were cut into the door, they were mostly made of brass, although gold, silver, and china were also employed. Produced in a wide variety of shapes– including round, oval, cartouche, and teardrop–many were fitted with pivoting covers, which were intended to protect the keyhole from accumulations of dust.

10 *This brass door hard-ware is late nineteenth century. The knob and keyhole escutcheon display raised relief patterns; the push plates show pierced fretwork vases and foliage.*

WINDOWS

The orchestration of window architecture affects not only the esthetic aspect and technical structure of the exterior, but also the interior proportions and the way light affects them. Mullioned and transomed windows–those with upright posts and horizontal bars–were common by the late sixteenth century, as was diagonal leaded glazing. The monastic trefoiled and four-centered arched windows of the early-Tudor window (*see* left) were superseded from the seventeenth century by square heads and panes. Later, casement windows were fitted within these with a variety of glazing patterns. Mullions and transoms were reduced in number and size as window proportions became taller and narrower. The first uncorded sash windows of the mid-seventeenth century had a fixed top half and sliding bottom half, but by 1700, sashes were counterweighted, allowing larger areas of glass to be moved vertically.

After 1709, windows were set back four inches from the wall face, and thereafter the reveals were often plastered and painted white. However, vernacular buildings retained casement windows and leaded panes for much longer. The Baroque period saw great sophistication in window design, and window surrounds included such features as decorative scrollwork or rustication, key stones, pedimentation, and curved window heads.

Pattern books affected the evolution of Georgian buildings and ensured structural integrity. The Venetian window is characteristic, with its arched section between two narrower side windows, adapted to suit classical fashion. Exterior embellishment included classical window pediments supported by console brackets or pilasters, cut brickwork, and stonework lintels. In America, these devices were heavier and more elaborate. Dormer windows were also popular, especially in America, where they carried the fenestration pattern into the deep-hipped roof line. Glazing variations included ornamental lattice or stained glass, and the arrangement of six-over-six panes. In Britain, the old, thick, hardwood glazing bars became more refined in softwood, and were always protected by white lead paint.

After 1774, frames were rebated within the wall face to meet the British fire-safety regulations, and Coade stone or rusticated surrounds on the first floor restored visual weight to hidden frames. Below the attenuated window line of the *piano nobile* the string course formed a unifying running sill and, by the 1780s, French doors gave onto balconies. Round-headed, Gothic, Venetian (sometimes with spider's-web tracery or squared with a pedimented heading) and, by mid-century, bay windows, were popular. By 1780, some windows were painted a darker color, usually gray, particularly with white stucco facades, but by 1800, brown paint was also fashionable.

The classical, mannered style of the 1800s loosened as the nineteenth century progressed. The Regency period is typified by tall, narrow French windows and delicate ironwork balconies and verandas. Windows had narrow margin lights, sometimes paned with colored glass, arched windows enlivened with Gothic tracery, and sophisticated bow windows. American style ca. 1800–50 is typified by attenuated moldings, Greek Revival surrounds, semicircular and oval windows on the upper stories, and Queen Anne or Empire-style dormers enhancing the roof line.

Glass was cheaper after 1850, and sash windows became plainer and had more glass, counterbalanced by decorative brickwork, stucco, and terra cotta decoration. Gothic, Queen Anne, Italianate styles, and stained and leaded glass had a following in Britain and America. Late-nineteenth-century windows favored small, square panes in the upper sash and plain glass below, or vernacular casements with leaded glass. Colored glass was extensively used in both countries.

Edwardian facades had more window space than Victorian, and bow and bay were popular. Multiple "Queen Anne" glazing divisions were often used in the top section only, and stained glass screened secondary windows. American turn-of-the-century style was more flamboyant, with Colonial Revival six-over-six paned tall windows, Italian Renaissance-style aedicules or pedimented heads, French classical arched or carved surrounds, and Spanish Revival ornamental iron grilles.

CASEMENT WINDOWS

Glass was so precious in the mid-fifteenth century that casement windows were considered separate pieces of furniture and not part of the house structure. They were commonly fitted into existing mullion openings of notable houses from the mid-fifteenth century, but they were not used in country dwellings until the second half of the eighteenth century. Stone houses had iron casements and timber houses had wooden ones. In urban areas theses initially opened inward to avoid the elements buffeting the fragile glass and because of the proximity of passing traffic. Casements again became fashionable in Arts and Crafts and Edwardian Tudor Revival houses, when they were inserted into the prepared brick or stone openings or wooden sub-frame, and embellished with decorative colored-glass transfers or stained-glass panes.

1 This is a mid-sixteenth-century eight-light window with typical four-centered headings. Casements were often inserted into older mullion and transom windows, but the size of the panes indicates that the glazing is seventeenth century.

2 This early-twentieth-century stone-dressed Tudor-style window also has four-centered arches and a stone mullion and transom, but it is glazed with plate glass, as the Edwardians preferred to have as much natural light as possible.

3 In this eighteenth-century château, the verticality of these narrow casement windows is accentuated by being divided into four separate panes. The panes are simply glazed and the frame is painted softwood.

4 Very small windows were generally found in rustic dwellings because glass was unavailable until well into the eighteenth century. Shutters, waxed paper, oilcloth, or skins were used to keep out the elements.

5 French windows, beloved in England from the 1780s, are seen here in their place of origin–a ca. 1765 Normandy château, which shows the exquisite attenuated lines of the window and architrave.

6 Bay windows had several periods of being in vogue, from medieval times to the mid-eighteenth century, and from the Regency to the Edwardian periods. Here, the metal casement windows and large area of glass indicate the latter.

7 This distinctive Gothic Revival window of the mid-nineteenth century has a typically ogee-shaped top and fragments of sixteenth- and seventeenth-century stained glass set in the heading.

8 Such a dominating element as this glorious Victorian stained-glass casement window should always influence the interior style. Here, the bathroom fittings are very well-suited to their style.

9 There were numerous movements during the nineteenth century inspired by rural life-styles. This lodge at Blue Mountain Lake, in New York State, has beautifully crafted wooden leading to hold the glass quarries.

10 In this Tudorbethan house, the casement windows have leaded lights that are arranged in a rectangular pattern, which is appropriate to the period and the vernacular tradition.

SASH WINDOWS

By the end of the seventeenth century, better glass-making techniques allowed larger quantities of glass to be used and, as a consequence, a completely new window composition was required. Probably introduced to Britain from France or Holland in about 1640, the first sash windows were kept open by means of pegs that were inserted into notches in the bottom frame's grooves, but from 1700 weighted sashes radically changed the face of architecture. The British fire-safety regulations stipulated that the wooden frames be recessed from the wall face, and this gave a lighter architectural profile while at the same time accommodating the weighted sash mechanism within the window jamb. These developments resulted in the ability to raise greater areas of glass and create a more elegant frame with increasingly narrow glazing bars. Endless permutations of glazing formations followed until, by mid-eighteenth century, the twelve-pane sash became standard in the majority of buildings. The next two-and-a-half centuries saw designers exploring the esthetic possibilities of the sash window in all its endless variety, as evidenced here.

1

1 These beautifully proportioned mid-eighteenth-century sash windows are in a Connecticut farmhouse, where they are complemented by simple but generous curtains. The number of panes, the size of glazing bars, and the placement of the pair of windows are indicative of the period.

2 Perhaps more than any other element, the tripartite Venetian window, adapted to suit the fashionable classical idiom, most clearly identifies the early-Georgian period. The window was employed to draw focus to the facade's center and, from the 1730s, the design was freely interpreted both in Britain and America.

4

3 Here, an imaginatively designed American "bay" window, dating from the second half of the eighteenth century, not only provides a window seat, but also lets in as much natural light as possible.

4 The six-over-six panes and louvered shutters of the ca. 1800 Gaillard-Bennett House, in Charleston, South Carolina, put it ahead of fashion. The green and cream paints are historically accurate.

2

3

5 In the windows of this ca. 1720 house in Spitalfields, London, there is the usual arrangement of panes and double shutters. The paneled room is painted a deep dusty red which, with the other dull, muted colors, is in keeping with the period.

6 Well-balanced window proportions and a corner position favor this elaborate American Empire-style interior treatment and luxurious fringed pelmet.

7 This mid-nineteenth-century Shaker house reveals the uncluttered symmetry, soothing colors, and unadorned furnishings that epitomize the Shaker ideology. The window is similarly plain and unembellished, and without any curtains or other types of covering.

8 The Victorians favored the double-story bay with two narrow windows set on either side of the larger one. However, they draped the interior heavily, thereby keeping out the natural light.

5 6 7

9 This mid-Victorian double-story bay arrangement, which is very much of its period, has a mixture of types of brick banding across the upper story, stucco piers, and a broad lower sill for holding a window box.

10 Here, a reproduction oriel window is used in an early-twentieth-century house of idiosyncratic design. It has a paneled base and blind covers and lead half-bell canopy, and permits a broad sweep of the fine views of the surrounding area.

8 9 10

WINDOW SURROUNDS

There were numerous exterior and interior treatments that influenced the look of a window's environment, both exterior and interior. Historically, this consideration was of great importance as it affected many aspects of design. For example, thought was given to the pediment detailing that was considered best-suited to the building's classical references—correct geometry was intrinsic to an eighteenth-century architect's rule book. Certainly, the choices were determined by the availability of materials, the skill and imagination of the craftsmen, and the vernacular architecture of the locality (it should be remembered that the fashion of the city was not the national standard). On another level, the designer's esthetic decorative quest could be satisfied when attention was given to the minute detail within the broader plan. Thus the type of questions that would have been addressed were as follows: Should marble or stone be used for a heading key stone? Which would be more pleasing and appropriate for a surround—quartered columns or pilasters? And should a mahogany cornice or material pelmet be employed for the window's embellishment? Robert and James Adam, the mid-eighteenth-century designers, excelled at marrying their dignified classical-exterior ensemble with interior decoration of exquisite refinement and, of course, the windows were of utmost importance, being the gateway between the two.

2

1 The interior view of the window surrounds at Wenlocke Abbey, in England, reveals a monastically austere atmosphere that has not been dissipated by modern overdressing. The trefoil surrounds have a tiny casement window, sturdy oak shutters strengthened with metal cross-bracing, and heavy carved-stone window headings. The deep window reveals have room enough for integral carved stone side sills, which may have been used as book supports, thereby making the best use of space and the available natural light.

2 In the ca. 1775 Home House, in London, Robert Adam used neoclassical style to provide the complete architectural vocabulary to richly decorate this room. The treatment of the window surround integrates the grand "hardness" of the architecture with the "soft" opulence of the green, gold, and black ornamentation.

3 The faux stone walls, the marble baseboard, and the classical artifacts and window surround re-create the American Empire style of Edgewater, in New York, ca. 1854.

1

3

4 The Nathaniel Russell House in Charleston, South Carolina, dates to 1808, and this window arrangement embodies several typical elements of the period. The long sash window is placed in a shallow arched recess capped by a key stone that is paired with the lintel design. The delicate balcony and a line of stone stringing provide a strong visual link between the windows, unifying the overall architectural geometry.

5 Reproduction mahogany brass-mounted cornices, with corded pennant valances of striped crimson moiré silk, give these floor-to-ceiling windows a balanced proportion and a period feel. Their corner position prohibits the use of curtains, which would, in any case, hide the architectural symmetry of the window surround.

6 This example illustrates a Victorian Gothic theme within a genuine medieval building. The window initiated the collection of numerous modern and antique pieces that do credit to the house's origins. Plain, mellow stonework makes a fine backdrop for artifacts, whether they are metal, wood, or richly colored materials.

PELMETS

Pelmets have been in and out of fashion since they first appeared in the sixteenth century in France. Pelmets and window cornices played a part in defining the proportions of a window, and giving decorative emphasis to the blank area of a room between the window and the ceiling. Careful choice of material, color, style, and embellishment will help to enhance the period feel of the room.

4

5

7 Grange, a late-nineteenth-century house in Philadelphia, Pennsylvania, has a charmingly ornate exterior. The carved Gothic tracery of the window pediment draws the eye toward a tiny circular window and "gingerbread" vergeboard beneath the eaves.

8 This American Italianate bay window in a house in Los Angeles is also late nineteenth century, and shows great complexity and craftsmanship in its quest to make a flamboyant statement.

6

7

8

SHUTTERS

Before glass was in widespread use, window openings were often covered in wood, waxed paper, oilcloth, or skins, and then sometimes in a primitive wooden shutter. Shutters were often needed both inside and out to eliminate light and drafts, protect privacy, and repel burglars. From 1620 they were fitted in pairs, each side having two hinged leaves. Esthetically, shutters could be used to play with the effect of light, and to protect precious furnishing materials from fading. Grand houses with sliding sash windows generally had shutters. Each pair was divided into two or three tiers, and closed vertically to fold away in the window embrasure which was either at right angles to the window or, increasingly in the Georgian era, splayed back in order to maximize light. Their paneling matched that of other woodwork, but toward the end of the seventeenth century, shutters began to be decorated en suite with the room, or painted in a darker color. Victorian softwood shutters, like those of the Georgian period, were always painted, while Arts and Crafts shutters and areas of other woodwork were mainly left unpainted.

1 Even a very basic shutter adds to the theatricality of this medieval interior. A similar shutter could quite easily be made from old floorboards or part of a door.

2 The windows' structure and the surrounding architecture indicate that curtains were never envisaged in this Empire-style New York apartment. The window opening is elegantly served by slender paneled shutters.

3 The architecture of the wall face is continued with these eighteenth-century shutters. The window rests comfortably on top of the dado, its outline continued to the floor, and the whole ensemble is united by period-gray paint.

4 The finely louvered shutters in the early-nineteenth-century Nathaniel Russell House, in Charleston, South Carolina, are multi-hinged and arranged in several tiers in order to manage the flow of air, heat, humidity, and light.

5 On the garden door of John Keats's house, in Hampstead, London, built ca. 1820, the shutters are set in shallow, splayed boxes, and the door retains its colored and acid-etched glass.

WINDOW HARDWARE

Seventeenth-century casement windows had several parts to their opening mechanism: the hinge, the wrought-iron handle for opening and closing, and the stay for holding the window open. In a domestic interior, decorative hardware allowed a noticeable element of status to the house and its occupants. The hardware, made by the local blacksmith, was beautifully crafted and came in a great variety, including cock's-head and zoomorphic-shaped designs. Some examples were highly sophisticated: they could twist, have a spring mechanism, or function as a simple latch. Brass was very expensive, and therefore it was the most desirable to the wealthy. Early sash windows, which were without counterweights, were very heavy and had wooden lifts until 1760, but weighted sashes, with more glass, required tougher brass or cast iron. As brass became cheaper, and decorations generally more ornate, the window hardware became more elaborate as well.

3 Apart from looking serviceable, there is a certain esthetic about the tangible chunkiness of this rustic window fastener, which is made of brass but has been painted over.

4 The first patent for a sash fastener–a barrel-type with a spring and screw– was registered in 1776 in Britain. This type (above) and the variation (below) reproduction brass examples are strong and very authentic looking.

5 The addition of a sash lift, which evenly distributes the upward draw, helps to protect the counterweight mechanism and paintwork. These reproduction Georgian examples are both made of brass.

1 Good reproduction casement hardware will be historically correct. For example, the wrought-iron fasteners and mortise plates (far left) are accurate for medieval and revival windows, while the brass catches and plates (left) are appropriate for the mid-1850s.

2 The top window stay is forged iron and is of a type used since the Renaissance, particularly in Jacobean Revival, Arts and Crafts, and vernacular houses. Brass superseded iron from the eighteenth century. The second stay is Georgian, and was used until the twentieth century; the third was employed from the late eighteenth to the early nineteenth centuries; the fourth is early twentieth century.

CURTAIN POLES

The fashion for hanging a curtain or curtains from a pole over a window or interior door has appeared in some form throughout the last five hundred years. The most frequently revived style is the Gothic, and today there is a great assortment of pole finials available reflecting that period's motifs. The one illustrated is a fleur-de-lis style made from cast resin. Today, curtain poles and finials are manufactured in a number of period styles and materials, including wood, brass, steel, and painted metal.

TAIRS

In terms of their constructional role, the basic components of a staircase have remained largely unaltered since the Middle Ages. Individual steps consist of an upper, horizontal surface known as a tread, the front edge (or nosing) of which rests on (and slightly overlaps) a vertical section, called a riser. On most staircases, the sides of a run or flight of steps are keyed into supporting diagonal members, known as strings, although on spiral staircases the narrow ends of the steps are keyed into a central newel post (*see* spiral stairs, right). The structure that runs up one, or both, side(s) of a flight of steps is known as a balustrade. This is made up of balusters, newel posts, and a handrail. Balusters are vertical posts that support the handrail and serve as a barrier to the open sides of the steps. If the bottom of the balusters are keyed into the strings, the staircase is referred to as closed-string; if they are keyed directly into the steps, and the latter are not enclosed by the string, the staircase is open-string. The balusters are flanked at each end of a flight of steps by a vertical newel post. Newels, which often bear decorative finials and, sometimes on floors above first-floor level, pendants, are much larger than balusters. They support the ends of the strings and the handrail(s), and are keyed into the floor or the landing–the latter being either a platform between flights of steps, or the floor at the top of the stairs.

The materials used to make these components include stone, metal (especially wrought and cast iron, but also steel) and, most commonly, wood. Apart from basic structural requirements–notably, the need to bear given loads under compression or tension–their form and decoration (carved or molded) has been determined by prevailing fashions. For example, vase- or columnar-shaped balusters are mostly found on staircases where the architecture of the house is influenced by Greco-Roman classicism, while newel posts capped with chamfered pinnacles are confined to Gothic or Gothic Revival staircases (*see* pp. 8–33 for the predominant historical styles of architecture and ornament).

Over and above variations in the shape and decoration of their component parts, staircases are divided into a number of basic categories or types. Straight flights, as the name implies, provide a direct, diagonal link between floors. Doglegs provide the connection via two straight flights, which run parallel in opposite directions to one another, have no space (or well) between their outer strings, and are joined, between floors, by an intermediate landing. A variation on the dogleg is the open-well, which has a wider landing and a space between the outer strings of the flights. Turning stairs link floors with a single flight of steps, but instead of the flight being straight, it is angled or turned at one or more points along its rise or descent. The angle of turn varies, but quarter-turns, half-turns, and three-quarter turns are most common. Spiral or newel staircases connect two or more floors and consist of angled steps wound around a large central newel post. A variation of the spiral is the framed newel, in which the inner edges of the steps are keyed into a timber-framed tower, rather than a solid, central newel, and the outer edges into the surrounding brick or stone walls of the stairwell. The final basic category consists of cantilevered (or "flying") stairs, in which only the outer edges of a flight of steps are keyed into and cantilevered from a straight or curved side wall–the inner edges having no visible means of support.

Other, less commonly employed types of staircase worthy of note include bifurcated, in which a single flight divides at a landing into two flights to the floor above, and a double-return, where a single flight joins a floor above, but divides and returns to the original floor in two flights. Both of these tend to be used as grand staircases in large houses. Also used, mainly prior to the nineteenth century, as the principal staircase in smaller houses, and secondary stairs in grander ones, were box-winders. Turning between floors, they were concealed within a narrow stairwell which, especially in American Colonial houses, was often sited next to a chimney flue, and accessed by a door in the fireplace wall.

STAIRCASE STYLES

Many types of staircase have been employed during the various historical periods from the Middle Ages to the end of the First World War. However, because most staircases (especially the main ones, rather than the secondary staircases that were primarily installed for the servants) have been conceived of as a domestic showpiece, reflecting the status of the house and the homeowner, the style of their construction and ornamentation has almost invariably followed prevailing fashions in architecture and ornament. For example, Gothic shapes and motifs dominate medieval staircases, and are combined with classical equivalents on Renaissance stairs. Similarly, classical forms and imagery dominate Baroque and neoclassical staircases–exaggerated and heavily sculpted in the former and more refined, symmetrical, and historically accurate in the latter. Victorian stairs can be characterized by the numerous reproductions and pastiches of almost all of the preceding period styles (*see* pp. 8–33) revived under the banner of "eclecticism."

1 Made of oak, this reproduction, framed-newel, closed-string staircase is of a type originally found in grander early- to mid-sixteenth century houses. It has carved and pierced flat balusters, their curvaceous shape inspired by strapwork. They were especially favored in English Jacobean houses, although turned columnar shapes were also popular. The square-section newel posts, topped with urn-shape finials, are quite plain for the period–more decorative examples were carved with motifs and imagery.

2 Dated to 1738–42, and installed at Drayton Hall, Charleston, South Carolina, this was probably the most elaborate staircase in the American Colonies at this period. Made of mahogany, open-string, and with three turned balusters to each tread, it has two double-dogleg flights, and is based on English Palladian models.

3 Built 1764–7 at Cliveden, in Philadelphia, Pennsylvania, this open-string American Colonial staircase is a very refined classical composition. Its turned balusters are elegantly attenuated, and the sawn tread ends display wavescroll profiles.

4 Like 3, this eighteenth-century American Colonial, open-string staircase is made of softwood, and painted in a Colonial color. The fielded side paneling, and plain, square-section newel posts and balusters–two of the latter to each tread–are typical of rural Colonial houses.

5 This painted "Gothick" staircase at Strawberry Hill, Twickenham, England, dates to ca. 1754. Closed-string, and with a balustrade of carved tracery, and caged, carved birds and animals on the newels, it is based on seventeenth-century models.

6 Cantilevered from the wall, this white-painted, open-string staircase is a reproduction of a mid- to late-eighteenth-century model. Its stained and polished mahogany handrails terminate in fashionable spiral forms on and around the classical, columnar-shaped newel posts. The fitted runners became common towards the end of the century.

7 The central stair-hall is typical of classically inspired, mid-eighteenth century American Colonial architecture. This example, at Hunter House, on Rhode Island (built ca. 1758) follows the characteristic pattern of a long hall, divided by a bracketed arch, and with an open-string staircase to the rear. A characteristic feature is the absence of a runner on the treads.

8 When the prestigious French decorator, Frédéric Méchiche, recently "transformed" his Parisian apartment, giving it the appearance of a late-eighteenth-century neoclassical, French Directoire-style town house, he installed a restored, original Louis XVI staircase. Closed-string and cantilevered, it has white-painted strings and risers, bare wooden treads, and an elegantly simple cast-iron balustrade–the latter painted black to be en suite with the striped upholstery.

1 Cantilevered into the wall of a stairwell, this curved staircase is an American reproduction of an early-nineteenth-century model. Made of stained and polished wood (with metal balusters), it is a good example of the flying staircases which became popular in many grander neoclassical houses during the late eighteenth and early nineteenth centuries. As with other examples, the main handrail, which is supported on balusters secured to the tread ends, rather than the tops of the treads, is supplemented with a secondary rail fixed to the stairwell wall. Also typical of the period is the central stair runner, which displays a pattern derived from the Oriental vocabulary of ornament.

2 & 3 Both of these cantilevered, winding staircases date to the first half of the nineteenth century, and are of a type much favored in larger American houses of the Federal period (see pp. 18–9). The example on the left rises from the ground floor to attic level at the Bartow-Pell Mansion, in New York, and dates to ca. 1842. Its tapering balusters are turned and reeded and, like the treads and handrail, are made of stained and polished mahogany. The equally fine example on the right is in Patrick Duncan House, Charleston, South Carolina, and dates to 1816. While it also features a mahogany handrail and treads, its thin balusters display the simpler and more delicate profile popular in early-nineteenth-century neoclassical interiors on both sides of the Atlantic.

4 This reproduction early-nineteenth-century English staircase is also curved, cantilevered, and open-string and, like staircase 3, has a balustrade of refined neoclassical simplicity. In contrast to staircase 1, its runner spans the full width of the treads, and is patterned with repeat floral motifs taken from the European, rather than the Oriental, vocabulary of ornament.

5 *Constructed ca. 1880, this majestic staircase rises from the center of a large stair-hall in an eighteenth-century English Georgian country house (with later and major Victorian modifications and additions). Quite often referred to as bifurcated–because its initial flight rises to a half-landing and then divides into two dogleg flights–it is made from stained and polished mahogany. The deep, shallow-rising treads, the closed-string balustrade, with robustly turned balusters, and the large urn, obelisk, and ball finials on the newel post, are typical mid-Victorian, as are the arched niches in the side paneling (which serve as bookshelves, and a storage closet).*

6 *In contrast to 6, this classic dogleg staircase is far more utilitarian in both its form and its decoration. Early-American Victorian, and sited in the hallway of a house in Galena, Illinois, it is open-string and has a simple, but elegant, balustrade, with a tapered newel post and balusters turned from walnut. The painted risers and the walnut treads are left bare, although in American houses of this period they could also be covered with a carpet or floor-cloth runner.*

CAST-IRON SPIRAL STAIRS

Spiral staircases–also known as newel, turngrece, vice, turnpike, winding, or cockle stairs–consist of a series of steps wound around a central pier or column (a newel). They have been used since the Middle Ages, but prior to the nineteenth century had to be enclosed, for supportive reasons, within a tower or a stairwell, so that the broad end of the steps could be keyed into a circumference wall–the narrow ends being keyed into the newel. However, by making the newel from inter-locking sections of heavy cast iron (rather than stone or wood), and by integrating a cast-iron step with each section, the Victorians were able to mass-produce free-standing spiral staircases. This example has been installed between two floors of a converted malt house, near Bath, England.

7 *Designed for the Red House (built 1859), in Bexleyheath, near London, England, by the architect Philip Webb (working with the house's owner, William Morris), this framed newel staircase is based on late-sixteenth- and early-seventeenth-century models. Like many staircases in Arts and Crafts houses, it is made of oak. Also typically Arts and Crafts are the solid balustrade, consisting of vertical, butt-jointed planks, and the faceted, medieval Gothic-style pinnacles on the newel post.*

STAIRCASE COMPONENTS

Before the widespread adoption during the nineteenth century of semi-automated cutting, carving, and routing machines, and of techniques for casting iron, staircase components were fashioned–mostly from stone, wood, and iron–by hand. This skilled, labor-intensive, and relatively expensive process meant that sophisticated decorative embellishments of items such as tread ends, balusters, newel posts, finials, and handrails were confined to wealthier households. There were a few exceptions. For example, in some quite humble houses, wooden newel posts might be elaborately turned and carved. Generally, however, it was only after the Victorians developed the techniques for mass-producing staircase components that costs were reduced and ordinary householders gained access to the wide and diverse range of ornamentation applied since the Middle Ages. However, what this development didn't change was the premium placed on skilled craftsmanship and design ingenuity, and the enduring status and cost of raw materials such as intricately veined marbles and finely figured hardwoods, over more abundant, cheaper, and less prestigious alternatives, such as softwood firs and pines.

1 The balustrade of this reproduction Jacobean, framed-newel staircase has been given the appearance of Gothic arcading by linking the tops of the chamfered balusters with pierced and carved, double-arch inserts. The square-section newel post– popular during the sixteenth and early seventeenth centuries– is topped with an urn-shaped finial, but ball, obelisk, and pyramidal shapes, of varying complexity, were also fashionable at this time.

2 The turned sections of the balusters on this early-eighteenth-century, open-string English staircase display the spiral-twist pattern that was much in vogue during this period. Also typical is the use of two balusters per tread; by the mid-eighteenth century, this was often increased to three per tread. The undulating profile and the carved details of the tread ends–like the expensive spiral-twist turnings, and thick mahogany handrail–are indicative of a fairly wealthy household. The columnar newel post reveals the strong influence of classical architectural forms in the modeling of many eighteenth-century staircase components.

3 The complexity of handrail and stair-end moldings reflected both the status of the house and the position of the staircase. The finely carved and pierced scrolling plant-form motifs on this mid-eighteenth-century American Colonial mahogany staircase are particularly elaborate.

4 The newel post and balustrade on this mid-Victorian staircase are made of cast iron. Their detailed and lavish ornamentation consists of forms and motifs primarily derived from the classical vocabulary of ornament, and includes rows of rosettes, rows of husks, bead molding, and scrolling foliate forms.

2

3

4

5 Fretwork decoration on this imposing mid-Victorian paneled balustrade is in the form of quatrefoils and, above and below, stylized floral motifs, derived from the Gothic vocabulary of ornament. The diagonal string beneath the intricately carved handrail displays a row of carved rosettes.

6 This superbly carved balustrade is in a François Premier-style house in New York (built 1899). Its dolphins and urn-shaped balusters, like the acanthus-leaf carving on the newel post, were inspired by Renaissance prototypes.

7 Substantial newel posts, exuberantly carved with floral, fruit, and foliate forms, and invariably topped with elaborate finials, are highly characteristic of Baroque staircases. This particularly splendid example is at Moulton Hall, in Yorkshire, England, and dates to ca. 1654–60.

8 Mounted on a carved, cube-shaped plinth, this American newel post is turned as a pair of vases, and carved with acanthus-leaf motifs. Made of stained and polished oak, it dates to the 1830s, and was almost certainly inspired by a seventeenth-century newel carved from stone.

9 Dated to the 1880s, this impressive, square-sectioned newel post is molded and carved from mahogany. Square, columnar-shaped newels were particularly fashionable during the late-Victorian era.

10 Turned and faceted wooden newel posts, modeled on medieval Gothic prototypes, were often employed in Victorian Arts and Crafts houses. This example has a faceted pinnacle, which is very typical of the style. However, some newels in the grandest of late-nineteenth-century Arts and Crafts houses were capped with electric lights.

5

6

7

8

9

10

1 Designed by the English architect George Aitchison in 1879–81, the principal staircase at Leighton House, in London, has stone treads and risers, which are keyed into a wood-paneled brick wall. Largely due to the costs of quarrying, transporting, and carving the raw material, stone steps were invariably much more expensive than wooden equivalents, and thus tended to be reserved for grander houses. The Oriental runner on the stairs is nineteenth century, but displays a re-creation of a "Tree of Life" pattern often found on rugs and carpets in the seventeenth century.

2 Like the balustrade, the treads of this open-string, cantilevered staircase in Richard Jenrette's American Empire-style house on the Hudson River, in New York State, are made of mahogany. Supported on painted softwood strings and risers, the centers of the treads are, as in many other imposing American Federal- and Empire-style houses, covered with a monochrome (dark green), woven-pile runner. This is secured to the risers with ornate, polished-brass stair rods, which feature wavescrolls–a favorite neoclassical motif of the late eighteenth and early nineteenth centuries.

4 Marble has retained its status since classical Greek and Roman times as one of the most prestigious building materials. Consequently, marble staircases have been almost exclusively confined to the grandest houses. This example, at The Elms, in Newport, Rhode Island, dates to 1895, and has steps and strings of contrasting-colored and figured marbles. The interlaced, stylized foliate forms of the wrought-iron balustrade are typical of American Beaux Arts mansions styled on classical French houses.

3 The knotted-pile central runner covering this reproduction, late-nineteenth-century wooden staircase is secured with plain, lacquered-brass stair rods. These slot into small clips screwed into the treads and the risers, and can be easily removed for cleaning. In order to protect the runner from excessive wear and tear, L-shaped brass strips have been screwed over the nosings of the treads. Although these metal strips were often applied over runners on grander staircases from the late-Victorian age onward, they were rarely used prior to this.

5 Like the balustrades and newel posts, the majority of treads and risers on late-nineteenth- and early-twentieth-century Arts and Crafts stairs were made of wood. The finest were polished hardwood (especially oak, as here), although in smaller houses, softwoods such as fir and pine were used, and were often painted. As with most other Arts and Crafts woodwork, the esthetic appeal of the steps resides in the quality of their construction, and the natural color, figuring, and grain of the oak (enhanced by polishing), rather than by any applied decorative detail.

6 The staircase, like the rest of the woodwork, furnishings and decorations, in this late-twentieth-century American house, is modeled on eighteenth-century prototypes found in the plank houses of Chester County, Pennsylvania. The simple, but well-executed, craftsmanship of the bare wooden treads, strings, and risers is echoed in the form and decoration of the chamfered newel post and molded handrail. These are painted with authentic Williamsburg green-blue milk paint to match the tongue-and-groove side paneling and window.

7 During the second half of the eighteenth and the early nineteenth centuries, it was fashionable to terminate handrails in a spiral– either a tight coil, as here, or a loose curve. The center of this reproduction mahogany handrail is inlaid with small cuts of mahogany that display contrasting figuring to that of the main body of the rail.

8 This cantilevered, winding stone staircase in an early-nineteenth-century American Empire house has painted, wrought-iron balusters with a matching handrail. Their very simple profiles indicate that this is a secondary, and not the main, staircase.

9 Wooden handrails have been made with a wide range of profiles, especially since the advent of automated cutting, carving, and routing machines in the nineteenth century. Most are copies, or adaptations, of moldings used in classical Greco-Roman architecture. Notable examples include torus, astragal, ovolo, scotia and, as here, bolection moldings.

10 This wall-mounted wooden handrail is part of a restored American staircase dated to 1889. Wall-mounted rails were rare prior to the late nineteenth century, and up until then mostly confined to the circumference walls of towers or stairwells surrounding spiral ("vice") stairs that wound around a central newel post. Thereafter, they were increasingly used as an additional safety feature, to supplement the main handrail on a balustrade.

11 The main staircase at Olana, built in New York in the 1870s, has a brass-pole handrail mounted on its wooden balustrade, and a matching brass finial on the newel post. While wrought- and cast-iron rails were in widespread use during the nineteenth century, brass ones were rarer, and mainly used in Esthetic and Arts and Crafts houses.

6
8
7
9
10
11

LOORS

Since the Middle Ages, the choice of flooring materials has been determined by a combination of geographic location, constructional restrictions, and degrees of affluence. For example, prior to the eighteenth century, inexpensive floors made of baked, dampened, and beaten earth (*see* pp. 92–3) were often employed in first-floor-level rooms by homeowners who couldn't afford, or didn't have access to, more durable and expensive tiles or stone. When tiles (*see* pp. 94–5) were laid, more costly, glazed, polychrome-patterned versions, as opposed to cheaper, unglazed monochrome types, were the preserve of wealthier households. Similarly, given the high cost of quarrying and then transporting heavy stone over long distances by boat or cart, superior stone flag floors–and particularly exotic, inlaid marble floors–were only used in ordinary houses in close proximity to local quarries, a restriction eventually eased in the nineteenth century by the development of extensive and efficient transportation systems (primarily the railways, but also better roads).

Wooden floors have been subject to similar constraints. The absence of properly ventilated spaces under the majority of houses built before the eighteenth century meant that any wooden floors laid in first-floor-level rooms were subject to damp and rot. Consequently, up to this period, they were confined in most houses to upper stories; thereafter, following the introduction of improved subfloor ventilation and damp-proofing, they vied with stone and tiles at first-floor level as a worthwhile flooring option. As with stone, the type of wood used was largely determined by availability and cost: durable hardwoods such as oak and elm were abundant before the late seventeenth century, and therefore in common use. However, as supplies dwindled, they were increasingly reserved for better houses, and generally supplanted by plentiful and cheaper softwoods such as pine and fir. In terms of how the wood were used for flooring, standard floorboards, whether hardwood or softwood (*see* pp. 88–9), have been the most prevalent, and intricate marquetry and parquetry hardwood block floors (*see* pp.90–1) the more exclusive.

While the styles of decoration applied to floors–particularly the patterns or motifs–have always closely reflected prevailing fashions in architecture and ornament at different historical periods (*see* pp. 8–33), the form they have taken was largely fueled, as before, by availability and cost. For example, stenciled or hand-painted motifs and patterns–especially popular in the United States from the late seventeenth to the end of the nineteenth centuries–were often applied to softwood floorboards either as an inexpensive simulation of costly or unavailable hardwood marquetry or parquetry floors, or of even more expensive stone or inlaid-marble floors.

Much the same principle has applied to different types of floor covering. For example, plain woven matting (*see* pp. 96–7) was in widespread use up to the late seventeenth century, primarily because during this period patterned woven carpets were either unavailable or unaffordable to all but the wealthiest house-holders. Even though flat-weave and woven-pile carpets, of Oriental or European manufacture, were increasingly employed in larger houses during the course of the eighteenth and early nineteenth centuries, they still remained well beyond the means of most people. Consequently, oil-stiffened canvas floorcloths, stenciled or hand-painted in imitation of fashionable carpet patterns (*see* pp. 96–7), were often used in ordinary houses–again, especially in the United States–as cheaper substitutes. Similarly, although the introduction of automated mass production during the second half of the nineteenth century helped to increase the supply and reduce the cost of woven carpets, less expensive alternatives were still required. The invention of linoleum (*see* pp. 96–7) in ca. 1860 largely fulfilled the demand. Made of solidified linseed oil, resin and gum, heat-bonded to a canvas or jute ground-cloth, linoleum was not only relatively cheap and very durable, but it was also made available in a tremendous range of finishes, including simulations of carpet patterns, woven matting, finely figured hardwood boards, marquetry and parquetry, as well as diverse tiled, stone-flag, and inlaid-marble floors.

FLOORBOARDS

Before the late seventeenth century, most floorboards were of irregular width–up to 14 inches–and cut from hardwood, notably oak or elm. Hardwood boards, of oak, teak, mahogany, maple, and cherry, enjoyed a revival during the Victorian and Edwardian eras. However, from the early eighteenth century, they were supplanted in most houses by softwood pine or fir boards, which became increasingly uniform in width, and gradually narrower–down to 4 inches–by the early nineteenth century. Most hardwood boards have been clear-waxed or varnished, while softwood boards have been either untreated (especially in the United States), or stained, flat-painted, stenciled, faux marbled, or wood-grained in imitation of hardwoods.

1 These butt-jointed and dark-stained pine boards are in an eighteenth-century London town house kitchen.

2 Oak or pine boards, unstained, unvarnished, and of random widths, are typical of American Colonial houses. These butt-jointed boards are in the "keeping room" of an eighteenth-century Rhode Island house. Home of Stephen P. Mack.

3 From the late seventeenth century onward, fir and pine boards (often imported from the Baltic) gradually replaced oak and elm boards in most English houses. As with these stained and varnished boards in a Georgian drawing room, they also became narrower and of a more regular width.

4 During the nineteenth century, pine and fir boards become narrower than in the eighteenth century, and now measured 7–9 inches. These varnished boards are in Lady Hertford's Regency-style bedroom at Temple Newsam, in Leeds, England.

5 Between 1780 and 1840, tongue-and-groove boards were commonly used in grander American Federal houses. Until the late eighteenth century, white pine was favored in New England; thereafter, there was a gradual switch to yellow pine, which had long been used along the Eastern seaboard and in the South. These yellow pine boards are in the Gaillard-Bennett House, built ca. 1800 in Charleston, South Carolina.

6 These plain pine boards, of regular width and irregular length, are typical of modest English Victorian houses.

7 While fir and pine boards gradually superseded oak boards in most English houses from the late seventeenth century onward, the latter remained popular in timber-framed houses that continued to be built in the vernacular tradition. These modern tongue-and-groove oak boards were installed in a restored cottage in Dorset, England.

8 Also made of oak, these wide-plank modern boards are cut to display the distinctive heart grain of the wood. Like many reproduction boards, they are finished with a clear matte sealant.

5   6   7

8   9

9 Primarily employed for their insecticidal properties, liming pastes and waxes were often applied to boards in Scandinavia and, to a lesser extent, in British and American rural houses up until the mid-nineteenth century. These limed boards are in the Hansmoen Farmhouse in Norway.

10 In many American Federal houses, pine boards in some rooms were often flat-painted and stenciled, rather than being covered with rugs or floorcloths. Diamond patterns made up of, as here, recurring leaf (or floral) motifs, were particularly popular

11 This more austere grid pattern is in an eighteenth-century English country house, and is hand-painted in an ox-blood red over pink-painted, butt-jointed wooden boards.

10   11

MARQUETRY AND PARQUETRY

Originating in Persia (now Iran), the technique of marquetry involves inlaying a base wood with contrasting-colored pieces of different woods, or materials such as ivory, bone, and various metals, to create decorative patterns. First adopted in Italy during the fourteenth century, it had become widespread in France by the seventeenth century, and thereafter was taken up throughout the rest of Europe and in America. As cutting the pieces was time-consuming and required a high level of skill (even after the introduction of automated cutting techniques in the nineteenth century), marquetry floors were very expensive, and therefore have invariably been confined to the grandest houses. They are primarily associated with late-Baroque, Regency, Victorian, and American Beaux Arts houses, with favored designs ranging from arabesques, to naturalistic floral patterns of Western origin, to geometric, organic, and pictorial imagery derived from the classical vocabulary of ornament. The technique of parquetry emerged in France during the seventeenth century, and involves arranging blocks of hardwood of different, or the same, species and colors of wood, to form geometric patterns. Cheaper than marquetry, parquetry flooring was used in Baroque, Regency, Victorian, Art Nouveau, Edwardian and Beaux Arts houses, either as a complete flooring or, from the Victorian era onward, as a border for a centrally placed carpet. Latticework patterns have been enduringly fashionable, as have cube, lozenge, diamond, star, octagon, and Greek key repeats, sometimes shaded to create trompe l'oeil, three-dimensional effects.

1 & 2 Parquetry floors, consisting of hardwood blocks laid in geometric patterns, were first employed in grander houses in France during the seventeenth century, and soon became popular in Britain, and later in the United States. Both of these eighteenth-century French floors are laid to a standard design, in which a large diamond-patterned grid, formed by long rectangular blocks, is infilled with repeated latticework patterns made up of smaller rectangular and square blocks.

3 Herringbone-pattern parquet floors such as this became particularly popular for the kitchens, hallways, and living rooms of suburban houses in the late nineteenth and early twentieth centuries. The best-quality versions were made up of 1-inch thick oak or teak blocks, and laid on a cement base covered with pitch. A cheaper alternative consisted of thinner blocks, ready-assembled in panels fixed to a cloth backing, and designed to be laid directly onto existing boards.

4 This close-up of some oak parquet reveals how the illusion of woven, three-dimensional latticework is created by alternating longer and shorter, butt-jointed rectangular blocks.

5 & 6 Some parquet floors feature wooden blocks of almost uniform pattern and color, and therefore rely for visual effect purely on the configuration of the blocks when they are laid down. However, many parquet floors also exploit the variations of figuring and grain of different woods, or in different cuts of the same wood, as in the American octagonal-pattern oak parquet in 5. Others utilize inherent color contrasts which, as in the English rectilinear-pattern oak parquet in 6, can also be artificially enhanced by selectively staining some of the blocks.

7, 8 & 9 Marquetry floors first appeared in the West during the Renaissance, and feature patterns and motifs created by inlaying contrasting-colored woods (or materials such as ivory or bone) into a more uniformly colored base wood. Floor 7 displays a neoclassical border of S-scrolls and anthemia composed of ash, mahogany, bubinga, and walnut. Neoclassical floor 8 has a rope and banding border, made of red oak, maple, and mahogany. The early-twentieth-century floral motif border in floor 9 is created with mahogany, maple, and American cherry.

5

6

7

8

9

10

10 Numerous and diverse geometrical and figurative patterns have been employed in marquetry floors. These range from figures and scenes from classical mythology, through stylized or naturalistic floral and foliate motifs, to "faceted" diamonds and stars. This classic interlaced, eight-pointed star motif is made of walnut, mahogany, red oak, and cherry.

EARTH, BRICK, AND STONE

The simplest type of first-floor-level flooring in general use from the Middle Ages until the end of the seventeenth century was beaten earth. These floors, sometimes enlivened with scratched designs or covered with straw, continued to be used in Georgian country cottages and the basements of poorer Georgian town houses, but thereafter were rarely employed. Throughout this period, floors made of bricks, laid on edge, were considered a better and more durable alternative to beaten earth; they were still laid in the cellars and service areas of many houses, on both sides of the Atlantic, well into the nineteenth century. Better still, and costlier, were stone floors. Most were laid as sandstone or limestone flags, although granite and slate–the latter usually cut to smaller, tile-size proportions–were also employed. Up until the eighteenth century, these stone floors were used in many first-floor-level rooms, but subsequently they were generally restricted to entrance halls, covered porches, and kitchens. The most prestigious and expensive, however, were stone floors made of marble. Employed in grander houses from the Renaissance onward, they could be laid either like other stone floors, in simple geometric patterns, or in more complex inlaid designs inspired by classical Roman prototypes, in which the contrasts of color and figuring inherent in different types of marble were exploited to enhance the basic symmetry of geometric patterns, and to enrich them with trompe l'oeil, three-dimensional, parquetrylike effects.

2 Brick floors were in common use on the first-floor level up until the eighteenth century, particularly in rural areas, and provided a cheaper alternative to stone flags. This floor is in an English farmhouse.

3 Stone tiles are mostly laid in traditional brick-work patterns, as with this eighteenth-century English floor. In addition to the mortar lines, patterns are often created by alternating different-colored stone tiles.

4 Although rare by the late eighteenth century, first- and basement-level floors made of stamped earth were often used in ordinary houses prior to that, and were less costly than brick or stone.

1 Large flagstones have been used on the first-floor level since the Middle Ages, but the high cost of transporting the stone over long distances meant that, with the exception of the most prestigious buildings, its use was restricted to areas where there was an abundant supply of the material. This flagstone floor is in the kitchen of a large house in London, England, but it is made up of stone pavers imported from Tuscany, in Italy, which also provides the source of inspiration for the neoclassical decoration.

5 Flagstone floors remained popular in hallways and kitchens well into the twentieth century, although they were superseded by suspended wooden floors on the first floor from the eighteenth century onward. In some houses, flagstones were laid onto a beaten earth or cement base, while in others, as here, they were laid onto boards supported on a grid of strong joists. The limestone pavers in this English Victorian hallway are laid in a traditional diamond pattern used since the Middle Ages.

6 & 7 *During the seventeenth and early eighteenth centuries, sandstone and limestone paved floors were often embellished with colorful marble inlays to create highly elaborate geometrical patterns. However, in the late eighteenth and early nineteenth centuries, simpler flooring patterns also came into vogue. These late-eighteenth-century English entrance halls have been paved with French limestone flags.*

8 *Contrasts of color and figuring between different types of marble (and within individual marbles) have often been exploited by architects and designers to relieve the rigidity of many traditional rectilinear flooring patterns. This marble flooring is in the bathroom of an early-nineteenth-century English house.*

9 *Checker-patterned stone or marble floors, consisting of regularly spaced squares of alternating colors, were popular in classical Roman architecture, and have subsequently been associated with medieval, early Renaissance, and Victorian houses. This black and white marble floor is in the hallway of a restored English Renaissance house. Red or green alternated with black or white as popular options.*

10 *The neoclassical geometric pattern of this hall floor is composed of contrasting-colored granite and marble inlays. Granites, like porphyries, are quarried from igneous rocks and, unlike many marbles, which are quarried from metamorphic rock, display an intricate, but broadly uniform, pattern across their surface.*

11 *Because marble can be prohibitively costly, it has often been simulated in paint over either a wooden or plain stone ground. This black and white faux marble floor is in the hallway of a Federal-style New York apartment. The pattern is neoclassical, and features a central fan motif encompassed by banding and four corner roundels–the latter displaying stars (one of the symbols of American independence).*

TILES

Floor tiles have often been employed since the Middle Ages, mainly at first-floor level, as an alternative to stone floors (*see* pp. 92–3). Made from fired clays, the simplest–particularly, but not exclusively, favored in rural areas–are unglazed quarry tiles, produced in natural clay colors ranging from off white to various shades of brown and red. Where other monochrome colors–notably, black, greens, and yellows–have been required, these are created by adding mineral dyes to a thin tin or lead glaze fired onto the surface of the tile. Made in basic geometric shapes, such as squares, rectangles, triangles, hexagons, and octagons, monochrome tiles have either been laid to intricate mosaic designs (*see* right) or, more often, in simple or complex, overall geometric patterns. More elaborate tiled floors, especially favored during the Middle Ages and the Victorian era, have been created by combining monochrome tiles with patterned encaustic tiles bearing inlaid and colorful motifs and imagery–the choice of the latter always reflecting the prevailing styles of architecture and ornament, but mostly medieval, classical, or Oriental in origin.

1 Smooth-surfaced and highly durable, encaustic tiles made of inlaid earthenware were often laid in the entrance halls and passageways of British and American Victorian houses. In a typical arrangement, the encaustic tiles in this English Victorian entrance hall feature a border that follows and defines the contours of the main architectural fixtures and fittings, namely the doors and the staircase. The recurring motif, in both the border and center of the floor, is a simple diamond or lozenge shape, set in a small square. Diamonds, either used as individual motifs or as diaper patterns, were very popular during the Victorian era.

2 Although far more intricate than 1, the pattern of this late-Victorian encaustic-tiled hallway is also highly symmetrical, and made up of basic square and triangular geometric shapes. However, in terms of imagery, it differs from floor 1 in the use of a number of floral-patterned tiles, sited at intervals along the border and at the center of the octagonal star patterns. Floral motifs were rarely used in the late eighteenth and early nineteenth centuries, but they came back into vogue from ca. 1860 onward under the aegis of the Esthetic movement and the influence of Oriental styles of ornament.

3 Hall Place was built in the mid-nineteenth century by associates of the influential British architect Sir Gilbert Scott. Like many other Victorian Gothic Revival houses, the hallway features a plain and patterned tiled floor in which the patterned tiles display heraldic and medieval-inspired Islamic motifs. Prominent among these are the stylized floral and foliate motifs, and the lions–the latter symbolizing, since Ancient Egyptian times, strength, courage, pride, fortitude, goodness, majesty, watchfulness, and victory.

4 This spacious entrance hall is in a Victorian Gothic Revival mansion built in 1855 in Galena, Illinois. The simple, but striking, geometric pattern of the tiled flooring comprises alternating diagonal rows of monochromatic burned-orange and buttercup-yellow octagonal tiles that are linked on the diagonals by smaller, rectangular, powder-blue spacer tiles.

5 The Calhoun Mansion was built in the 1870s in Charleston, South Carolina. The encaustic tiles in its entrance hall are laid in a geometric pattern, and display motifs inspired by classical Romanesque prototypes. These include bands of white and blue guilloche, enriched with small rosettes, naturalistic floral forms and, at the center, anthemia and gently scrolling foliage.

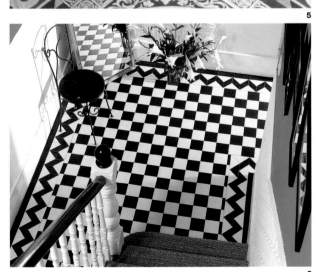

6 The classic black and white checker pattern at the center of this Victorian hallway is bordered with a black-on-white chevron pattern. V-shaped chevrons were an ancient symbol of both water and lightning. Usually strung together to form a zigzag pattern, they were often used in Romanesque, Gothic, and Renaissance architecture, and also in their nineteenth-century revivals.

7 Small, black diamond-shaped tiles mark the intersections of the larger, octagonal-shaped, "white-vein" marble tiles in a late-nineteenth-century English bathroom. The overall pattern of the tiles (like the basin in the alcove) is French in origin, and known as carreaux d'octagnes. It was very popular in both Europe and America throughout the eighteenth and nineteenth centuries.

8 Terra cotta tiles have been used as a flooring material for centuries, especially in the rural areas of Europe. Made by firing a mixture of clay and sand, and usually unglazed, they range from a pale-orange hue to a deep reddish-brown, depending on the color of the local clay. Mostly square, they are traditionally laid, as here, in a simple, rectilinear grid pattern.

MOSAIC TILES

Classical Roman and Islamic Middle Eastern mosaic floors, in which geometric, floral, foliate, or pictorial patterns are created from up to thousands of small, plain tiles in contrasting colors, provided much of the inspiration for the elaborate mosaic flooring laid (usually at first-floor level) in grander houses from the Renaissance onward. Mainly employed in entrance halls, passageways, and bathrooms, mosaic floors were particularly popular in early-nineteenth-century Regency and mid- to late-Victorian houses. This early-nineteenth-century example is modeled on a classical Roman design.

FLOOR COVERINGS

Woven rush matting was the almost universal floor covering before the late seventeenth century, and lighter equivalents made of sisal, coir, or jute were often favored in late-Colonial, Federal, and Arts and Crafts interiors. Floorcloths made of oil-stiffened canvas, and stenciled or hand-painted with patterns, were used in the eighteenth and nineteenth centuries, notably in the United States, as a cheap substitute for carpets. Inexpensive, homemade, rag, shirred, and hooked rugs were also popular at this time, especially in rural American homes. Expensive Oriental carpets were only used to cover tables before the mid-seventeenth century. Thereafter, along with Western-made, flat-weave and woven-pile carpets, they were used on floors in grander houses and, following the mid-nineteenth-century development of automated production, in ordinary houses as well. Linoleum, made of solidified linseed oil, resin, and gum bonded to a canvas or jute backing, was developed in 1860. Durable and inexpensive, it was mainly used in hallways, kitchens, and bathrooms.

1 & 2 Woven rush or straw matting was often employed as a floor covering in grander houses from the Middle Ages to the early seventeenth century. It could either be laid on a damp plaster screed (fusing to the floor when the plaster dried) or, as in the Elizabethan manor house in 1 and Jacobean manor house in 2, loose laid in strips on stone flags or wooden boards, then stitched together and nailed or stuck down.

3 & 4 Made of canvas or other stout cloths, and stiffened with linseed oil, floorcloths first appeared in the seventeenth century, and provided a cheaper alternative to flat-weave or woven-pile rugs and carpets. Employed on both sides of the Atlantic, but especially in the United States, well into the twentieth century, they have invariably been decorated with either stenciled or hand-painted patterns. The floorcloths shown here are English, and date to ca. 1892. Floorcloth 3 is stenciled to simulate a geometric-pattern tiled floor, while 4 is inspired by an Oriental mosaic design. Other popular patterns include various faux marbles and fake marquetry and parquetry flooring.

5 Homemade rag, shirred, and hooked rugs were often laid on top of either rush or sisal floor coverings, or bare wooden floorboards, in rural houses during the eighteenth and nineteenth centuries, and were very popular in American houses. In this bathroom, the larger of the two rugs is a Victorian rag rug, and the smaller is a twentieth-century French hooked rug of ethnic design.

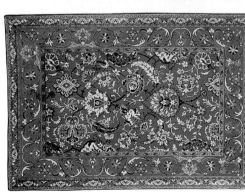

6 Up until the late seventeenth century, Oriental rugs such as this were too rare and expensive to be laid on floors, and were mainly used as table coverings. Later used on floors, they also inspired cheaper, Western-made copies–known as "turkeywork."

7 Although European pile carpets were popular in the reception rooms of grander houses in the late eighteenth and early nineteenth centuries, Oriental rugs were also used. This Persian rug is in a Regency drawing room.

8 An Empire-style drawing room in the Calhoun Mansion, in Charleston, South Carolina, has a knotted-pile carpet patterned with small, stylized floral motifs, and a guilloche border enriched with naturalistic floral sprigs.

7

8

9

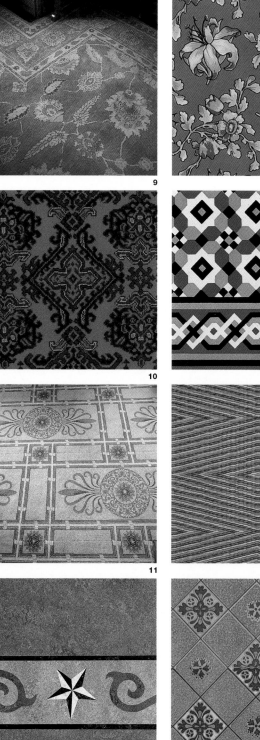

10

11

12

13

14

15

16

9 A British Victorian carpet, custom-made to fit the contours of a room, and patterned with naturalistic floral and foliate motifs of Eastern origin.

10 A nineteenth-century European copy of a Turkestan carpet, with a symmetrical pattern typical of the region, and made up of geometric motifs based on stylized foliate forms.

11 Anthemia and pateras with floral motifs are incorporated in a neoclassical geometric pattern in this early-nineteenth-century American woven-pile carpet.

12 A detail of a late-nineteenth-century faux marble American linoleum, with an alternating curlicue and star border.

13, 14, & 15 English linoleums, all dated to ca. 1892: 13 is based on a naturalistic floral carpet pattern; 14 is an "inlaid" linoleum (in which the colors penetrate to the full depth of the material), simulating encaustic tiling; 15 is patterned to resemble woven matting.

16 Similar to, but less durable than, linoleum, this English cork carpet is modeled on plain and stylized floral-patterned ceramic tiles.

CEILINGS

Before the mid-seventeenth century, first-floor ceilings in the majority of houses were made up of the structural timbers (beams and joists) of the floor above, together with either the exposed undersides of the floorboards or, in better houses, lath-and-plaster infills between the joists. In single-story dwellings, and in the upper-story rooms of other houses, ceilings consisted of the structural timbers of the roof and the underside of the roof covering–the latter made of woven matting, wooden boards, or lath-and-plaster infills. In the reception rooms of grander houses, the beams and joists were often arranged to divide the ceiling into a grid of symmetrical compartments (or coffers). Decoration of the beams and joists–reflecting the status of the room, the household, or both–ranged from simple chamfering, to carved motifs (notably of birds, animals, flowers, and foliage), to the application of carved ribs or straps in compartments, and carved pendants where the timbers intersected. Sometimes, painted decoration was also used: the simplest, white limewash, was applied to lath-and-plaster infills (and occasionally to the timbers, primarily to protect against insect infestation), while the most flamboyant had polychrome stenciled or hand-painted medieval, heraldic, or Renaissance motifs and imagery.

Exposed timber ceilings continued to be used well into the twentieth century, notably in vernacular timber-framed, and Arts and Crafts and Renaissance Revival, houses (*see* pp. 100–2). However, from the sixteenth century onward in many grander houses, and from the mid-seventeenth century in most other houses, they were generally supplanted by suspended ceilings. These ceilings fall into three basic categories: wooden-boarded, tin-paneled, and plaster. Wooden-boarded ceilings, made up of painted, butt-jointed, or tongue-and-groove planks, nailed to the undersides of the joists, were employed in some American Colonial, Federal, and Victorian houses, and embossed tin-paneled ceilings, also nailed or screwed to the joists, were installed in some nineteenth- and early-twentieth-century houses. However, in most houses, suspended plaster ceilings were those most commonly used.

In its most basic form, the plaster ceiling consists of a smoothed coat of plaster bonded into a network of wooden laths that are nailed to the undersides of the joists, and trimmed around the perimeter, at the junction with walls, with a decorative cornice molding (*see* pp. 102–3). From the eighteenth century to the present day, plain plaster ceilings–usually flat-painted and often embellished with a central ceiling medallion (*see* pp. 103)–were used throughout most houses, and in the secondary rooms of larger homes, but more ornate versions have also been favored, especially in the reception rooms of grander houses. For example, some Renaissance and Baroque ceilings were covered with plaster moldings, such as bosses, pendants, ribs, medallions, and rectilinear and foliate strapwork which, during the course of the seventeenth century (and under the prevailing influence of classicism in architecture and ornament), became increasingly systematic in the manner in which they compartmented the ceiling. These heavily ornamented plaster ceilings continued to be employed in many grand reception rooms on both sides of the Atlantic up until the early twentieth century, with the moldings sometimes highlighted (notably in Victorian houses) with polychrome painting, and gilding, against flat-painted monochrome grounds.

Fashionable additions, or alternatives, to plaster moldings on elaborate ceilings included polychrome hand-painted (and gilded) imagery, and patterned papers. The former are particularly associated with early-Georgian, Rococo, and neoclassical interiors. For example, many of the compartmented ceilings designed or influenced by Robert Adam during the late eighteenth century feature painted figures and scenes from classical mythology in plaques, cartouches, or roundels, set in a combination of flat-painted and plaster-relief moldings. During the nineteenth century, sets of printed polychrome papers, bearing pictorial imagery and trompe l'oeil simulations of plaster moldings, were used to create much the same effect and, following the development of machine-printing, provided a cheaper option.

CEILING TYPES

Particular types of ceiling are strongly associated with specific historical periods or styles of architecture and decoration. Ceilings in which most or all of the structural timbers–such as beams, joists, and braces–of the floor or roof above are exposed were commonplace in the Middle Ages, and continued to be used in most houses until the mid-seventeenth century. Thereafter, they were largely confined to vernacular, timber-framed dwellings–particularly the Arts and Crafts houses of the late nineteenth and early twentieth centuries–as well as some nineteenth-century Gothic and Renaissance Revival houses. Suspended ceilings made of jointed wooden boards or panels were used in many late-Colonial and some Federal and late-Victorian American homes. However, having first appeared in the grandest Renaissance and Baroque houses, suspended plaster gradually superseded all of the above in the majority of houses from the 1650s onward. The simplest–mono-chrome-painted flat plaster–has been widely used since then in most secondary rooms. However, in reception rooms and some main bedrooms, especially in larger houses, more ornate treatments dividing the ceiling into compartments have been favored. Most of these have been created with plaster moldings–systematic and gridlike on late-Baroque, early-Georgian, neoclassical, Victorian, and Edwardian ceilings, and more organic or fluid on Renaissance and Revival ceilings. Alternatives include polychromatic painting and stenciling, notably in neoclassical houses, and the application of printed papers–the latter much favored during the Victorian age.

1 The dining room at Frog Pool Farm, in Avon, England, dates to the early sixteenth century. Its gridlike coffered ceiling consists of heavily molded oak beams, infilled with painted lath-and-plaster panels. On many earlier coffered ceilings the undersides of the floorboards above would have been exposed, rather than concealed under plaster panels. More ornate ceilings had carved motifs on the beams, and molded bosses or pendants at the intersections.

2 The oak coffering of this sixteenth-century English manor-house ceiling is denser that that of 1. The joists of the floor above, supported on the cross-beams, are left exposed, and only the undersides of the floor-boards are covered with plaster paneling.

3 A series of arched oak braces and horizontal oak purlins supports the painted lath-and-plaster vaulted ceiling in this Elizabethan dining room. Such ceilings enjoyed a revival during the early twentieth century.

4 Coffered wooden ceilings were sometimes used in the eighteenth century. This example is in a pine-paneled English library that dates to the reign of George II (1727–60). The gridlike pattern and the profiles of the molded beams recall late-medieval coffered ceilings, and typify a mid-eighteenth-century revival of interest in medieval "Gothick" architecture. However, the modillion cornice used to define the ceiling's perimeter– and derived from the Corinthian, Composite, and Ionic Orders–also illustrates the prevailing influence of classicism during the period.

5 In the sixteenth and early seventeenth centuries, plaster ceilings in grander reception rooms were frequently embellished with a maze of ornament. During the second half of the seventeenth century, the ornament, although still profuse, was applied within a gridlike system of compartments, which usually radiated out from the center of the ceiling to the corners. However, by the late seventeenth century, as on this English Baroque dining-room ceiling, the grid was often omitted, leaving only the ovals or circles of ornament surrounding a large, usually plain, expanse of painted flat plaster.

4

5

6

6 This compartmented, polished-hardwood ceiling is in an American Victorian mansion in Newport, Rhode Island. The combination of arched ribs around the perimeter of the ceiling and the diamond and quartered-octagonal paneling in the center was much in vogue during the second half of the nineteenth century.

7

7 & 8 Both of these plaster ceilings display the structure and type of ornamentation that were the height of fashion in neoclassical houses of the late eighteenth and early nineteenth centuries. Ceiling 7 is Roman-inspired, and divided into a regular grid of diamond- and octagonal-shaped coffers, embellished with rosettes. Ceiling 8 has a plain field bordered with recessed coffering, containing pateras. Both ceilings are "supported" by purely decorative, rather than structural, classical columns.

8

1 This plaster ceiling is in a small drawing room at Drayton Hall, built ca. 1740, near Charleston, South Carolina. The liveliness and refinement of the plasterwork, in which scrolled foliate motifs are compartmented by classical moldings, are characteristic of the best mid-eighteenth-century Palladian-style American houses.

2 Neoclassical ceilings designed by Robert Adam were segmented and embellished with either plaster moldings, painted decoration, as here, or both. This centerpiece of a ceiling at Newby Hall, built in the early 1770s in Yorkshire, England, features a central roundel painted with scenes from classical mythology. Notable among other popular neoclassical motifs are rings of guilloche and wavescrolls, as well as candelabra forms incorporating anthemia and husks.

3 This detail of an English Victorian ceiling reveals the edge of the papered field, bordered with an ornate plaster molding displaying rosettes and gently scrolling foliage. Foliate-pattern papered fields, in realistic colors such as browns and greens, were a popular choice in Victorian interiors.

4 Proportion and symmetry underpin the decoration of this Adam ceiling at Home House, built ca. 1775 in London. As was often the case with neoclassical ceilings, the ground color and most of the motifs are painted onto the plaster, while the figurative plaques and roundels are painted onto paper, which is then glued in place.

5 Small and colorful compartments of decoration, which combined stenciling with painted and gilded plaster moldings, were fashionable in American Victorian mansions.

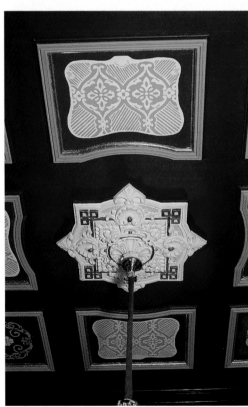

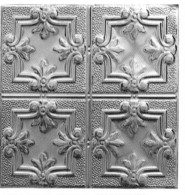

TIN AND STEEL CEILINGS
During the nineteenth century, stamped-tin ceilings were often used instead of traditional plaster or wooden ceilings in American houses. Produced in a range of historical styles, assembled from separate panels, and often painted in situ, they were fireproof, and supposedly "nonabsorbent and free from bacteria." In the early twentieth century, they were generally supplanted by pressed-steel versions, which also proved popular in some English Edwardian houses.

CEILING MEDALLIONS

A focal point of the majority of plastered ceilings since the early eighteenth century, especially during the Victorian period, ceiling medallions have been fashioned in all the predominant architectural styles. Originally, they were made of plaster, but nowadays resin is also used. Their circumference and degree of ornamentation have traditionally been related to, respectively, the size of the ceiling and the status of the room for which they are intended.

1 This plaster ceiling medallion is in the dining room of an American Empire-style house in New York State. Its rings of foliate motifs are typical neoclassical forms of ornament.

2 The medallion in the drawing room of the same house is a rosette and a ring of caulicoli. Set in a recessed coffer, it is encircled by a plain molding, and framed with four corner fans and key-pattern moldings.

3 Fruit and, as here, vegetable motifs have often been employed on ceiling medallions, to symbolize fertility, wealth, or abundance.

4 Of a type that is found in eighteenth-century "Gothick" and nineteenth-century Gothic Revival houses, this ceiling medallion draws on medieval Gothic forms and motifs. Notable elements include cinqfoils and lozenges containing naturalistic flowers and foliage, and a brattished (crested) perimeter embellished with alternating ball flowers and fleurs-de-lis.

5 On this segmented Robert Adam ceiling, ca. 1770s, the central medallion is a fluted, circular fan, topped with a rosette and a ring of foliate forms. Set in a recessed, octagonal compartment, the medallion is encompassed by a circular, scoop molding, and by strings of husks swagged from ribbons. The white, blue, and cream color scheme is a modern restoration of the original decoration.

6, 7, & 8 As with these reproduction Victorian examples, most ceiling medallions made from the early eighteenth to early twentieth centuries were decorated with stylized or naturalistic floral and foliate motifs.

CORNICES

Because of their purpose and prominent position–to disguise and ornament the junction between ceilings and walls–cornices have played a significant role in establishing the architectural and decorative style of interiors. They were rarely employed with the timber-framed ceilings in widespread use prior to the seventeenth century, and in many houses built in the vernacular tradition thereafter, because the perimeters of these were usually defined by wooden beams (supporting cross-beams or floor joists), or by full-height wainscoting. However, they have invariably been used with plaster and wood-paneled ceilings. Mostly made of plaster or wood, but also of stone, papier-mâché and, nowadays, resin, the extent of their molded or carved ornamentation usually reflects the type of room for which they are intended– generally, more elaborate in reception rooms and principal bedrooms, and plainer in other rooms. The simplest ones consist of concave or convex profile moldings–such as ogee, ovolo, torus, scotia, bolection, and *cyma reversa* and *recta*– and are mostly derived from the Classical Orders. More elaborate examples combine these with key and scoop patterns, dentils, and modillions; repeat motifs such as egg-and-dart, bead-and-reel, and ribbon-and-rosette; or devices such as vases, urns, cartouches, plaques, and human and animal forms. However, the most enduringly fashionable imagery has been stylized or naturalistic representations of plant forms.

4 *The cornice and its accompanying frieze are part of an elaborate curved ceiling designed by Robert Adam in 1772. The cornice contains a continuous band of guilloche, set above a strip of bead molding. The frieze is dominated by pateras and aegricanes, linked by swagged strings of husks, and is painted in Pompeiian colors.*

5 & 6 *The foliate motif that dominates these reproduction cornices is the acanthus leaf. The most widely used foliage ornament from the Greco-Roman era to the end of the Victorian period, it is based on the leaves of the Mediterranean species Acanthus spinosus. Generally, acanthus-leaf moldings inspired by Greek prototypes are sparser than their heavier, droopier, and more elaborate Roman-inspired equivalents.*

1 *Carved from oak, this American Victorian cornice features alternating rose and stylized English Tudor flower motifs, set above a rope molding.*

2 *This double-bolection cornice molding is of a type that was widely used in the eighteenth and nineteenth centuries. Made of pine, it would have almost invariably been painted to match the ceiling, or other woodwork in the room.*

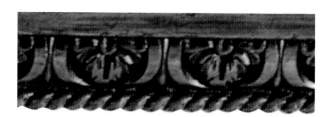

3 *Neoclassical imagery here includes plaques of foliage and trophies-of-arms, wreath heads, and egg-and-dart molding.*

7 *Waterleaf or stiff-leaf is the motif that is used in this neoclassical plaster cornice. Feather-shaped in appearance, this foliate motif was often employed by the architect Andrea Palladio to enrich moldings on Ionic, Corinthian, and Composite Orders, and also by Robert Adam as an alternative to acanthus leaves on columns, friezes and, as here, cornices.*

8 *The modillions on this classical cornice are inspired by the consoles that support the cornice in the Corinthian and Composite Orders.*

9 *Also derived from the Corinthian, Composite, and Ionic Orders, dentil moldings have often been applied to cornices in classical interiors, notably in the eighteenth century.*

10 *This neoclassical modillion cornice is early nineteenth century. The modillions are fluted, alternated with recessed rosettes, and set above egg-and-dart molding.*

11 *This painted-plaster cornice-frieze is in the oval Music Room of Nathaniel Russell House, built 1808 in Charleston, South Carolina. It incorporates strings of husks, guilloche, scoop moldings, and lozenges and cartouches filled with floral ornament.*

12 *The pomegranate was a popular motif in Oriental and Greco-Roman ornament, and also used in plasterwork and wood carving during the Renaissance and the eighteenth- and nineteenth-century classical revivals. A symbol of fertility, it is here surrounded by leaves in the formalized vegetal pattern that dominates this American Greek Revival cornice.*

14 *Apart from acanthus, the most popular leaf motifs for cornices have been vine, laurel, lotus, ivy, oak, palm and, here with its fruits, lime.*

15 *Prominent features in this American Victorian cornice are a Greek key-pattern molding along the bottom, a series of modillions around the center, and rosettes along the top.*

16 *This cornice-frieze is in a Victorian drawing room. Its center is made up of a deep, concave scotia molding and, above that, scrolling foliage interspersed with rosettes. Flanking these are parallel bands of stylized leaf ornament. To highlight all the prominent motifs, the green paint has been rubbed back on raised areas to expose a muted gold ground color–a decorative finish very similar in appearance to aged or distressed gilding.*

13 *This plaster cornice is in a mid-nineteenth-century Gothic Revival house in New York. The upper section is an ogee molding; the lower a series of trefoil arches, alter- nating with smaller, flowerlike quatrefoils. Trefoil and cinqfoil arches were often used on Gothic Revival cornices, sometimes embellished with spikelike pendants.*

CORBELS

Used in classical and Gothic architecture, corbels are projecting stone or wooden blocks or brackets that are attached to a wall and used to support beams, arches, and cornices. S-shaped corbels, such as this reproduction Renaissance example, are called consoles. Like many, it is carved with scrolling forms and foliate motifs, here derived from the classical vocabulary of ornament. A series of small, blocklike consoles regularly spaced along cornice's length, and usually more decorative than functional, are known as modillions (*see* cornices 8 and 10).

WALLS

Internal walls fall into one of two broad stylistic categories: those in which the basic structural components are either wholly or partly exposed, and those in which they are clad with various materials. The first category is comprised of stone, brick, and half-timbered walls. The latter consist of a gridlike network of vertical posts and studs, horizontal cross-rails and, in some cases, curved or arched braces. The spaces between these exposed, structural wooden components are traditionally infilled with either limewashed lath-and-plaster panels, or bricks laid in various decorative patterns (notably chevron or herringbone). Such walls were in widespread use in timber-framed medieval and Renaissance houses, and continued to be employed in some vernacular timber-framed houses thereafter–mostly in rural areas of England, but also in early-American Colonial homes, and in some Arts and Crafts houses of the late nineteenth and early twentieth centuries. Exposed stone walls were also much in evidence during the Middle Ages and the Renaissance, but generally were confined to residential castles and palaces. Subsequent use was mainly restricted to the entrance halls, passageways, and stairwells of neoclassical, and Gothic- and Classical Revival houses of the eighteenth, nineteenth, and early twentieth centuries, although in many cases faux stone (including marble) effects painted onto flat plaster were employed instead of real stone. Apart from in basements, internal walls with exposed structural brickwork have been much rarer than half-timbered and stone walls. However, exceptions include inglenooks in British and American houses built prior to the early eighteenth century, and inglenooks and some projecting chimney breasts in Arts and Crafts houses.

Walls in which the structural components are covered have been far more prevalent than their exposed equivalents. One fundamental reason for this has been because they help to minimize the loss of heat from the interior of the house. For example, from the eighteenth century onward, most walls in American timber-framed houses were clad with boards or paneling to insulate against the harshness of the winter climate. However, architectural and decorative considerations have also influenced the choice. The impact of classicism on European, and later American, architecture from the Renaissance onward saw walls increasingly divided, horizontally, into three sections. These were a frieze at the top (see pp. 112–3), a field in the center (see pp. 114–5), and a dado at the bottom (see pp. 116–7), with the relative proportions of each of these derived from the architrave, column, and base of Classical Greek and Roman Orders. This tripartite division was much easier to create if the structural elements were covered, and various materials and decorative techniques have been employed to this end.

Polished hardwood, or painted softwood, paneling applied to the full height of the wall has often been used (see pp. 108–11), and the distinction between frieze, field, and dado created with applied moldings or carved detail. Alternatively, frieze-height paneling has been combined with a flat or molded plaster frieze, or dado-height paneling has been surmounted by a painted or papered plaster field–with the latter usually separated from the plaster frieze by a picture rail or similarly positioned lengths of wooden or plaster molding.

Where wooden paneling has not been employed, flat plaster has been applied over the entire surface of the wall, and the tripartite division marked by rectilinear baseboards, and dado and picture rails–the last two usually of wood or plaster, but sometimes stenciled, hand-painted trompe l'oeil simulations, or thin strips of patterned wallpaper. These horizontal divisions have then been further defined by infills of either applied plaster moldings (usually painted or gilded), hand-painted motifs, fabrics stretched over battens, and wallpapers, or ceramic tiles–with the latter mainly applied to dadoes from the nineteenth century onward. In all cases, the motifs and patterns that were employed–whether carved, molded, stenciled, hand-painted, or printed–have invariably reflected prevailing fashions in decoration and ornament (see pp. 8–33).

PANELING

In grander medieval and Renaissance houses, oak paneling was often applied to brick, stone, and timber-framed walls–either to full-height or frieze or dado level on the brick or stone type, and always to full-height on the timber frame. Polished oak or walnut paneling, as well as pine or fir paneling painted in imitation of finely figured hardwoods, marbles, or even tortoiseshell, was also prevalent in larger Baroque houses, and was regarded as furniture that could be dismantled and taken to a new house when the owner moved. Having remained in vogue in early-Georgian and American Colonial homes–mainly in the form of flat-painted, sometimes gilded, and wood-grained or faux marbled softwood–it generally fell out of fashion (apart from on some Federal fireplace walls), until it enjoyed a resurgence of use beginning in the 1830s. Full- or frieze-height paneling was then often employed in hallways, studies, and dining rooms. Victorian paneling was dark-stained and polished hardwood; Arts and Crafts was polished hardwood or flat-painted softwood; while Art Nouveau was of painted or lacquered softwood. In the late nineteenth and early twentieth centuries, Tudorbethan- and Georgian-style paneling was also used throughout Edwardian homes, as was Renaissance-, Baroque-, and Colonial-style paneling in larger American Beaux Arts houses. Much of this paneling, as with its forerunners, bore elaborately carved decoration (*see* right).

1 & 2 *From the late fifteenth to the early seventeenth centuries, oak wall paneling was often used in grander houses. Fashionable carved decoration included linenfold patterns and, later in the period, arabesques, strapwork, foliage forms, busts, and roundels. The linenfold paneling in 1 is in an Elizabethan manor house, and in 2 in a Jacobean manor house. The latter, topped with a foliate frieze, provides a backdrop to paneled cupboard doors decorated with shieldlike cartouches with portraits of knights, clerics, and patrons of the arts.*

3 *The influence of classical Renaissance architecture is evident in this fine quality, carved wall paneling at Parham House, an Elizabethan manor house in Sussex, England. Made of oak, and limed, the ornately carved paneling flanks an arched doorway, and features fan-arched niches, fluted pilasters, and an entablature bearing corbels and scrolling foliate forms. (The tapestry hanging in the doorway is typical of the period.)*

4 Like many other Jacobean houses, the oak wall paneling here is more elaborate on the fireplace wall than on the other walls of the room. While the latter have an unadorned, grid-like configuration, the former incorporates the fire surround, shelving, and a central panel with a double, blind arch and a pair of pilasters.

5 As in 4, this fireplace at Drayton Hall, built ca. 1740 in Charleston, South Carolina, is conceived as an extension of the wall paneling (and vice versa). The whole ensemble is Palladian in style and, as in many Colonial houses, has been painted. Notable features include the low chair rail, and a triglyph and metope frieze just below the egg-and-dart molding of the cornice.

6 Also painted, this wall paneling features fielded panels. The rigid symmetry of their rectilinear configuration, together with the absence of ornament, is typical of eighteenth-century American Federal interiors.

7 Made of pine, the paneling and doors in this Adam-style room are embellished with corner pateras and rope and transverse scoop moldings. The painted frieze is Pompeiian style.

4

7

8

5

6

9

8 The rectangular wall panels, like the chair rail and the tops of the baseboards in this neoclassical room, are made up of simple, classical rectilinear moldings, highlighted in white against a lilac ground. Additional definition is given to the panels by using a darker tone of lilac (also used on the frieze) than on the rest of the field.

9 Fluted pilasters and rectangular and oval panels define the walls of the neoclassical style Music Room in Lillian Williams's eighteenth-century French château. Made up of wooden moldings, they are decorated in a yellow and gold color scheme that was fashionable in late-eighteenth-century European reception rooms.

1 *In some nineteenth-century timber-framed American houses, the walls were paneled with horizontal tongue-and-groove planks. In this restored cottage near Houston, Texas, the planks have been stripped of layers of paint to reveal the original stenciled frieze. Stenciled decorations such as this–especially foliate patterns–were very popular in the United States, and are mostly attributed to itinerant artists and craftsmen of German and Scandinavian origin.*

2 *When wall paneling was employed in British Victorian houses it was usually confined to halls, studies, and dining rooms. The paneling here is at Cragside, built in 1870 in Northumbria. It is made of oak, has a castellated cresting, incorporates sunflower and animal carvings in the upper panels, and is topped with a floral-patterned wallpaper.*

3 *In this American Victorian house, the dado level in the oak wall paneling is defined at intervals by fretwork, in this case a latticework pattern with rosettes on the overlaps. Latticework (a type of diaper pattern) was very popular in eighteenth-century "Gothick" houses, and enjoyed a notable revival during the Victorian age.*

4 *Full-height or, as here, three-quarter height wall paneling, was often used in the hallways of late-nineteenth- and early-twentieth-century Arts and Crafts houses. Oak, stained and polished, was the hardwood of choice. However, softwoods, usually painted ivory white, sage green, or olive green, were also employed. This oak paneling incorporates a large pair of bifold double-doors leading to a reception room. Because the simple rectilinear panels on the walls and the doors are the same, the latter are "concealed" within the former when closed–a popular architectural convention in Arts and Crafts houses.*

5 *While flat-painted or wood-grained pine was used for wall paneling in the majority of American homes during the second half of the nineteenth century, more expensive, stained and polished native American hardwoods were usually employed in grander houses. This elaborate, full-height mahogany paneling dates to the 1880s. The larger panels at dado level are carved with a linenfold pattern. The panels in the field above feature mahogany veneers inlaid to form geometric patterns, which incorporate recurring star motifs.*

6 This superbly paneled library is in an American Queen Anne-style house. It features fan niches, fretwork-style panels, and interlaced glazing bars–all high-lighted with gilding to contrast with the painted green ground.

7 Designed 1902–3 in Art Nouveau style by C. R. Mackintosh, the hallway at The Hill House, in Helensburgh, Scotland, is lined with black-stained pine paneling. The vertical straps are enlivened at the frieze height with small, pink-painted, fluted panels. The latter flank stenciled motifs (of stylized organic forms) applied to the white-painted plaster panels framed by the straps.

8 This mahogany-lined inglenook at the Gamble House, in Pasadena, California, dates to 1908–9, and is inspired by sixteenth-century European inglenooks. However, the horizontal emphasis and the relatively plain surfaces of the paneling identify this as a twentieth-century composition.

9 Built in the vernacular tradition of the Southern states, this twentieth-century house in Florida has pine-boarded walls. It is distinguished from its predecessors by a plain, white-painted finish, without, as in 1, stenciled decoration.

CARVED DECORATION

While decorative geometric shapes applied to wall paneling have mainly been created with wooden moldings, figurative embellishments have either been painted or carved in relief. Carved decoration has been employed from the Middle Ages to the early twentieth century, most extensively and elaborately in medieval Gothic, Renaissance, Baroque, Gothic Revival (as in the panel above), American Beaux Arts, and Edwardian Tudorbethan houses. However, the finest and most flamboyant carving was produced in English Baroque houses by Grinling Gibbons during the late seventeenth century. His incredibly naturalistic carved animal, marine, and plant-form imagery was much copied but it has never been surpassed.

FRIEZES

Derived from the Classical Orders (*see* p. 107), friezes have mainly been defined at the tops of walls in houses where classicism or neoclassicism has influenced the overall style of architecture and ornament (*see* pp. 8–33). For the same reason, the patterns and motifs used to decorate the frieze have primarily been classical Greek or Roman in origin, although Gothic and Oriental imagery have also been employed–the former in the early Renaissance, and during the late eighteenth, nineteenth, and early twentieth centuries. Favored materials and forms of decoration have included carving–where wooden paneling was employed (*see* pp. 108–111); painted plaster moldings–sometimes gilded, often combined with hand-painted imagery, and especially favored in neoclassical interiors; stenciling–notably in Colonial, Arts and Crafts, and Art Nouveau houses; and hand- or machine-printed strips of wallpaper–the latter increasingly common from the Victorian era onward.

1 *This early-1770s neo-classical painted plaster frieze is at Newby Hall, Yorkshire, England. It has bands of interlaced foliage and rosettes against a Wedgwood-blue ground, and scrolling flowers and foliage, interspersed with Greek urns and winged chimeras, on a Pompeiian red ground.*

2 *The painted and gilded frieze in this domed niche is at Home House, designed by Robert Adam ca. 1775. It has a row of anthemia above strings of husks–the latter flanked by urns and swagged around a row of pateras.*

3 *This French Empire-style frieze is at the Morris-Jumel Mansion in New York. Made of paper, it displays neo-classical urns, lyres, and flower and foliate motifs.*

1

2

3

4 *Also at Home House, this Adam frieze features a thin band of pateras, linked by strings of husks and anthemia, and alternating plaques and roundels showing figures and scenes from classical mythology.*

5 *This paper frieze is in a reception room in the Eastlake-style Durfee House, built ca. 1880 in Los Angeles, California. The upper section is patterned with scrolling foliage and flowers, and the lower section with a two-tone checker pattern sandwiched between rope and bead motifs.*

4

5

6 In a recreation of a nineteenth-century Shaker interior at the American Museum in Bath, England, the painted plaster walls are divided into a field and deep frieze by a wooden peg rail. Simple wooden moldings such as this are a feature of Shaker houses.

7 This reproduction cornice-frieze (which can also be used as a pelmet) is carved from oak, and has a limed finish. It is modeled on an eighteenth-century plaster-on-wood original used in an Irish castle.

8 Carved from oak, this reproduction Jacobean cornice-frieze displays small rosettes set in a band of guilloche.

9 Although inspired by a Victorian original, the combination of rosettes and gently scrolling foliage on this oak cornice-frieze is derived from seventeenth-century carving.

10 Also inspired by a seventeenth-century original, this cornice-frieze features acanthus leaves that are carved in deep relief.

11 Similar to, and often used interchangeably with, hop plants and ivy, grapevine imagery has been used on architectural ornament since Ancient Egyptian times. This cornice-frieze is based on an eighteenth-century original.

12 The repeat floral motifs on this frieze molding are palmettes (formalized palm leaves). A feature of Etruscan ornament, they are a recurring motif in neo-classical and Classical Revival architecture.

13 & 14 These turn-of-the-nineteenth-century picture rail moldings have repeat floral motifs.

15 This torus picture-rail molding is of a type used in the eighteenth and nineteenth centuries.

FIELDS

While various types of wooden paneling (*see* pp. 108–11) have often covered the fields of walls since the Middle Ages, many other forms of decoration have also been favored. In medieval, Renaissance, and Baroque houses, pictorial tapestries or painted cloths were hung over limewashed flat plaster, or the latter was embellished with hand-painted or stenciled imagery. In early-Georgian and Colonial homes, flat-painted plaster was most prevalent, although faux marble and other painted stone effects, silk and woolen fabrics stretched over a network of battens, and, more rarely, hand-printed or flocked wallpapers, were also used in grander houses. All of these treatments continued to be widely employed in late-Georgian, Federal and Empire, and Regency homes. However, in reception rooms, much greater use was made of stretched fabrics, especially damasks and brocades, and increasingly of patterned wallpapers. The introduction of cheaper, machine-printed papers in the mid-nineteenth century saw patterned-papered fields become commonplace thereafter even in ordinary houses, although alternative finishes were never supplanted. In addition to flat-painted plaster, notable examples included a revival of tapestry hangings in Arts and Crafts and Renaissance Revival houses; colorwashed flat plaster in Art Nouveau-style interiors; and ceramic-tiled fields in most bathrooms, but also in some hallways designed under the aegis of the Esthetic movement.

1 Walls decorated with painted simulations of stone and marble blocks were employed in many grand Renaissance, Baroque, and neo classical houses. These faux marble walls are in the study of Richard Jenrette's American Empire-style house on the Hudson River.

2 Flat-painted plaster fields have been employed in many houses since the Middle Ages. The painted field in this fan-arched wall niche is at Home House, London, designed ca. 1775 by Robert Adam.

3 Apart from in kitchens and bathrooms, tiled fields have rarely appeared in British and American houses. However, largely due to Oriental influence, they were fashionable in the entrance halls of some grander houses during the late nineteenth century. This tiled field is in Leighton House, built in the late 1870s, in Kensington, London.

4 In the eighteenth and nineteenth centuries, in the rural areas of Europe and America, stenciling was cheaper than costly wallpapers. This flower and foliage pattern, in an English country house hallway, is copied from an eighteenth-century bedroom at the American Museum in Bath, England.

5 & 6 Stenciled and hand-painted decoration overpainting plank fields is highly characteristic of timber-framed American and Northern European rural houses built during the late seventeenth, eighteenth, and nineteenth centuries. The "pattern-box" stenciling in 5 was applied in the late nineteenth century by itinerant German painters on the plank walls of a cottage near Houston. Its stylized foliate forms are taken from the classical vocabulary of ornament. The hand-painted decoration in 6 was produced ca. 1796–1820 in a Norwegian country house. It consists of a garland of roses entwined around a rectilinear trompe l'oeil molding.

5

6

7 Hand-painted grisaille (monochrome trompe l'oeil) has been used to decorate plaster fields since the Renaissance. Set in a plaster panel, this bouquet of fruit and flowers is in a bedroom of a mid-Victorian house in London, England.

8, 9, & 10 Due to the cost of hand-printing, wallpapered fields were confined to grander houses prior to the mid-nineteenth century, but following the advent of cheaper machine-printed papers, they came into common use. Paper-paneled field 8 is in an American Federal house. The "Chinese Garden" paper in 9 is in a ca. 1800 Georgian room, and has imagery from Audubon's The Birds of America. The colonnaded paper field in 10 is in the American Empire-style Morris-Jumel Mansion, in New York.

7

8

9

10

DADOES

A wide range of materials and decorative techniques have been used to define dadoes on walls since the Middle Ages. In houses where full- or three-quarter-height wooden paneling was applied (*see* pp. 108–11), the distinction between the dado and the field above was often made within the overall composition of the paneling by applied rectilinear moldings or bands of carving, which could also be highlighted with contrasting-colored paints, or by gilding. An alternative treatment for full-height paneling composed of butt-jointed or tongue-and-groove planks was the application of hand-painted or stenciled dado rails–a decorative convention much favored in eighteenth- and nineteenth-century rural American dwellings. In some Renaissance and early-Georgian houses, and many late-Georgian, Regency, Federal, Victorian, Arts and Crafts, Art Nouveau, Edwardian, and American Beaux Arts homes, wooden paneling was simply extended up only to dado or chair-rail height, and the contrasting plaster field above painted or covered with fabric or wallpaper. Where paneling was not used, definition of the dado has been achieved by the combination of chair and dado rails above and wooden baseboards below, infilled with painted or papered plaster; by the use of tripartite wallpaper sets (which include separate dado strips); and by ceramic tiles–the latter particularly popular in bathrooms, kitchens, and hallways from the mid-nineteenth century onward.

1 In most American Federal houses built ca. 1780 to 1830, wall paneling was taken to dado level only– the exception being on fireplace walls where, as in the Colonial period, full-height paneling was often used. This painted wooden paneling is in a hallway of the American Empire-style Morris-Jumel Mansion, in New York. The classical moldings framing the center panel are typical of the period. However, more ornate beading, guilloche, and gouge-work were also used, as were painted neoclassical motifs on the center panels.

2 Set above a mahogany baseboard, this Victorian dado panel is painted over flat plaster. The bands of flowers and foliage have been stenciled over a painted faux sienna marble.

3 Dated to ca. 1822, the dado on the plank walls of this farmhouse is divided from the blue colorwashed field above by a hand-painted floral border and a contrasting red colorwash.

4 & 5 Tiled dadoes became more common in bathrooms, kitchens and, to a lesser extent, hallways, in the last third of the nineteenth century (and thereafter). As here, rectangular tiles in one or two colors were usually laid in traditional brickwork patterns, and topped with bands of patterned and three-dimensional tiles, the latter profiled as classical moldings.

6 The dado in this late-Victorian hallway is covered with Anaglypta. Invented in 1886, made of cotton-fiber pulp, and incorporating relief patterns made by hollow molding, it was always painted, and it provided a lighter and cheaper alternative to Lincrusta.

7 Invented in 1877, Lincrusta was made of linseed oil, gum, resins, and wood pulp spread over canvas, and had embossed patterns created with engraved metal rollers. This Art Nouveau Lincrusta dado is painted to resemble ceramic paneling.

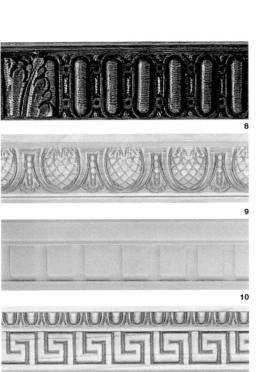

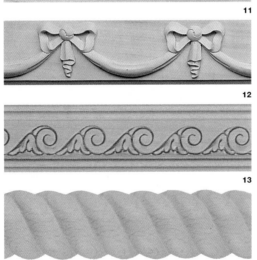

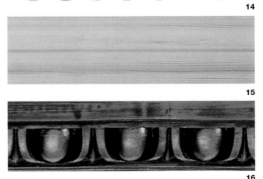

8 A reproduction dado rail with a Tudor-style reeded pattern, carved from oak and based on a sixteenth-century original.

9 A reproduction dado rail with alternating pine-apple and dart motifs, based on an eighteenth-century original.

10 A classical dentil-pattern dado rail, carved from whitewood. Based on eighteenth- and early-nineteenth-century rails.

11 A Greek key pattern dado rail, with egg-and-dart border, based on an early-nineteenth-century Greek Revival original.

12 A reproduction neoclassical dado rail, with repeat swagged ribbon motifs carved in deep relief.

13 A wavescroll pattern dado rail, of a type used in Classical Revival and neoclassical houses since the Renaissance.

14 A rope (or cable) molding dado rail, of a type used in neo-classical, and especially Regency, houses.

15 A reproduction classical astragal molding, common in the seventeenth, eighteenth, and nineteenth centuries.

16 A classical-style egg-and-dart molding, carved in oak and copied from an eighteenth-century plaster original.

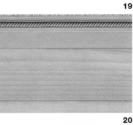

17 A reproduction oak baseboard, of a type often used under carved linenfold wall paneling. Available in different depths to suit the proportions of the room.

18 A whitewood base-board topped with a bolection molding–the latter is directly above a band of classical egg-and-dart motifs.

19 A pine baseboard topped with a stained band of naturalistic leaf motifs–the latter set above a classical concave torus molding.

20 A classical base-board featuring a fielded band set underneath a thin rope (or cable) molding, and topped with a repeat bead-and-reel molding.

21 The molding on top of this baseboard is a variant of the concave and convex ogee mold-ing in widespread use from the seventeenth to the nineteenth centuries.

22 Also popular from the seventeenth to the nineteenth centuries, a pine baseboard topped with a classical convex astragal molding (with a chamfered top edge).

23 Another variant of the classical convex torus molding topping a baseboard. Torus profile moldings were very fashionable in the late nineteenth century.

FIREPLACES

Prior to the late fifteenth century, an open hearth in the center or near one end of the main living room of a house–its smoke allowed to meander up through a hole in the roof–was the most common form of fireplace. However, the introduction of wattle-and-daub or wooden canopies above the hearth, designed to channel smoke more efficiently out of the room, increasingly led to the relocation of the fireplace to one of the walls–it being easier to support the canopy there, rather than from a wooden stand or the ceiling. From the early sixteenth century, the open hearth and canopy was, in turn, largely superseded by the enclosed wall fireplace, consisting of a brick or stone stack (a chimney) with a hollow center (a flue) designed to conduct smoke up from a hearth (recessed in the base of the stack) and out via a louver in the roof. Most hearth openings were rectangular and spanned by a stone or wood lintel, but in some grander houses they were shaped as a Gothic four-centered arch. Lintels and arches could be plain, chamfered, or carved and painted or gilded with decorative motifs–the extent of this reflecting the wealth of the household.

Despite its new position and its increased ornamentation, the early-sixteenth-century fireplace was, in many respects, treated as just part of a wall. However, it rapidly thereafter became not only a dominant feature in its own right, but also the architectural focus of most rooms–an effect primarily due to the development of the fire surround (or mantelpiece). Initially devised in Italy during the Renaissance, and inspired by the Classical Greco-Roman Orders of architecture, the surround took the form of a pair of jambs (flanking the hearth) linked (just above the hearth) by an entablature; the jambs could be columns, pilasters, carved figures, or simple architectural moldings, while the entablature was essentially a decorative frieze. The surface of the chimney breast above was also invariably subject to a decorative treatment–in the form of a wooden or stone overmantel, consisting of either a large, projecting smoke hood, an architectural structure mirroring the surround below or, more usually, carved, or painted and gilded, paneling.

This basic model for the fireplace has survived to the present day, although it has inevitably been subject to numerous technical and decorative changes over the intervening centuries. Notable among the former are canting of the sides of the hearth to help project heat into the room; reductions in the size of the hearth and the flue (and also the depth of the chimney breast) to increase the draw of air and improve combustion; the invention of, in turn, dog, hob, and register grates designed to burn coal, rather than logs–the latter traditionally burned on firedogs (*see* pp. 134–5); and the introduction of enclosed stoves and heaters as alternatives to open fires (*see* p. 136). Significant decorative developments include lining the areas between the sides of the jambs and the hearth or grate with marble, slate, or ceramic tiles (*see* pp. 123 and 133); incorporating a picture panel or, from the late seventeenth century, a mirror-glass within the overmantel structure (*see* pp. 138–9), or dispensing with the overmantel and hanging a picture or mirror on the chimney breast; and, during the nineteenth century, increasing the depth of the mantelshelf to accommodate clocks, candles, and numerous decorative artifacts. Nevertheless, esthetically, the most pronounced changes have occurred in the style of the fire surround. Made of stone, slate, and brick (*see* pp. 120–3), marble (*see* pp. 124–7), wood (*see* pp. 128–31), or cast iron and copper (see pp. 132–3), they have always closely reflected changing fashions in architecture and ornament.

During the twentieth century, the fireplace suffered a demise in popularity, largely due to the widespread adoption of central-heating systems (*see* p. 137). Indeed, in the 1960s and 1970s, many fire surrounds were ripped out and their hearths boarded up, thereby removing the architectural focal point of the room. Fortunately, this trend has now been reversed by numerous homeowners intent on restoring the architectural equilibrium and period authenticity of their properties, and by the many reclamation companies and manufacturers now supplying a diverse range of restored original and fine-quality reproduction fireplaces.

STONE, SLATE, AND BRICK

Many of the earliest fire surrounds, dating to the late fifteenth century, were cut and carved from stone, a material that has proved enduringly fashionable for this purpose ever since. Like marble (*see* pp. 124–7), stone has always been expensive to quarry and transport, and therefore usually reserved for more prestigious surrounds, although reconstituted stones, such as the Coade stone developed in the eighteenth century, have provided cheaper alternatives. Their appeal to architects and craftsmen largely resides in the receptiveness of most types–notably various limestones–to carving and chamfering. Consequently, numerous examples have displayed elaborate decorative embellishments on their jambs, lintels, entablatures and, where deployed, hoods or overmantels. However, many stones are equally prized for their variations of color and figuring, which range from the largely monochromatic off white and yellow limestones, and black and gray slates (very popular during the nineteenth century), to the polychromatic purple, brown, white, and red porphyries–the latter often used as decorative inlays set in plainer stones. Variations, and particularly subtle gradations, of color also explain the visual appeal of bricks. Unsuitable for carving, they have not often been employed (except in later Arts and Crafts houses) to make fire surrounds as such. Yet, because of their load-bearing qualities, and their resistance to high temperatures, they have been regularly used since the Renaissance to construct hearths, chimney breasts, and inglenooks. Their esthetic qualities (which also include different patterns of mortaring) have often been exploited by leaving them exposed, rather than cladding them with materials such as cement, plaster, wooden paneling, or ceramic tiles.

2 Large smoke hoods, as on this neo-Gothic limestone fire surround, were often employed in medieval, Renaissance, and Baroque houses. Here, late-medieval decoration includes the coat-of-arms on the hood, stylized floral roundels along the frieze, clerics' heads on the pilasters, and a four-centered arched hearth.

3 The drawing room in Plas Teg, a Jacobean mansion in North Wales, retains its original seven-teenth-century stone fireplace. Its columnar jambs, four-centered arch, and breakfront mantelshelf were carved as separate sections and assembled on site.

1 Hand-carved from limestone, this fire surround is modeled on fifteenth-century English Tudor style. Essentially classical in form, it also incorporates lingering elements of the medieval Gothic style– in this case a pointed arch over the hearth. The latter features a cast-iron fireback with lion and unicorn motifs, and a cast-iron, swan's-nest firebasket flanked by a pair of black-iron and brass firedogs.

4 Modeled on an original Queen Anne stone fireplace, this modern reproduction displays the robustness and simplicity of line that characterized many turn-of-the-seventeenth-century fire surrounds–qualities consolidated during the eighteenth-century Georgian era. Available in Portland, Bath, or reconstituted stone, it is shown here with a cast-iron insert.

5 Classical ornament is evident in the pair of turned roundels, and in the reeded pilaster jambs and frieze, of this reproduction, late-Georgian fire surround. Roundels and reeding were fashionable forms of decoration on early-nineteenth-century Regency fire surrounds. Classical flower and bead motifs are employed on the arch-top, cast-iron insert.

7 This reproduction of a classic Louis XV carved-stone fire surround, with its serpentine-profile frieze and mantelshelf, and scrolling motifs, is very characteristic of late-eighteenth-century French neoclassicism. Intended for use with a free-standing dog grate, surrounds such as this one were exported in considerable numbers to both Britain and the United States.

7

4

5

8

6 Classical decoration on this late-eighteenth-century English Coade stone fire surround is far more ornate than on 5. The bacchanalian figures on the pilaster jambs, Pomona and Flora, are inspired by murals found ca. 1738–65 during the excavations of Herculaneum. They are surmounted by myrtle wreaths, bows, and quivers, and these flank a frieze that is embellished with a trailing vine heavily laden with grapes.

6

8 Carved from a creamy colored limestone, this reproduction of a mid-nineteenth-century fireplace displays the minimum of applied or carved decoration. As such, the emphasis is clearly on pared-down classical architectural form, rather than as with many other Victorian fireplaces, on classical ornament. The matching limestone slips and infill frame an extremely plain cast-iron insert–a combination that would sit happily in many twentieth-century Modernist rooms. However, when installed in a Victorian-style interior, a more appropriate insert would feature simple classical motifs, such as reeding, strings of husks, individual rosettes, and rows of acanthus leaves.

1 *Reproduced from a mid-nineteenth-century model, this fire surround, like the similarly austere example 8 shown on page 121, relies for effect on its classical architectural form and simple linear moldings, rather than on any applied or carved ornament. However, decoration of sorts is present in the subtle mottling and gradations of color inherent in the stone itself. Moreover, the color contrast between the elegant beige surround and the black-leaded, arch-top grate that it frames makes a strong visual impact, and thereby consolidates the fireplace's position as the architectural focal point of a Victorian room.*

3 *Designed in 1870 by the influential Arts and Crafts architect Richard Norman Shaw, this monumental stone fireplace has carved columnar jambs surmounted by a pair of massive corbels. The latter are intricately carved with foliate and bird motifs, and support a deep frieze bearing a homely Victorian motto. Unusually, the mantel-shelf is made of finely figured marble. The tiled slips are Islamic, and the wrought-iron fire-back bears images of medieval chivalry—a military theme extended to the armorial brass shields on the firedogs.*

2 *This Arts and Crafts fire surround dates from the late nineteenth century and is made from Welsh slate. While the surround itself is unornamented, the contrasting-colored blue ceramic tile slips display subtle but decorative mottling, and the hood of the one-piece, cast-iron insert features Islamic-inspired fretwork. It is also worth noting that the insert is polished, rather than black-leaded, as was usually the case during the second half of the nineteenth century.*

4 *Located in an eighteenth-century American Colonial house, this is very much a working fireplace designed for open-hearth cooking. Framed by a simple, painted wooden surround, the jambs, lintel, and back of the hearth are constructed from mortared bricks. Also highly characteristic of the period are the pair of wrought-iron firedogs and the swivel-crane—the latter designed to support pots and kettles over the burning logs. Home of Stephen P. Mack.*

5 In an American Colonial house on Rhode Island, this brick fireplace is framed by a painted wooden surround made of simple rectilinear moldings, which blend into the surrounding raised-and-fielded, painted wall paneling. In the grandest eighteenth- century American Colonial houses, it was not unusual for all of the walls of some reception rooms to be similarly paneled. In most houses, however, paneling was confined to the fireplace wall. Home of Stephen P. Mack

7 Designed in 1859 by the influential Arts and Crafts architect Philip Webb, for the Red House, in Bexleyheath, near London, this mortared, red-brick chimney breast incorporates a pointed arch and curved lintel infilled with herringbone-pattern brickwork. The cast-iron grate is bordered with a lattice-work pattern, and flanked by English delft tile slips. It also features an adjustable brass smoke canopy, which augments the iron hood (with rosette motif) directly above the grate.

6 Large, brick-built, inglenook fireplaces enjoyed a revival during the second half of the nineteenth century, especially in substantial Arts and Crafts houses. As in many sixteenth- and seventeenth-century houses, the larger inglenooks sometimes, as here, incorporated a small bake oven set into the rear wall to one side of the main hearth. However, the primary purpose of the inglenook was to provide bench seating, keyed into the side walls, in close proximity to the fire. Typically, the wooden lintel and mantelshelf above it are used to store and display mugs, jugs, bowls, and other useful household wares, as well as many other decorative artifacts.

EARLY TILE SLIPS

During the seventeenth and early eighteenth centuries, Delft tiles (made in the Netherlands), and English delft tiles, were often used to decorate fireplace slips–the areas between the fire surround and the front of the hearth. Popular in Europe and the American Colonies, they were produced with tin-glazed polychrome or blue-on-white motifs and patterns. The latter (and most fashionable) were inspired by Chinese export blue and white porcelain wares. Some simply had corner motifs, such as oak leaves or fleurs-de-lis, but most featured a decoratively bordered central picture of either ships, windmills, landscapes, figures, or moral or religious themes.

MARBLE

Marble has been one of the most prestigious building materials since classical Greek and Roman times, and since the late sixteenth century have been used to make the finest fire surrounds, especially in houses where the design and decoration has been primarily inspired by the classical Greco-Roman vocabulary of architecture and ornament (*see* pp. 10–33). The esthetic and constructional reasons for this are manifold. First, all types of marble instantly convey an air of solidity, formality, and opulence–the latter due to the considerable cost of cutting and polishing marble from dense metamorphic rock, and transporting it from quarries mainly located in Italy, France, and Belgium. Second, some varieties, notably the almost pure white statuary marble from Carrara, in Italy, are very receptive to elaborate and finely detailed carving. And third, numerous other types of marble are highly decorative, displaying subtle or bold gradations of color, mainly in the form of crystalline deposits, such as turquoise, opal, and quartz. Typical examples of these variegated marbles, which are either used in their own right, or employed as decorative inlays within paler and more monochromatic marble surrounds, include serpentine, onyx, sienna, breche violet, red levanto, and bois jordan.

1 Made from contrasting plain and finely figured marbles, this grand Palladian fireplace dates to ca. 1720–30. Its composition is characteristically bold, and includes numerous decorative devices derived from the classical Roman vocabulary of ornament. Notable features include the "earred" egg-and-dart molding framing the jambs and lintel; S-scroll brackets (bearing gilded pateras) flanking the jambs; a dentil cornice along the top of the stepped frieze, the latter bearing, at its center, a projecting sculpted mask; and, on top of the mantelshelf, a triangular-shaped pediment.

2 The curving sculptural forms of this reproduction, early-eighteenth-century Louis XIV fire surround are seventeenth-century French Baroque in style, but they also herald the lighter French Rococo style of the eighteenth century. Characteristic Gallic features include splayed pilaster jambs, and the serpentine-profile mantelshelf and frieze. Both are embellished with simple linear and curved moldings and, more prominently, scrolling, spiraling, and splayed acanthus leaves, and "abstract" architectural scrolls. The reeding of the surround's inner perimeter further defines the hearth's opening.

3 Dated to the reign of George II (1727–60), this fire surround has a "bracketed" mantelshelf. Bracketed surrounds were very fashionable during the first half of the eighteenth century. Here, each bracket is carved with three long, straplike, feather-shaped leaves. These foliate motifs are usually referred to as waterleafs, and were often used in both Palladian and later eighteenth-century neo-classical architecture. Apart from the carved bust on the frieze, the other particularly notable feature is the use of contrasting plain and fossilized marbles.

4 *This is a reproduction of a late-eighteenth-century English neoclassical fire surround. Hand-carved from marble, its frieze and pilaster jambs are fluted. The latter have capitals derived from the Ionic Order of architecture, and which surmount stiff-leaf acanthus carving. The frieze is also embellished with a central plaque displaying an urn and lightly scrolling foliage carved in shallow relief. This, in turn, is flanked by a pair of corner brackets which are carved with ribboned drinking vessels and lend additional support to the mantelshelf.*

4

6

5 *Designed by the Adam brothers ca. 1776, this white marble fireplace is in Home House, in London. Neoclassical ornament includes fluted columnar jambs, a reeded frieze, a frieze plaque with a ribboned urn, and mantelshelf brackets with roundels. The surrounding walls are painted faux marble to match the contrasting-colored and stridently figured marble slips.*

5

7

6 *Modeled on a French neoclassical fireplace at the Fontainebleau Palace, this reproduction surround is carved from the finest white statuary marble. Its flat pilaster jambs feature carved acanthus leaves surmounted by rosette motifs on the corner blocks of the frieze–the latter is also embellished with splayed branches tied with a ribbon.*

7 *Dated to the early 1830s, this American Greek Revival fireplace is in a house in New York. It is carved from gray-and-white-veined black marble–one of the most fashionable colors for surrounds in mid-nineteenth-century Greek Revival houses. The columnar jambs are derived from the classical Greek, rather than Roman, Ionic Order* *of architecture. Their austere, unadorned forms are echoed in the sparse ornamentation of the rest of the surround. The cast-iron grate, which is framed by a marble insert modeled on the surround itself, is shown with its cast-iron, pierced-fretwork cover– the latter intended for installation during the summer months when the fire was out of use.*

3 The most prominent architectural feature of this reproduction early-Victorian marble fire surround is the pair of scrolled consoles (or corbels) flanking the flat frieze and supporting the mantelshelf, each of which surmounts a demi-oval paterae. The elegant arched insert is trimmed with a string of husks, crested with floral and foliate motifs.

4 Similar to 3, this reproduction marble fire surround is copied from a model that was initially popular during the reign of William IV, but remained in fashion well into Queen Victoria's reign. It is shown with a black marble hearth slab. Contrasting black and white marbles were very popular during the first half of the nineteenth century.

1 Ornamentation of this reproduction Regency marble fire surround is confined to fluting on the flat jambs and frieze, and to roundels on the corner tablets.

2 Inspired by classical temple-front porticoes, this early-nineteenth-century marble surround is topped with a broken pediment. The fluted frieze and flat pilaster jambs are bordered by an egg-and-dart molding. The frieze plaque displays scrolled foliage, and the corner tablets show rosettes.

5 This fireplace is in the drawing room of a mid-nineteenth-century Greek Revival-style house in Connecticut. It is constructed from lightly veined white marble, although its columnar jambs are in fact painted a contrasting and more stridently figured black and gold faux marble. Typical Greek Revival motifs include carved aegricanes (sacrificial goats' heads) on the corner tablets, and scrolling acanthus and a Greek vase, filled with fruits and flowers, on the frieze plaque.

6 Made from Belgian black and gold marble, this Greek Revival fire surround dates to the 1860s. Its columnar jambs are derived from the rather austere, Classical Greek Ionic Order of architecture. The spiral scrolls which form the capitals of the columns are known as volutes, their shape supposedly derived from the horns of goats or rams. The cast-iron, arch-top register grate is designed to burn coals, but is shown fitted with its summer cover. This is decorated with intricate pierced fretwork, in the form of stylized, interlaced foliage patterns, known as arabesques.

6

7 This plain Victorian marble fire surround dates to ca. 1892. As with many late-nineteenth-century fireplaces, its glazed ceramic tile slips are monochrome (green), rather than patterned, although they display subtle mottling across their surfaces. Rather than being individually mortared, tiles such as this were often supplied as ready-made panels that slotted into a cast-iron framework around a register grate. The latter incorporates a smoke canopy, which has a serpentine profile and bears a large, stylized floral motif with lightly scrolling foliage.

7

8

9

8 This late-nineteenth-century American Beaux Arts fireplace consists of a tabernacle of carved and polished mahogany, enclosing an overmantel and fire surround made of contrasting-colored and patterned marbles. The entire composition is a hybrid revival of French and Italian Renaissance designs.

9 Contrasting-colored and patterned marbles are employed in this late-nineteenth-century Arts and Crafts fire surround. The blue and white ceramic tile slips display motifs and imagery inspired by the Victorian pre-Raphaelite school of painting.

WOODEN

Fire surrounds made of wood have been in widespread use from the late Middle Ages onward, and have been produced in all the major styles displayed in their stone and metal equivalents. Wooden surrounds can be divided into two basic types: those made of hardwood and those made of softwood. Because most hardwoods, such as oak and mahogany, are esthetically pleasing in their own right, the surrounds made from them have often been stained and waxed or varnished to accentuate the natural figuring and grain of the wood; these woods have also proved particularly suited to carved decoration. On the other hand, softwoods, such as fir and pine, have always been more abundant and and much less expensive, but they are blander in appearance. Thus, softwood surrounds have tended to be wood-grained in imitation of hardwoods, or painted to simulate the appearance of other prestigious materials, such as marble; these surrounds have also often featured applied, rather than carved, decoration, usually in the form of composition moldings.

1 The integration of the fire surround with wooden wall paneling was common practice in the reception rooms of eighteenth-century American Colonial houses. This example is in Hunter House, on Rhode Island, and dates to 1758. Its original overmantel picture panel has survived, as have the imported Dutch Delft tile slips. As in many Colonial houses of this period, the paneled surround is made of softwood (probably fir or pine) and wood-grained in imitation of more expensive mahogany.

2 Flat-painted wooden fire surrounds are also typical of eighteenth-century American Colonial interiors and, as in this Rhode Island house, were often painted the same color as the surrounding woodwork. The simple moldings that define the jambs, frieze, and mantelshelf are also characteristic of the Colonial period. Home of Stephen P. Mack.

3 The ornamentation of the painted wooden fire surround–restricted to the leading edge of the mantelshelf–in another room of the Rhode Island house is even plainer than on the surround in 2. The flat-painted, sage green finish, like the buttermilk yellow in 2, is from a Colonial color palette based on earth and vegetable dyes. Home of Stephen P. Mack.

4 A notable feature of this reproduction of an early-eighteenth-century wooden fire surround is the linear molding that runs up the sides of the marble slips and then projects outward at 90 degrees, before continuing up the sides and then across the top of the marble lintel. This geometrical configuration, known as "earring," was a fashionable embellishment of late-seventeenth- and early-eighteenth-century fire surrounds.

5 The painted motifs, such as anthemia, scrolling foliage, husks, masks, urns, and mythological figures, on the frieze and jambs of this Adam fire surround, which dates to the 1770s, are derived from the Etruscan vocabulary of ornament. Ancient Etruscan, Greek, and Roman ornament was very popular in late-eighteenth-century neoclassical interiors.

6 Like 5, this Adam-style fire surround also dates to the 1770s, and is decorated with painted and gilded neoclassical motifs. Their color schemes–pale blue, off white, and gold in 6; raw umber, white, and off white and gold in 5–are typical of late-eighteenth-century neoclassical interiors, as was Pompeiian red, black, and white.

7 Painting softwood fire surrounds, made of inexpensive pine or fir, to simulate expensive and prestigious Italian white statuary marble was a well-established decorative convention during the eighteenth century. This reproduction of a late-eighteenth-century neoclassical surround has fluted pilaster jambs and a dentil cornice below the mantelshelf. The swags-and-tails and the urn on the frieze are applied composition moldings.

8 In contrast to the neoclassical surrounds shown on this page, this detail of a painted wooden fireplace from Strawberry Hill, a house in England, illustrates the "Gothick" style of ornamentation–a revival of late-medieval Gothic forms–that also came into vogue during the second half of the eighteenth century.

9 Typical Adam-style motifs–urns, anthemia, husks, caulicoli, ribbons, bead molding–ornament this late-eighteenth-century flat-painted wooden surround.

1 This reproduction wooden fire surround is copied from an early-nineteenth-century model. The vigor and precision of the hand-carved decoration are evident in the scrolling foliage, swags, and a rosette on the frieze; the egg-and-dart molding around the figured marble infill; and the fluting on the pilaster jambs.

2 Dated to ca. 1808, this American neoclassical wooden fire surround is carved from softwood and painted a cream color in imitation of a plain marble. Its reeded consoles support a dentiled mantelshelf, and the frieze plaque displays bacchanalian figures set against a contrasting-colored, Wedgwood blue ground.

3 This white-painted wooden fire surround is early nineteenth century, and is in an Empire-style reception room of the Morris-Jumel Mansion, in New York. Ornamentation is restricted to the rather bulbous classical moldings on the frieze and on the "earred" jambs. In contrast, the stridently figured, black and gray marble slips and lintel that frame the hearth are far more obviously decorative, as is the pair of brass-finialed firedogs on the stone hearth slab.

1

2

3

4

5

4 Copied from an early Victorian fire surround, this stained and polished reproduction is carved from mahogany. The decorative details are primarily classical in origin. They include fluting and S-scrolls on the jambs; naturalistic buds, fruits, and foliage on the frieze plaque; and rope molding on the leading edge of the mantelshelf. The cast-iron insert is partly black-leaded and partly burnished. Bordered with palmettes, the insert has vases and scrolling plant forms on the slip panels, and budding shoots surrounding a highly stylized rosette on the smoke hood.

5 Integrating a wooden fire surround into the surrounding wooden wall paneling is an architectural convention which has its origins in the grander Jacobethan houses of the fifteenth and sixteenth centuries. It was subsequently employed in many late-Colonial and Federal American houses during the seventeenth and eighteenth centuries. Here it is revived in a late-nineteenth-century interior. The lighter, post-Victorian look is evident in the use of pine, rather than darker-stained oak or mahogany.

6 This highly elaborate Victorian Gothic Revival fireplace is made of carved, stained, and gilt-painted mahogany, but some decoration is gilded composition or plaster. The pair of carved inset panels flanking the mantelshelf clock were salvaged from a seventeenth-century Dutch fireplace. The Gothic and heraldic imagery–coats-of-arms, arcading, and tracery– is supplemented with some classical motifs, notably Ionic capitals and rosettes on the columnar jambs.

7 The decoration on this very plain, reproduction Victorian fire surround, which is made of antique pine, is restricted to reeding on the flat pilaster jambs and the mantelshelf.

6

9 The pink marble insert with a Moorish arch is the most striking feature of this late-nineteenth-century American Arts and Crafts hardwood fire surround. Various stylized floral motifs– inlaid on the frieze, carved on the spandrels of the arch, and painted on the tile inserts in the base of the jambs– provide the decoration.

10 Classical scrolling foliage is used with the sinuous and elongated organic forms of Art Nouveau in this reproduction, late-nineteenth-century, hand-carved mahogany surround.

9

7

8 Fire surrounds with integrated overmantels became increasingly popular toward the end of the nineteenth century. This American example, made of pine and with an inset mirror and display shelving, is very characteristic of the type and period. The grate, framed by relief-tiled slips depicting hunting scenes, has its pierced fretwork cover installed for the summer.

8

10

CAST IRON AND COPPER

One of the major developments in fireplace design during the nineteenth century was the introduction of metal fire surrounds, the most popular and numerous being those mass-produced in cast iron from the mid-century onward. Due to the abundance and cheapness of iron, and the efficiencies of the industrial casting process–which automatically replicated elaborate decorative details that had to be laboriously hand-carved on scarcer and more expensive marbles or hardwoods– cast-iron surrounds proved affordable to the rapidly expanding middle classes of the period. Moreover, as casting techniques improved, and construction and decoration therefore became more sophisticated, these surrounds proved to be an acceptable alternative in many wealthier households to those made of prestigious marble and finely figured hardwoods. Usually made with a built-in cast-iron register grate, and in some cases an integrated overmantel, cast-iron surrounds were produced in all of the historical-revival and innovative styles in vogue from the mid-nineteenth century onward (*see* pp. 24–33). Fashionable finishes included white paint (in imitation of statuary marble) and wood-graining. More popular, however, were black-lead and burnishing. The latter, which gave the iron a subtle reflective appearance and thus emphasized the metallic qualities of the fire surround, had an esthetic appeal similar to those fashioned from hammered and press-molded copper produced under the aegis of the Arts and Crafts and Art Nouveau movements of the late nineteenth and early twentieth centuries

1 Small, modest fire surrounds such as this one were designed to be installed in secondary rooms, especially small bedrooms. Dated to the mid-nineteenth century, it is made of cast iron and painted white to simulate expensive white statuary marble. Decoration–classical in origin–is confined to thin pilasters on the jambs and a small, ribboned wreath on the deep frieze. Like the shallow, overhanging mantelshelf, the plain, beige-colored tile slips framing the hearth are typical of "lesser" Victorian surrounds.

2 Stylistically, this typical cast-iron, mid-Victorian fireplace, which dates to the late 1850s, is highly eclectic. Architecturally it is classical in form– its flat pilaster jamb topped with a deep mantelshelf and flanking a decorative frieze. Classical influence is further evident in the strings of husks on the jambs and in the scrolling foliage on the frieze. However, Gothic ornament is also used, notably in the pair of quatrefoils (the stylized four-lobed floral forms) on the smoke hood.

3 Made from beaten copper, this distinctive turn-of-the-nineteenth- century fire surround was made by George Walton. Although it is essentially Arts and Crafts style, the sinuous interlacing plant-form motifs on the frieze and jambs reflect the style of the Art Nouveau movement that became popular in the last decade of the nineteenth century. The free-stand- ing, cast-iron firebasket was designed by C. F. A. Voysey, and is framed by a slate-lined lintel and matching slips.

4 With its slender, flat jambs and columnar mantelshelf brackets, and its characteristically elongated organic motifs, this early-twentieth-century fireplace is quintessentially Art Nouveau. As with many Art Nouveau surrounds, the cast iron is burnished rather than black-leaded, as with example 2.

5 This fireplace was designed by Charles Rennie Mackintosh in 1902–3 for the main bedroom in The Hill House, in Helensburgh, Scotland. It has a burnished cast-iron frieze and jambs, framed by a simple concave molding, and built-in overmantel shelving. The frieze is decorated with inset colored-glass mosaics of highly stylized organic motifs.

6 Painted off white in imitation of stone, this Edwardian fireplace combines classical with late-medieval ornament. The former is evident in the fluting and tiny swags on the frieze and the beading on the mantelshelf; the latter in armorial shields on the jambs and a Tudor-style hearth.

VICTORIAN TILES

Having been widely supplanted by marble fascias during the late eighteenth and early nineteenth centuries, ceramic tile slips again became popular in the 1840s, and remained very fashionable throughout the Victorian era. Some were hand-painted, such as those made under the aegis of the Esthetic and Arts and Crafts movements. Most, however, were mass-produced, and often in the form of ready-made panels for slotting into the one-piece, cast-iron inserts of register grates. The vast range of pictorial, floral, and other organic patterns and motifs was inspired by the diverse historical styles in vogue during the period, notably the Gothic, Renaissance, Baroque, Rococo, and neoclassical revivals.

7 One-piece, cast-iron fireplaces and register grates were often fitted with tile slips (see left), but panels made of burnished or black-leaded cast iron, or of brass, were sometimes used instead. These panels depict the Greek goddess Hestia, symbol of fire. Other popular motifs included urns, vases, scrolling foliage, and Electra, goddess of hearth and home.

133

FIREDOGS AND GRATES

Since the Middle Ages, four basic devices–firedogs, and dog, hob, and register grates –have been utilized to burn wood or coal in open hearths. Firedogs (or andirons) are pairs of iron bars used to support the ends of logs and raise them above the hearth. Employed almost exclusively until the late seventeenth century, and for most log fires thereafter, they have been made of both wrought and cast iron, with more decorative examples featuring brass or silver finials, typically in the shape of balusters or globes. Free-standing, wrought-iron dog grates (or firebaskets) appeared in the late seventeenth century, and were designed to contain and burn coals, although small logs could also be burned. Although they continued to be used in some larger hearths, they were generally superseded in the 1720s by the cast-iron hob grate, which took up the full width of hearths made narrower to promote the greater draw of air required for the efficient combustion of coal. During the second half of the eighteenth century, hob grates became highly decorative, and displayed a wide range of classical, Rococo, and "Gothick" motifs. Their coal baskets were also moved forward, and their sides canted, to minimize heat loss up the chimney and reflect more heat into the room. However, in the 1820s, these were superseded by even more efficient register grates. Cast in one piece, and forming the sides and back of the hearth, they had a damper plate to control the supply of air to the coals, another damper in the chimney, and were usually embellished with built-in tile slips.

1 The hearth of this reproduction sixteenth-century stone fireplace, with its carved wooden overmantel, has an arch-top, cast-iron fireback, and a wrought-iron grate. The fireback bears an heraldic armorial device–a coronet-crested achievement-of-arms–flanked by naturalistic foliage. The front of the dog grate is in the form of a medieval portcullis. Dog grates, which only came into general use at the end of the seventeenth century, were better suited to containing and burning coals than fire-dogs (see right).

2 The hearth of this late-eighteenth-century Adam-style fireplace contains a particularly elegant dog grate. Made of polished steel, it has a built-in, arch-top fire-back, and a pierced, serpentine-profile front, supported on columnar legs with urn-shaped finials. A type only found in the grandest houses of the period, it displays in its form and classical decorative detail an exceptionally high level of craftsmanship.

3 Set in the hearth of a fine marble fireplace with splayed and fluted, quarter-column jambs, this large Regency register grate is made of cast iron and is equally suitable for burning coals or logs. The absence of decorative detail on the grate indicates that it was not intended for use in the finest reception rooms.

4 This reproduction Regency dog grate is made of cast iron and is notably sculptural in form. Neoclassical details include the splayed scrolled legs and feet–the former embellished with strings of husks–and small, brass, urn-shaped finials. The reproduction surround is carved from white statuary marble.

5 *The smoke hood of this black-leaded, cast-iron Edwardian register grate is decorated with thistles and other stylized organic motifs popular during the late nineteenth and early twentieth centuries. The grate has a damper below the bars to regulate the draft and thus the combustion rate.*

6 *The hearth of this late-nineteenth-century black marble fireplace has a pair of brass-finialed firedogs designed for burning logs rather than coals. The primary purpose of the brass fender is to stop burning logs rolling onto the surrounding carpet.*

5

6

7

7 *Set in a nineteenth-century American Rococo Revival stone surround, which features exuberantly carved foliate motifs typical of the style, this arch-top,*

cast-iron register grate is fitted with its summer cover. The intricacy of the pierced foliate motifs decorating the cover echoes those on the fire surround.

8 *This late-Victorian, one-piece register grate and fire surround are made of cast iron, and are burnished, rather than black-leaded, like grate shown in 5.*

8

HEARTH ACCESSORIES

Since the Middle Ages, most hearths have been equipped with a basic set of tools–tongs, billets, shovels, brushes, and bellows–that is used to prepare, manage, and clean log and coal fires. However, a variety of other implements have also been sited in the hearth to make use of the heat. These include bottle and jug stands for warming wine and, as here, plate warmers made of tin, cast iron, brass, or copper.

STOVES

During the course of the eighteenth century, enclosed wood-burning stoves made of cast iron became increasingly common in continental Europe, Scandinavia, and America, although far less so in Britain. Throughout this period, most models were employed in houses with combined kitchen and living areas, and incorporated one or more hot plates for heating food and liquids. In this respect they supplanted earlier open-hearth methods of cooking, and were precursors of more sophisticated cast-iron cooking ranges that gradually came into widespread use during the nineteenth century (*see* pp. 152–3 and 158–9). While hot plates were retained on nineteenth-century stoves sited in kitchens, they were usually removed from models installed in other rooms for purely heating purposes. Further developments included a substantial increase in the number of stoves designed to burn coal (and, near the end of the nineteenth century, gas); the introduction of fireproof glazed doors; and a much greater emphasis on decorative detail, such as brass hinges and knobs, and molded geometric and organic patterns and motifs.

3 Copied from a nine-teenth-century French model, this reproduction fireplace heater can be fueled by logs, coal, or gas. Smoke and waste gases pass up the chimney flue via a domed ventilator on the top. The naturalistic plant-form imagery on the arched frame surrounding the glazed door is typically French, and is echoed in the splayed feet, which are modeled as stylized leaf forms.

5 Many Victorian heaters had elaborate cast-iron casings. Architectural in form, this reproduction model features a pair of engaged fluted pillars on the two "show" corners, and a stepped plinth edged with rope molding and highly stylized palmettes. Further decoration derived from the classical vocabulary of ornament includes a string of husks on the door frame and, above that, swags of foliage.

1 This reproduction, coal-burning English stove has a black-leaded, cast-iron casing with glazed doors. Features include a warming plate, double-doors with arched glazed windows, and a sliding soot and cinder tray on the underside. The duck motifs on the doors are typical of the floral and faunal decoration often applied to these stoves.

2 Late-nineteenth-century, and also made of cast iron, this large, free-standing heater is designed to burn logs, although coals could also be used. Mounted on castors, it can be moved to anywhere in the room, provided that flue can be set up to carry the smoke and waste gases up through the roof to the outside of the house.

4 Highly versatile, this American, black-leaded, cast-iron stove–known as a "potbelly"–could be enclosed in a hearth or inglenook, or placed out in a room, provided the flue could be run through an opening cut *in the roof. Either log or coal burning, most potbellies have a warming plate on top. This model has rather elaborate cabriole legs that are decorated with foliate motifs and end in paw feet.*

RADIATORS

Central-heating systems, servicing rooms via a series of cast-iron radiators linked by hot-water pipes running from a coal-, wood-, or gas-powered boiler, were first installed in grander American and European houses during the last quarter of the nineteenth century, but substantial installation and running costs meant they were beyond the means of most homeowners until after the Second World War. Consequently, in order to supplement coal- or wood-burning open fires or cast-iron stoves with central heating in houses built prior to the late nineteenth century, owners have had to compromise period authenticity for greater domestic comfort. The most visually effective and commonly used solution has been to disguise modern steel radiators with either purpose-built cabinets designed in the style of the woodwork, or pieces of carcass furniture (such as chiffoniers or window seats), appropriate to the period of the house. Many owners of late-nineteenth-century, and later, houses have also adopted this practice, but today's availability of reproduction cast-iron period radiators provides a more historically accurate option.

3 Made to simulate a Regency chiffonier, this painted wooden radiator cabinet features fluted pilaster jambs topped with shell motifs, and latticework door panels. Plainer and more decorative models are made in various other period styles from materials such as limed oak and mahogany.

4 Instead of being concealed them in purpose-built cabinets such as 3, radiators can be disguised within the basic architectural features of a room. For example, in this corner of a late-nineteenth-century French neo-classical-style interior, a modern panel radiator has been made an integral part of the dado by framing it with simple wooden moldings. The baseboard disguises the pipework; vertical panels, like those on the door, conceal the valves; and a dado rail-like shelf conceals its top, leaving the center exposed as reeded dado paneling.

5 As an alternative to boxing-in and disguising radiators esthetically ill-suited to pre-late-nineteenth-century interiors, some modern architects and designers make a feature of them. This usually involves adapting the basic design to create a pastiche of a classical architectural form—the engaged fluted column or pilaster, as here. The success of this approach invariably depends upon the radiator's position—in other words, whether it is sited where you would normally expect to find a real column or pilaster.

1 & 2 The two radiators shown above are made of cast iron. The one on the left dates to the early twentieth century; the one on the right is a modern reproduction. They both display minor variations on a standard design that has been employed on both sides of the Atlantic, but especially in Europe, since the turn of the nineteenth century. The earlier example is slightly more decorative, in that the individual pipes are molded in low relief with stylized foliate motifs. Its feet, which supplement concealed wall brackets, are also more prominent and ornamental than those on the more recent model. A notable, and substantial, variation was the free-standing circular types first made at the beginning of the twentieth century. These could be dismantled into two semicircular halves designed to fit around a pillar or column.

OVERMANTEL MIRRORS

When the fashion for placing a mirror above a fireplace began in the late seventeenth century, most mirror-plates were produced from blown glass–a process that limited their size and made them very expensive. Consequently, until the second half of the eighteenth century, when the perfection of casting techniques facilitated much larger and cheaper plates, such mirrors were the preserve of the wealthy, and invariably took the form of a small centerpiece in a large architectural overmantel. The latter, made from wood, stone, or plaster, usually consisted of an entablature and flanking columns or pilasters designed as an integral part of the fire surround beneath. Integrated, architectural-style overmantels with inset mirrors continued to be employed during the nineteenth and early twentieth centuries, when they often incorporated shelves and niches for the display of artifacts. However, from the late eighteenth century onward, larger mirror-plates framed independently of the fire surround proved more popular. Fashionable shapes included rectangular, oval, round, cartouche (scroll-shaped), and convex. Framing materials–notably, gold, silver, copper, plaster and, more commonly, gilded, painted, or polished wood– were fashioned in diverse styles, ranging from simple rectilinear moldings to more elaborate compositions incorporating geometric, mythological, or floral and faunal motifs primarily derived from the classical or Gothic vocabularies of ornament.

1 Made of painted wood and plaster, this elegant overmantel mirror is in a boudoir in a late-eighteenth-century château in France. It illustrates the lingering influence of Rococo-style decoration during the early years of Louis XVI's reign (1774–92), when neoclassical styles of architecture and ornament gradually supplanted the Rococo. The latter is seen in the delicately carved flowers entwining the mirror frame. However, the much plainer moldings used to panel the fire-place wall establish the more austere rectilinear style of neoclassicism.

2 Surmounting an 1820s' neoclassical marble fire surround with herm jambs, this overmantel mirror is quintessentially Rococo style. Typically, the delicately carved flowers and foliage entwine a curvaceous giltwood frame that incorporates a series of S- and C-scrolls.

3 This nineteenth-century overmantel has a triptych-style mirror-glass, and a bronzed giltwood, pillared frame decorated with classical motifs, such as rope and egg-and-dart moldings.

4 Giltwood overmantel mirrors framed with simple rectilinear moldings of classical origin were fashionable throughout the nineteenth century, but especially in earlier and later Victorian interiors.

5 Sited above a carved-stone fireplace, this Baroque Revival-style overmantel mirror has a typically ornate and sculptural black and giltwood frame. The decoration is in the form of boldly carved S- and C-scrolls interspersed with flowers, foliage, and berries. The artifacts in front include a bracket clock with temple-front portico case and a pair of torchères.

5

6 This nineteenth-century American giltwood overmantel displays many of the architectural forms and decorative motifs of the Gothic Revival. Notable features include pointed arches, tracery, a trefoil, finials, crockets, and carved, naturalistic plant forms.

7

7 Carved from stone, the frame of this modern overmantel mirror draws on the Imperial Roman forms of architecture and ornament that were revived and adapted in the Empire style of the late eighteenth and early nineteenth centuries. It initially emerged in France under the patronage of Napoleon Bonaparte, and later spread throughout much of Europe and then to America. In addition to the wreaths of laurel or oak leaves on this frame, Empire style was characterized by the use of motifs such as lances, arrows, figures of Victory and Fame, chimeras, griffins, eagles, lions, winged torches, stars, and anthemia.

6

8 Wall-hung, oval-shape overmantel mirrors first appeared in France during the eighteenth century. They were very popular in Regency interiors, but were also hung, as here, in many Victorian houses. This example has a flat mirror-glass. However, some were fitted with convex glass, and known as girandoles. Decoration of this giltwood frame includes bead molding, strings of husks, and a crest of scrolling foliage.

8

9 During the second half of the nineteenth century, large over-mantels became more fashionable and remained so well into the twentieth century. Usually architectural in form and modeled as an extension of the fire surround below it, they invariably incorporated a panel of mirror-glass. In this late-nineteenth-century example, the inset mirror is framed by a pine surround. The latter features carved stylized floral motifs, a pair of turned pillars, and a pair of tabernacles (canopied niches) intended for the display of decorative artifacts.

9

BATHROOMS

From the Middle Ages to the middle of the nineteenth century, very few houses had rooms specifically designed, or set aside, as bathrooms. Portable chamber pots were used inside the house, mainly in bedrooms, and toilets (privies) were usually sited in small wooden, stone, or brick "houses of easement" above a cesspit at the end of the yard or garden. Everyday washing took place in bedrooms or dressing rooms, using jugs and basins, and bathing–infrequent by today's standards–was mostly carried out in portable hip baths placed in front of a fire (the baths were often hung on the back of a door when not in use). One of the main disadvantages of these facilities was that they were very time-consuming. Basins and bathtubs had to be filled by hand, with buckets of water either carried from a well or water butts outside the house or, more rarely, from crude wooden pipes that brought water, at very low pressure, into the first floor or basement. Moreover, when hot water was required, it had to be first heated over the kitchen fire or range before being toted around the house. Equally arduous was the task of emptying basins and baths. However, it was not as onerous as having to empty chamber pots into stinking cesspits that often overflowed after a heavy rainfall, and sometimes fouled the fresh-water supplies, causing diseases such as cholera (of which there were two major outbreaks in Europe during the mid-nineteenth century).

Labor-intensive, and too often unhygienic, these sanitary arrangements became increasingly unacceptable to the rapidly expanding urban populations of the Victorian age. Fortunately, the widespread desire to improve standards of hygiene was matched by the necessary technological innovation, industry, and prosperity to make it possible. The resulting series of major public and private works–initially in the towns and cities–from the second half of the nineteenth century onward saw the installation of extensive sewerage systems, the introduction of mains water under pressure (via lead and iron pipes) into many homes, and the development of more efficient methods of heating water–in the form of coal- and gas-fired boilers. Inevitably, these technological improvements were mirrored in the development of much improved sanitary fixtures and fittings. Mass-produced, enameled cast-iron baths (*see* pp. 142–3) and ceramic basins (*see* pp. 144–5) were plumbed into pressurized or gravity-fed hot-and-cold-water systems (controlled by reliable metal faucets–*see* pp. 148–9) and, like "self-flushing" toilets (*see* pp. 146–7), could be emptied via waste pipes directly into the sewers. And, because it made ergonomic sense to run most of the internal waste and water pipes to one area of the house, all these fixtures and fittings were increasingly installed either in a single room–a bathroom–or in an adjoining bathroom and toilet.

As the vast majority of houses built prior to the second half of the nineteenth century had not been designed with such a room (or rooms) in mind, most early bathrooms were converted from existing bedrooms, dressing rooms, or storerooms. Partly because of their original use, and partly to allay lingering Victorian fears about the hygienic merits of bringing toilets inside the house, they were often furnished as other rooms in the home, and the sanitary equipment "concealed" in furniturelike wooden encasements. The decorative convention of encasement lasted in many households for much of the second half of the nineteenth century (and enjoyed a number of revivals during the twentieth). However, as reticence to indoor toilets receded, and particularly after architects began to design houses with purpose-built bathrooms in the late nineteenth century, sanitary fixtures and fittings gradually came "out of the closet" and bathrooms acquired their own decorative genre. This could be characterized as a more stream-lined, functional, and hygienic look. Floors were covered with tiles or linoleum (*see* pp. 94–7), rather than carpet; dadoes were tiled (*see* pp. 116–7) or flat-painted; curtains were replaced with "frosted" glass; and the design and decoration of baths, basins, toilets, faucets, and towel rails, toilet-roll holders, and soap dishes (*see* pp. 150–1) was governed equally by changing fashions and ease of cleaning.

BATHS

Before the Victorian era, most domestic bathing took place in portable hip baths, made from sheet lead, copper, tin, or zinc, placed in front of a bedroom, scullery, or kitchen fire, or in a privy, and filled and emptied by bucket. However, during the course of the second half of the nineteenth century, hip baths were gradually supplanted by fixed baths which, following the introduction of pressurized mains-water supplies and improved drainage systems, were plumbed in and usually installed upstairs, in either what was formerly a bedroom or in a bathroom. Although copper and zinc baths were still used, mass-produced, roll-top-rimmed, cast-iron baths increasingly became the preferred choice in most households. Lined with vitreous enamel, they were often encased in wooden frames. However, from the last quarter of the century onward, they were more often raised above the floor on ornamental feet, and their exposed sides were either flat-painted (and often stenciled), or painted in imitation of marble or other decorative stones.

1 Combined bath-and-shower units began to be installed in some grander houses during the latter part of the nineteenth century, following the technical improvements made to hot-water boilers and pressurized water systems. The example shown here consists of a vitreous-enameled, cast-iron, roll-top bath (on lion's-paw feet), plus an overhead douche, and a shower compartment–also vitreous-enameled, fixed to the bath's rim, and housing horizontal "needle" sprays. The douche, pipework, and capstan-headed faucets are all chromed, and the latter allowing the bather instantly to divert hot and cold water from the bath to the douche, or to the needle sprays, or to both at the same time.

2 Finished in white porcelain, this late-Victorian, cast-iron, roll-top bath stands on elaborate ball-and-claw feet. These are modeled as harpies–the beasts of Greek and Roman mythology, with wings and claws of a bird, and the head of a woman.

3 This late-Victorian, cast-iron, roll-top bath is finished in vitreous enamel, and its exterior painted sage green. The ball-and-claw feet are caricatures of mythical birds, and highlighted with gold paint.

4 Before cast-iron baths became fashionable in the late nineteenth century, most baths were made from sheet lead, copper, or zinc. This French example is copper, has a roll-top, and dates to the mid-nineteenth century. The hot and cold water is supplied by a late-nineteenth-century, wall-mounted, bath-shower mixer faucet, made of brass, and with elegant shell-shaped spouts.

5

6

6 *The decorative convention, instigated by the Victorians, of encasing sanitary fixtures with woodwork has been partly adopted in this modern bathroom to give it a period feel. In many Victorian bathrooms, the bath, basin, and toilet would all have been encased; here, only the cast-iron bath is recessed within, and side-paneled to match the painted sea-green wall paneling.*

7

7 *Portable hip baths were common up to the late nineteenth century. With a high, sloping back to support the neck and shoulders, and a tapered end to save water, they were originally placed in front of a fireplace, and filled and emptied by bucket. However, this enameled, cast-iron reproduction has a plumbed-in waste, and is filled via a floor-mounted bath-shower mixer faucet.*

5 *Like baths 3 and 4, this enameled and painted, cast-iron bath is a "double-ended" turn-of-the-century reproduction. Positioned with one side, instead of one end, against a wall, double-ended baths receive their water supplies from faucets or bath-shower mixers mounted on either the wall, an infill panel inserted between the bath and the wall or, as in this example, a flat section (a "deck") fashioned into the rim.*

8

8 *Fashionable painted finishes applied to the outside of nineteenth-century, enameled, cast-iron baths included faux marble and, as here, repeat motifs stenciled over a flat-painted monochrome ground.*

9 *The roll-top rims of Edwardian, enameled, cast-iron baths, as on this reproduction model, were generally less bulbous than their Victorian counterparts.*

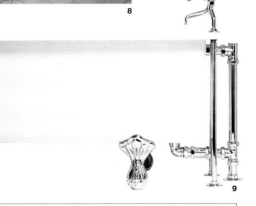

9

SHOWER SETS

Combination bath-and-shower faucets (or shower sets) evolved during the latter part of the nineteenth century, although their use was initially confined to those wealthier households, whose boiler was sufficiently powerful to pipe hot water to the faucets at roughly equal pressure as that of the cold water supplied from the tank. One of their main attractions was that they allowed the homeowner to bathe and shower in the same tub. They also helped reduce condensation in the bathroom by mixing the hot and cold water to a comfortable temperature before it was exposed to the atmosphere. Moreover, by linking a hand-held shower to the main body of the faucet with a flexible, rubber-core, metal-link hose, they gave the bather complete control over the spray's direction. The early-twentieth-century model shown here is particularly sophisticated, in that it combines the bath faucets and hand-held shower with a fixed, overhead douche, and also incorporates a soap and sponge rack on the riser pipe. Examples of shower sets without over-head douches are shown above, opposite, and on page 150.

BASINS

Plumbed-in basins were a rare luxury prior to the last quarter of the nineteenth century, and where they were installed–in only the grandest of houses–they often took the form of a small fountain recessed in a niche in the wall. In the vast majority of households, daily washing was carried out using ceramic basins and jugs, which were filled and emptied by hand and, together with various other bowls and dishes (designed to hold soap, perfumed water, toothbrushes, and shaving equipment), were placed on top of washstands. Sited in a bedroom or dressing room, most washstands were made as free-standing wooden dressers, and were usually fitted with a durable marble top. However, following the introduction of pressurized water systems controlled by metal faucets, and more efficient drainage systems, washstands, now made of wood or cast iron, were fitted with inset, plumbed-in, ceramic or enameled-metal basins. Around the turn of the century, these were generally superseded by ceramic pedestal basins, which were screwed to the wall and further supported on columnarlike, ceramic plinths.

1 Before the advent of separate bathrooms, and the installation of running hot-and-cold-water systems during the latter part of the nineteenth century, daily ablutions in most houses were carried out in bedrooms, using hand-filled jugs and basins. Here, in a bedroom at Ulysses S. Grant's house in Galena, Illinois, the Warwick china jug and basin are part of a set that also includes a slop pail, a chamber pot, and various other toilet accessories. They are sited on and around a marble-topped, mahogany washstand, dated to ca. 1860.

2 Many Victorian and Edwardian basins were wall-mounted on brackets, instead of being encased in a washstand. Here, white-painted, plain tubular brackets are used under a reproduction ceramic basin. Because of the preoccupation with hygiene during the late nineteenth and early twentieth centuries, water and waste pipes were often left exposed in order to aid cleaning.

3 This architectural, cast-iron washstand is late Victorian, and has an inset, transfer-printed ceramic basin, and an integral shelf and mirror. It is embellished with molded and painted floral motifs, which are primarily derived from the classical vocabulary of ornament.

4 Classical influence is also evident in the plain, columnar plinth and the serpentine profile of the leading edge of this reproduction Edwardian basin. As well as supporting the basin (which is additionally secured by screws to the wall), the hollowed-out plinth disguises the presence of the waste and water pipes.

5 Washstands with inset basins enjoyed a notable revival during the late twentieth century, and are now more usually referred to as vanity units. This example features chromed pillar faucets, and consists of a top and basin made of synthetic marble, on a plinth-mounted cabinet with fielded-panel doors. Stylistically, it is broadly modeled on an encased Victorian basin. However, the bluish-gray tones of the distressed paint finish applied to the softwood cabinet are more in keeping with the color schemes favored during the second half of the eighteenth century.

5

6

6 While most Victorian ceramic, and enameled-steel, basins were manufactured in plain white, cream, or an ivory color, brightly patterned models were also very fashionable, especially during the last quarter of the nineteenth century. Set in a marble-topped washstand, this reproduction ceramic basin is embellished with cherubs and sprigs of flowers and foliage.

7 Located in one of the bathrooms at the Rockcliffe Mansion in Hannibal, Missouri, this ceramic basin dates to 1898–1900. Neoclassical in style, it is supported on a pair of baluster legs, and features a serpentine-profile front, sides, and rim-mounted back-splash. The faucets, soap dishes, towel hook, and waste and water pipes are all original.

7

8

8 Installed in a recently remodeled attic bath-room, this original Victorian washstand is made of cast iron, and has an inset ceramic basin. The latter features a raised back and sides, designed partly to stop soap sliding off onto the floor, and partly to protect the wall and floor from splashing.

9

9 This late-Victorian corner washstand is made of mahogany, inset with floral-pattern ceramic tiles, and has a matching backsplash. Its ceramic basin is mounted on a pair of lugs set in the marble top. These allow the basin to be swiveled upside down so that water can be emptied into the waste pipe via a funnel in the cabinet.

TOILETS

Prior to the mid-nineteenth century, most houses had outside privies, which were usually composed of a wooden seat placed over a shaft leading to an ash- or cesspit–the latter periodically cleared by laborers. Inside the house, chamber pots were used, and were sometimes built into a small piece of movable furniture, known as a "close stool," which, in large houses, could be permanently housed in a small closet. While chamber pots were retained in many European bedrooms well into the twentieth century, the introduction of pressurized mains-water supplies and sophisticated sewerage systems during the Victorian era resulted in all other facilities being replaced by the internal, plumbed-in water closet (or toilet). Sited in its own room, or a bathroom, the toilet went through various stages of technical development, culminating in the 1890s in the perfection of the "wash-out" model. Still used today, it consisted of a ceramic bowl (with a fitted seat), whose contents were flushed through an S-bend gas trap by a downrush of water from an overhead cistern–the latter usually operated by pulling a chain.

1 Encasing the toilet in a chair- or thronelike enclosure was common during the nineteenth century, and was largely done to help overcome initial reticence about installing toilets inside (rather than outside) the house. This grand reproduction enclosure is made of stained and polished oak. Notable features include turned pilasters, drop pendants, linenfold carving and, on the seat lid, a carved portrait roundel–all primarily modeled in the English Tudorbethan style of the late fifteenth and sixteenth centuries.

2 High-level cisterns, which produced a powerful downrush of water to flush the toilet, were introduced in the nineteenth century. Many were hidden behind paneling, but more decorative models, such as this striking, burnished cast-iron example, were specifically designed to be displayed on the wall.

3 In this Gothic Revival bathroom, the columnar toilet bowl is flushed by a concealed high-level cistern–operated by pulling the chain handle in the arched niche in the wall paneling.

5 While most ceramic Victorian toilet bowls were produced in plain white (like basins, see pp. 144–5), transfer-printed-patterned models were also made. This original Victorian bowl displays a blue floral pattern on a white ground. The bold naturalistic flowers are typical of the mid-nineteenth century; smaller, more delicate floral patterns were favored during the late-Victorian period. The ceramic seat, which bears the maker's emblem, is bordered with bead and stylized floral motifs.

4 The toilet bowl in this original Edwardian bathroom suite is flushed by a high-level, chain-operated, ceramic cistern mounted on painted, cast-iron wall brackets. Ceramic cisterns became increasingly popular in the early twentieth century, although cast-iron versions continued to be produced in great numbers during this period. Most were plain white, but some bore transfer-printed patterns. The finish on the down-pipe from the cistern is lacquered brass, and matches the towel rails and the faucets on the bath and basin. The toilet seat is mahogany; other fashionable woods included oak and pine– the latter sometimes painted, usually white.

6 & 7 Both of these modern toilets are styled on Edwardian models. The one on the right has a separate cistern, which is mounted much lower on the wall than its high-level Victorian (and some Edwardian) predecessors (see 2 and 4). The example on the left, although Edwardian in profile, and also lever-operated, has a close-coupled cistern. These cisterns were introduced much later in the twentieth century, and rely on a plunger instead of gravity to push water out through the holes under the bowl's rim. Although not strictly authentic to Edwardian (and earlier) interiors, they are often used in them nowadays, as they allow the toilet bowl to be sited under a window.

FAUCETS

Although crude faucets made of wood and metal were in use before the 1850s, mechanically efficient metal faucets were not perfected until the second half of the nineteenth century, when pressurized mains-water supplies, storage tanks, hot-water boilers, and plumbed-in basins and bathtubs were gradually introduced to ordinary households. Apart from various stylistic changes, which included numerous different designs and finishes, many of them being reproduced today by specialist suppliers, the basic types of faucet developed by the Victorians have been employed ever since. These include pairs of bibs and globes (connected to separate hot-and-cold water pipes in the wall above a bath or basin); pairs of pillars (mounted on the rim of a bath or basin); mixer faucets (wall- or bath/basin-mounted, and mixing hot and cold water in the body of the faucet before delivery via a single spout); and combination bath-and-shower mixers.

3 Basin-rim-mounted, these reproduction Victorian pillar faucets are "antique" nickel-plated and have X-head handles. Capstans and X-heads are among the most enduringly fashionable types of handle since the mid-nineteenth century, despite the fact that lever handles are easier to operate.

1 Reproduced from a classic turn-of-the-nineteenth-century utilitarian design, this pair of pillar faucets supplies hot and cold water separately and is mounted on the rim of a basin. They feature capstan handles and have a nickel-plated finish. ("Antiqued" nickel-plated reproductions are also available.)

2 These pillar basin faucets are finished in chrome, and have ceramic "quick-turn" lever handles and curved spouts. Although reproduced from a mid-nineteenth-century Victorian design, they are compatible in style with late-eighteenth-century Georgian and early-nineteenth-century Edwardian bathrooms.

4 This Edwardian-style, wall-mounted bath mixer with X-head handles is finished in "antique" gold. Alternative finishes include chrome, nickel, and gunmetal.

5 The nickel-plated globe faucet shown here is modeled on a ca. 1890 prototype. Although its four-point capstan handle is a traditional Victorian design, its streamlined spout pre-empts Modernist designs of the twentieth century.

6 This basin mixer faucet is early twentieth century. Chrome-plated, it features a single spout (with an integral pop-up stopper) connected beneath the basin rim to a pair of capstan-headed mixer handles.

7 This monobloc basin faucet premixes hot and cold water in the same way as the bidet faucet shown below right. However, its truncated, swan's-neck spout is not adjustable. The finish is chrome, with contrasting brass detailing on the capstan handles, popup stopper, and spout end. Mixed-metal styling such as this dates from the early twentieth century.

7

8 In contrast to basin mixer faucet 6, this polished-brass example has "quick-turn" lever handles (with ceramic inserts), and a swan's-neck spout. Brass faucets have been popular since Victorian times. This is a modern reproduction, but many restored nineteenth- and early-twentieth-century originals are still available through specialist suppliers.

8

9 Finished in burnished brass, this bath-shower mixer is a reproduction of a traditional Victorian design. The shower handle and the diverter lever (which diverts the flow of premixed hot and cold water from the spout to the shower head, and vice versa) are ceramic, although many reproductions have plastic handles, and some Victorian originals had ebony or white- or black-painted wooden handles.

9

10

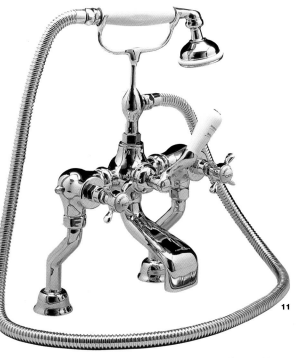

11

10 This reproduction Victorian, polished-brass bath-shower mixer, with ceramic shower handle and diverter lever, is designed to be used with matching brass supply and waste pipes. This allows free-standing, roll-top baths (which cannot support rim-mounted faucets) to be sited in the center of a room, or adjacent to a wall structurally unsuitable for mounting faucets or concealing pipework.

11 The S-shaped hot-and-cold supply pipes of this early-twentieth-century-style "antique" chrome bath-shower set can be swiveled prior to fixing to adjust the spout's position in relation to the bath's rim.

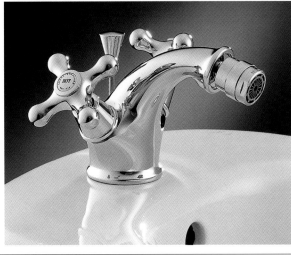

BIDETS

The bidet was first introduced during the early eighteenth century, in France. The earliest models took the form of portable, hand-pumped sprays. This more efficient, plumbed-in, chrome-finish bidet faucet is a reproduction of an early-twentieth-century design. Known as a monobloc or center-set bidet mixer, it has a pair of capstan handles, which allow the user to premix the hot-and-cold-water supplies in the body of the faucet, and an adjustable (swivel) spout for controlling the strength and arc of the spray. The back of the faucet also accommodates a plunger which, via two connecting rods, operates a pop-up stopper in the base of the ceramic bowl.

BATHROOM ACCESSORIES

A diverse range of bathroom accessories has been created for the convenience of bathers. Most of them were initially introduced by the Victorians during the latter part of the nineteenth century, especially after more and more houses had rooms (mostly bedrooms) either converted for use as bathrooms or, from around the turn of the century onward, were built with dedicated bathrooms. Notable examples include slatted racks, designed to hold soap, sponges, and washcloths, and be either wall-mounted next to baths or showers, or supported on the rims of baths; soap dishes, wall-mounted on metal brackets above basins or baths; wall-mounted and free-standing toothbrush holders; toilet-roll stands and holders; bathrobe hooks; adjustable mirrors; wall lights (*see* pp. 168–9); and towel rails– the latter either free-standing, or floor- or wall-mounted, and either heated or unheated. Favored materials for their manufacture have included, depending on the item, softwoods and hardwoods (the former often painted, the latter usually varnished, to insulate against moisture); glazed earthenware and porcelain; and various metals, notably brass, cast iron, and chrome- (and even gold-) plated brass and steel. In terms of design, all of these accessories have been fashioned or embellished in a range of period styles, including the numerous Victorian and Edwardian classical and Gothic revivals, as well as the Art Nouveau and embryonic Modernist styles of the late nineteenth and early twentieth centuries.

1 Metal bathracks have been in use since the Victorian era, and are divided into a series of compartments (slatted for draining) designed to hold soap, shampoo, loofahs, sponges, and various other cleansing paraphernalia. Rested on, rather than fixed to, the side rims of the bath, their position can be easily adjusted to provide optimum access to the contents. This example is chromed, but racks are also available in lacquered-brass and gold-plated finishes, as well as in varnished hardwoods, such as beech or mahogany.

2

1

2 & 3 The majority of wall-mounted soap dishes are designed to be positioned above or next to basins, but they can also be sited over baths. The one on the left is a reproduction Edwardian model with a cut-crystal dish bearing stylized floral motifs, and mounted on a chromed-metal holder. Also reproduction Edwardian, the example on the right is made of bone china, and set in a lacquered-brass holder. Both of these dishes can be instantly lifted and upturned to empty accumulations of water.

4 Floor-mounted, hot-water towel rails, piped into the central-heating system, became increasingly common during the early years of the twentieth century, and were styled on the free-standing, unheated, wooden clotheshorses used in many Victorian bathrooms. This double-rail, with ball joints, is finished in lacquered brass. Single rails are also produced, and other popular finishes include polished brass, chrome, and painted or gold-plated iron.

4

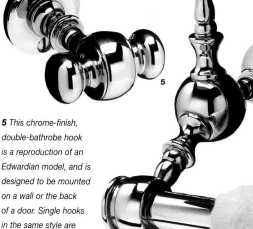

5

6

5 This chrome-finish, double-bathrobe hook is a reproduction of an Edwardian model, and is designed to be mounted on a wall or the back of a door. Single hooks in the same style are also available.

6 Unheated, chromed, and designed to be wall-mounted, this double-towel rail is reproduced from an Edwardian rail dated to ca. 1910. Its lower rail is projected further away from the wall than the upper rail in order to create a ventilation space between drying towels.

7 *Designed to be mounted above a basin, extendable shaving mirrors are available in various sizes. They can be pushed against the wall when not in use and, unlike fixed wall mirrors, pulled out and swiveled to the most desirable position when shaving. This chromed model has a standard mirror on one side, and a magnifying mirror on the other.*

8 *Like bathracks (see 1), wall-mounted, slatted metal shower racks are employed to provide ease of access to soap, shampoo, washcloths, and sponges. This is a reproduction Edwardian model with an "antiqued" chrome finish.*

9 & 10 *Toilet-paper holders have been produced in numerous styles during the nineteenth and twentieth centuries. The wall-mounted example on the left is late Edwardian, finished in chrome, and designed to hold rolls of toilet paper. The chromed, floor-standing model on the right is reproduction Edwardian, and also designed to hold toilet rolls. Wall-mounted, "letterbox" models are also made to hold wads of individual sheets of paper. All are available in polished or lacquered brass, gold plate, and varnished soft- and hardwoods.*

11 *This reproduction Edwardian toothbrush and toothpaste holder is wall-mounted, and consists of a white bone-china tumbler set in a chrome-ringed bracket. The tumbler can be lifted out for cleaning. The bracket is also available in brass and gold-plated finishes.*

12 *Also reproduction Edwardian, this tooth-brush stand is fitted with slotted ceramic disks mounted on an "antiqued," gold-plated stand with a decorative ball finial. It is intended for use on a washstand, or a shelf wall-mounted above the basin.*

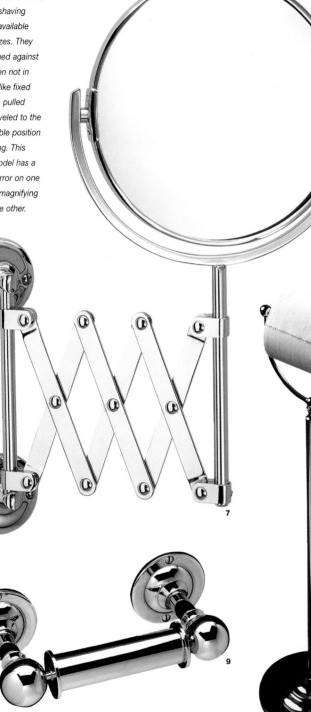

KITCHENS

Technology has had a more profound effect on the evolution of kitchen design than on any other room in the domestic interior. It touches every aspect of the preservation, preparation, cooking, and presentation of food. Storage, working surfaces, the *batterie de cuisine*, the means of cooking, and the efficient provision of water, fuel, and ventilation are all vital considerations. Not only must the modern kitchen comply with a practical need, but it must also embody the kind of comfort and character that make it the heart of the home.

Only in our very recent history have kitchens become the hub of the household, having both a social and decorative role. In the past, the kitchen was usually the servants' domain and a place of work, and hence the room was largely bereft of the frivolities of ornamentation. In grander houses, the kitchen was often placed in the basement. In 1570, the Italian architect, Andrea Palladio, described the service areas of the house as "the less comely parts," advocating that "somewhat underground, may be disposed the cellars, the magazines for wood, pantries, kitchens, servants' hall, wash-houses, ovens, and such like things necessary for daily use." His description illustrates how the kitchen environment was unlike the modern arrangement as we know it. Because most of the storage, preparation, cooking tasks, and washing were carried out in side rooms, the main kitchen served as the central "engine room," and usually contained a huge work table, dressers for holding sets of china, serving plates, and mixing bowls, hanging racks for frequently used items, drying racks for plates, a pantry for storing food, and a large and often cumbersome cooking range. In middle-class homes, all of these items would have been housed in only one or two rooms.

The evolution of cooking systems made slow progress in three principle steps, namely the open hearth, the open-fire range, and the enclosed range. The basic "down hearth" served as the means of cooking until the use of coal necessitated the creation of a draft by containing the fuel in a metal basket that was raised over the fire. This developed into a more-or-less standard facility that was constructed with an arrangement of horizontal bars and vertical posts. From 1567, iron "jacks" had been installed in the chimney, which in time became a sophisticated mechanism based on up-draft or ratcheted wheels that provided a means of turning roasting meat. The hob grate, first introduced in the 1750s, ousted the less efficient basket grate, and the period between 1770 and 1820 saw an increase in the use of cast-iron stoves incorporating an oven into the roasting range, and a back-boiler for hot water. This "closed range" dominated cooking methods from the late eighteenth century, and was even used until the 1920s. Despite being at the cutting edge of technological invention when it was introduced, in reality this range was a nightmare–dirty, temperamental, and in daily need of dedicated servicing and polishing. The mid-nineteenth century saw the arrival of the cast-iron gas stove and, while oil stoves remained popular, it took another fifty years before gas superseded the solid-fuel range. In turn, the first Edwardian electric stoves were deemed expensive, unglamorous, and slow to heat up.

Over the centuries, there have been many influences on the kitchen's metamorphosis. Global trade brought wealth, cultural changes, the introduction of new foods, and ways of using them. The Industrial Revolution resulted in a large urban population with related domestic needs. The inventiveness of the Victorians resulted in a plethora of ingenious kitchen equipment and labor-saving devices, and the two world wars had a profound effect on the way food was produced and on the kitchen's social environment.

The kitchen corner shown opposite is in a house in Rhode Island, and is the work of Stephen P. Mack (*see* page 187). Its unpolished stone sink, simple open shelves, and rustic woodwork illustrate how historical reference to detail creates a characterful setting. In combination with today's technology and lifestyle, the kitchen has finally become a place of physical and spiritual nourishment at the center of family life.

SINKS

Early-eighteenth-century sinks were very basic: wide and flat, they were usually made of stone, or of lead sheeting over a wooden framework, with a large vessel (a copper) to heat water brought in from a well. From the early nineteenth century, water provision started to improve. A single faucet, usually located on the wall above the sink, fed by the public water supply or a tank, gave cold water, which was still heated in a copper. In America, during the Federal period, only the grandest houses had running water; more modest houses continued to use well water that was brought inside. Sinks were usually made of stone or metal, and included a faucet and a hand pump to pump in water. In Britain, shallow earthenware sinks began to be mass-produced in the pottery towns. By the mid-nineteenth century, wooden sinks lined in beaten lead or copper were popular, but too expensive for most households. The Victorians used a variety of sinks for specific jobs, installing them in the kitchen's "domestic offices" away from the main cooking area. These included porcelain-glazed sinks such as the Belfast, "pot," butler's, and gamekeeper's sinks–so named because of their shapes and original uses. Teak sinks were used in the butler's pantry for washing fine glass and china. Arts and Crafts sinks were utilitarian, consistent with the movement's ideology. The early twentieth century saw a vast improvement in hot-water systems, resulting in sinks being supplied with both hot and cold water.

1 This heavy, rough stone sink, which needed to be supported on brick, stone, or concrete piers, is of a type that would have been in general use in America in the 1820s. The sink is huge and shallow, with only basic drainage. The large hand pump, sitting on what would now be considered a draining board, was a great improvement on fetching water in a bucket from a well in the kitchen's yard.

2 A Victorian ceramic butler's sink is housed in a Palladian-style wooden framework. Details such as the choice of "drab" paintwork, old-fashioned faucets and soap holder, and stone jars and other kitchen paraphernalia, serve to enhance the period illusion.

3 This type of long, shallow, Victorian-style ceramic sink is usually known as a gamekeeper's sink for the obvious reason that it was roomy enough to deal with the cleaning of his catch. Its weight requires solid support, as here, where it is held up on brick piers. In the modern kitchen such a sink has the advantage of being able to accommodate large pots and pans.

4 *This reproduction Victorian Belfast sink has been installed on an attractive country-style pine base, leaving enough space underneath to display decorative cooking pots. It would be suitable in an informal kitchen that has free-standing mix-and-match units.*

5 *A huge "pot" sink is supported in the traditional manner on sculptured plaster piers, which give it presence, and provide a convenient storage cubbyhole beneath. The draining boards on either side of the sink have a sensible slope and overhang.*

6 *Traditional materials and modern convenience are brought together in the design of this space-saving ceramic sink, with its built-in Iroko-wood drainer and polished chrome swan's-neck mixer taps.*

7 *This unusual double "pot" sink, with its wall-mounted faucets, would originally have been installed on plaster piers in the scullery, where all the dishwashing was done. Here it takes pride of place set in the middle of simple yellow-painted cupboards with a cutaway front.*

4

6

7

9

8 *Set within a cutaway cupboard unit with wrought-iron hinges and handles, this butler's sink has brass swan's-neck mixer faucets, which make an elegant contribution to the country style and period detailing.*

9 *This plain modern double sink is set within a wooden unit with rectilinear moldings. The period-style faucets and the plate rack above give it a more old-fashioned look. he sinks are flanked by teak drainer–teak being the most resilient wood for the purpose.*

5

8

FAUCETS

The majority of early sinks did not have faucets; instead, water for washing dishes, utensils, and pots and pans was brought in from wells outdoors. The few faucets in existence were primitive, and made of wood or metal, although in grander houses pumps brought in water to feed the sinks. In the mid-nineteenth century, there was a great improvement in water supply, and faucets became more common. From the Victorian era to the 1920s, cross-head or capstan pillar faucets were the most frequently used, and these were usually wall-mounted in pairs. Mixer faucets first appeared during the Victorian period, some with "quick-turn" lever handles.

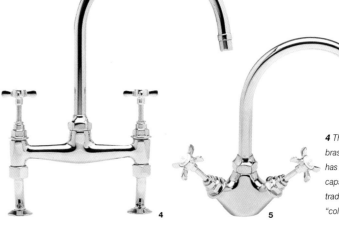

4 This elegant, polished-brass pillar mixer faucet has a swan's neck, capstan handles, and traditional "hot"-and-"cold" tops.

1 This reproduction chrome faucet with a cross-head dates to the Victorian era, and is intended to be mounted on the rim of the sink.

2 A wall-mounted faucet such as this chunky chrome copy of a mid-nineteenth-century style is suitable where there is no available connecting hole in a sink.

3 Brass pillar mixer faucets with porcelain handles are a handsome choice for a period sink. This example has a swan's neck, which is a traditional style that has been employed since the 1850s. The high neck allows large pots to be cleaned or filled easily, and the lever handles can be pushed off with an elbow when both hands are occupied.

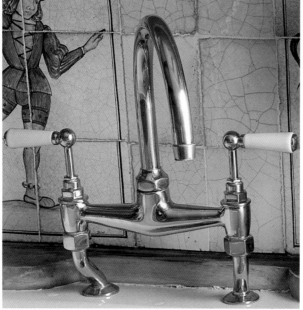

5 This brass mixer faucet has a swivel nozzle and angled handles. It is suitable for a period sink with a single outlet.

6 This unobtrusive wall-mounted flat chrome mixer faucet, with lever handles, goes well with the rustic decorative effect of pique-aisette ("crackle") tiles and granite sink surround.

7 Of classic American design, this pair of wall-mounted faucets is especially suitable for older sinks that cannot use modern fittings.

8 Similar to 7, these faucets have an upstanding mixer spout in chrome. Brushed or polished nickel and brass are alternative finishes.

WORKTOPS

Until the nineteenth century, kitchen furniture and work surfaces were kept to a minimum. As the century progressed, however, cooking methods became more elaborate, and there was a greater awareness of hygiene, resulting in the need for a variety of different types of working surfaces. The kitchen's mainstay was the central work table, usually made of pine, and standing quite low to aid kneading bread and pastry dough. The processing of dairy produce required an ultracool environment, and in the largest houses, marble, or even alabaster, were the favored surfaces. Shelves would sometimes be made of slate with a marble trim. In modest households, stone would be used. The late-nineteenth-century wet larder housed all the food not kept in the housekeeper's dry storeroom—meat, vegetables, bread, cheese, and fruit. Shelves were made from slate and marble several inches thick, and embedded deep in the walls. Fish and vegetables, covered in cheesecloth, would be laid on these slabs. Meat would be chopped on a strong wooden dresser, and there would be stone troughs for salting. The pastry area or room had marble slabs for kneading and rolling out dough.

3 An unusual and attractive worktop can be made from ceramic or quarry tiles, providing a cool surface on which to work, and having the the added bonus of being easy to clean. Here, the tiles are edged with a wooden girdle for support. Their rustic quality and color are well suited to the kitchen's earthy tones and textures.

4 In this imaginative kitchen, a piece of marble has been cut to fit an old Gothic-style cupboard, and used for preparing dough.

5 Oak and marble make naturally good-looking partners in this period-style kitchen, and are a practical combination for food preparation. The central table is also used to prepare food, and for dining.

1 This well-worn butcher's block mounted on a purpose-built console is an excellent work surface, and it also provides a warmly patinated quality that matches the decor in this kitchen. Butchers' blocks are traditionally made from maple or beech, and cut across the grain to ensure even wearing and minimize warping, although for decorative effect, the wear and tear is part of their charm.

2 Here, oak covers both the sink area and the dresser counter, and allows sufficient working space for the cook. The honeyed color of this traditional wood lends this kitchen a special glow.

RANGES, HOBS, AND OVENS

The cooking stove has always represented the biggest single investment in the kitchen, and has certainly been the most exploited item in search of the perfect culinary performance. A ca. 1869 article in *American Woman's Home* enthusiastically describes a multipurpose cooking range that kept 17 gallons of water heated at all times, baked pies and cakes in a warm oven, heated flat irons under the one cover, boiled a kettle and a pot under another cover, baked bread in the oven, and cooked a turkey in the tin roaster, as well as providing a heated flat surface for cooking in pans. Although the cooking skills and implements improved in the Victorian era, the rudimentary design of the kitchen, with its massive black cast-iron range and basic furniture arranged to a rigid formula, remained little changed until the social modernization of the early twentieth century. The hardware store was a great influence on commerce and fashion during the Victorian period, selling anything from saucepans to cooking ranges, illustrated in splendid catalogs, to the burgeoning building industry. The greatest influence on the development of the cooking range was the introduction of the "closed" range which, as the name suggests, had an enclosed fire grate, and was used in one form or another until the 1920s.

1 Even in its most basic form, the solid-fuel range has a retrospective charm given the right setting. This early-twentieth-century English example is made of black-leaded cast iron, and has a single-domed hotplate. Its predecessor was invented by Count Rumford, who designed ranges with flues and a heavily insulated stove system. The idea of the "social kitchen" is a relatively recent one, and a traditional oven can help to enhance the room's role as the heart of family life.

2 In contrast to the utilitarian style of its twentieth-century decendant, this majestic late-nineteenth-century American cast-iron range has a more ornamented finish than its British counterparts, and is typical of the Beaux Arts era. The American kitchen was generally less segregated from the living areas of the home than in Europe, and therefore warranted more embellishment.

3 This impressive modern version of the traditional range makes its own design statement. Influenced by the early-twentieth-century concept of an island unit combined with the high-tech of professional ranges, this brass and enamel oven has been set in the center of the kitchen, taking the place of the traditional Victorian work table.

4 The Aga, which is synonymous with the traditional English country kitchen, was designed in the early 1920s by the Swedish scientist Gustav Dalen, and was first marketed in Britain in the 1930s in its solid-fuel form. Today, it can be run on oil, gas, or electricity, and comes in different sizes and colors. Here it makes an appropriate choice for a period-style country kitchen.

5 *This dark blue Aga is framed by ceramic and slate tiles, bricks, and limed wood. Agas have been adapted worldwide to suit many different domestic environments, and have been used not only in a romanticized rural setting, but also in the refined high-tech urban home. Their imposing and serviceable good looks make them perfect partners to a variety of materials and styles.*

5

6 *This 1920s free-standing, vitreous-enameled American gas oven incorporates a large and a small oven, both thermostatically controlled, a four-ring cooktop, an overhead pot rack, and a built-in backsplash. Generally, the United States was well in advance of Britain in its kitchen equipment designs, and their gas ovens had become more streamlined by this period. This example, however, has the gray finish and charmingly old-fashioned cabriole legs of earlier models. Similar ovens can still be found and restored by experts to their original condition.*

6

7 *Of an American utilitarian design, this old-fashioned and compact gas oven is in a galley kitchen in California. It has chrome-plated finishing detail and curved edges and corners.*

7

8 *The coming of the electrically-ignited gas oven was a great advance in convenience and safety, and the introduction of a combined gas and electric range was the best of both worlds. The lean and clean lines of this example are reminiscent of earlier ovens.*

8

9

10 *The newest type of ovens cleverly combine a deceptively old-fashioned body, including "rivets" and faucet-style knobs, with a high-tech approach to cooking. This early-twentieth-century-style oven and cooktop incorporates forced-air cooking, variable broiling, removable double-glazed door, and integral cooling fan.*

10 *This is a heavy-duty version of 7, but with a four-ring cooking top, twin ovens, and broiling and heating drawers in its base.*

10

KITCHEN ACCESSORIES

In Britain and America, the greatest development in kitchen equipment came after the mid-nineteenth century, when the enclosed cooking range inspired more sophisticated cooking techniques. One of the first commercial fairs–the 1851 Great Exhibition in London–galvanized huge interest, resulting in the mass production of every kind of kitchen accessory. Until this period, cookware was made from cast iron, superseded by steel and aluminum, and, after 1840, enamelware or graniteware. Expensive copper pans lost popularity by the 1900s. In remote areas of Britain and America, traditional bakestones and griddles were used well into the twentieth century, while the Pennsylvania Dutch fashioned decorative trivets, ornate tin workwork, and carved hardwood spoons. Storage items ranged from locking tea caddies, earthenware or wooden salt holders, Victorian wirework egg baskets, American stenciled flour tins, plate racks, spice boxes, and more.

2 The wall-mounted plate rack came into use in the late eighteenth century and has been employed ever since. It is practical to have the rack near the sink to dry and safely store plates in constant use, while keeping the draining board uncluttered. It is also a decorative way of displaying a collection of plates. Usually found in pine, plate racks also look attractive when painted to harmonize with the kitchen style.

2

1 By the late-Victorian period, the batterie de cuisine had become extensive due to hugely elaborate cooking and presentation methods. Here, an eclectic collection of copper and brass equipment is hung decoratively from a rack over the kitchen table, an idea adopted from late-nineteenth-century professional kitchens, where it hung from hooks on a frame above the cooking range.

1

3 The Victorian kitchen usually had only open shelves and hanging racks around its walls, so that all the pots, pans, and other cooking equipment were easily available. The same idea can be used today with a more decorative intention. The unpainted wooden rack shown here is crammed with brown and cream pottery storage jars and other colorful china.

3

4 A traditional pine display board, hung up against a background of old blue-and-white tiles, is the rustic version of an overhead hanging rack. Here, dried herbs and flowers, scissors, copper pans, sieves, and graters are simply hooked onto nails hammered into a pine board that has a carved top.

4

5 This French 1920s utensil rack, which also has a drip tray, would have held a set of three utensils. Earlier versions of the 1850s were made in wrought iron, then enameled, and later, like this one, in stamped sheet aluminum. This example has echoes of Art Nouveau in its embossed design.

6 This food safe kept cheese, butter, and bacon safe from vermin. Earlier meat safes were hung from the ceiling in a cool, well-ventilated place. Made in inexpensive softwood, this one would have been sold unpainted, and then painted at home.

7 On the right is a French ca. 1900 soda box, which held soda washing crystals. On the left is an allumette (match) container of the same period, which would usually have a striking strip on the top. Even such utilitarian objects have been finished with stamped decoration and bright enameling.

8 Containers for precious spices were first made in the seventeenth century. As here, they were often in the form of small wooden cabinets with drawers or a small chest-of-drawers, which stood on a table or were hung on the wall.

9 This Dutch spice container is of a type produced from the mid-nineteenth century onward. With its naive-painted decoration and unusual combination of spices, it may have been made in a Dutch colony.

10 Beeswax candles have always been expensive, and were often kept safe from damage by being stored in a sturdy wooden box hung in a convenient place. This nineteenth-century example has been converted to hold a roll of paper towels.

LIGHTING

These days, we take our constant, clean, and user-friendly electric light for granted. In comparison, the beeswax candle has historically been a luxury beyond the means of common man. Animal-fat tallow candles, oil or pitch, or rushes dipped in sheep fat sufficed during the sixteenth century. In the seventeenth century, ornate candelabra and chandeliers in brass, gilded wood, and wrought iron, and silver candlestands and sconces on the wall were only for the wealthy.

In the Georgian period, lighting indicated status and wealth; grand reception rooms had low-hung chandeliers of wood, metal, or glass, with three or more pairs of curved arms. Oil lamps–often whale oil in America–were confined to hallways and outdoors. Modest American houses were lit by rush lamps or Betty lamps that burned oil, lard, or tallow. However, even these utilitarian items were sometimes touched by the elegant classicism of the period.

Progress in lighting was achieved by the invention, in 1784, of a colza (rapeseed) oil lamp by Aimé Argand, a Swiss physicist. The ventilated reservoir, wick, cylinder, and glass chimney produced a light ten times brighter than previous oil lamps, with no smoke. This lamp underwent many improvements after 1800, including a hanging-light version. Candlelight still remained the dominant lighting method, with the finest glass chandeliers being imported to America from Britain and France, neoclassical silver candelabra and sconces with reflecting plates, and *girandole* brackets either side of many grand chimney pieces. Lanterns for inside and out copied the lines and ornamentation of the late-Georgian period. Kerosene's availability from the mid-nineteenth century improved cleanliness and odor.

In Britain, Sir John Soane and Sir Walter Scott were among the first to install domestic piped gas in 1823–4, and it was generally available by the 1850s. The first gas lights–often large, clumsy creations–threw a savage light, and were criticized for dulling diamonds, making complexions look sickly, and fading colors. Colored-glass shades softened the light it and, by the 1830s, pulley systems and telescopic feeding mechanisms allowed easier access and positioning. The Victorians favored many sources and styles of lighting in one room, and happily combined candle, kerosene, gas and, when available, electric light. The chandelier (*see* left) epitomizes the exuberantly elaborate fashion of the late nineteenth century, with its gilding and deeply fringed shades.

Although Thomas Edison had invented the incandescent electric light bulb in 1879, electricity was not generally domestically available until the well into the twentieth century. Early electric carbon filaments emitted a harsh, inefficient light that needed a shade to soften it; these were first made in copper and brass, and then in etched glass to diffuse the light, and pleated silk for shading. With improvements in filaments, flower- and flame-shaped bulbs were used without shades.

Louis Comfort Tiffany produced his first stained-glass shades in 1895, intending to bring "harmonized decoration" to the masses. Other Art Nouveau options included metal pendant fixings in sinuous imitation of plants, and pewter or copper sconces. Gas and electric light should have given creative scope, but designs were usually based on earlier gas lights or period styles such as Georgian candelabra or seventeenth-century lanterns, hall lanterns in the vernacular style of black metal with small panes of glass, and Georgian Revival sconces and glass bowl lights hung from chains for reception rooms. Dining required more muted illumination, so pink-shaded wall lights and silver candlesticks with silk shades and beaded fringes were in vogue. From this period, lighting fixtures acquired their own character. American fashion adopted many revivalist styles, promoting wrought-iron, wheel-like chandeliers, Georgian glass, Queen Anne brass or ornate branched chandeliers, and Italian Renaissance bronze or gilded-metal chandeliers.

The early twentieth century saw a simplification of lines into clean-cut shapes, and this produced glass wall sconces in fan or shell shapes, vellum and parchment fixtures, and globe ceiling lights in chrome and glass.

CENTRAL LIGHTS

Providing a safe, long-lasting source of light in the communal areas of a house has always been an important consideration. When candles were the only lighting source, this was an impossibility, and so the introduction of oil lamps in the 1780s was a welcome innovation–even if the earlier types were inefficient, smelly, and dirty. During the nineteenth century, candles and oil lights continued to be most commonly used, but toward the middle of the century new types of burners–kerosene–and more efficient wicks and lamp chimneys were introduced. By the end of the century, gas "chandeliers" with glass-bowl diffusers were in common use, and these were made more convenient by their "rise-and-fall" mechanisms. The advent of electricity not only changed people's lives dramatically, but it also inspired designers to create new lighting fixtures, which changed the way light was diffused, casting it downward where it was needed. Generally electric light was employed only in the communal areas, as early bulbs gave little more light than gas.

1 In the hallway of Lars Sjoberg's renovated ca. 1770 Swedish country house, this glass and metal candle-lamp hangs from the wooden ceiling. It is appropriate to the period and the situation of this rustic house, which retains many of the original features and decorations.

2 Oil lamps have been in general use since the middle of the Georgian period. They came in all shapes and guises, but the hanging light in this German house is typical of a continental design. The interior of the shade is white in order to reflect as much light downward as possible.

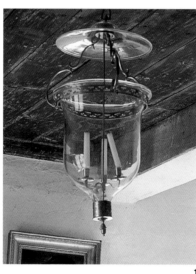

3 Of a classical rectilinear shape, this hanging lamp is in a small studio apartment in Greenwich Village, New York, that has been decorated in American Empire style.

4 The dining-room table of Thomas Calloway's mid-nineteenth-century house in Los Angeles, renovated in the Spanish Colonial style of Mexico, is lit by a simple kerosene hanging lamp of a type that was used throughout modest American homes of this period.

5 This kerosene lamp adds a touch of period authenticity to this recently refurbished French cottage. Made of brass and opaque glass, it complements the pale-painted walls.

6 Here, a late-nineteenth-century hanging globe is used in an American house of that period. It illustrates the Tiffany style of lamp, with a richly colored leaded-glass shade, suspended by a chain.

7 The Edwardians favored pendant lights with an opaque glass bowl and bronze chain and detailing, hung from a central ceiling medallion. This copy has an acrylic diffuser and "antiqued" bronze trim.

8 This is a more ornate version of the pendant light shown in 7. The sinuously shaped opaque diffuser was designed to add extra illumination. This type of design would have been suitable for lighting the common parts of a house–the hallway or landing, for example.

9 Of the Art Nouveau period, this highly decorative light has geometric leaded stained glass, and is appropriate for lighting a dining-room table. Such lamps were known as "rise-and-fall" lights as they came with a pulley-and-weight mechanism for altering the height, making the manipulation of lighting much easier. This particular example does not have this mechanism, and hence it is hung low over the table.

10 This modern electrified version of a Victorian candle-lamp has a spring-clip holding mechanism attaching the shade. The etched, translucent "storm glass" allows the light to be moved safely from place to place around the house.

11 Tiffany shades were first sold in 1895, and were immediately fashionable. This fine copy of an original pendant light has hand-cut opalescent glass, held in place with copper foil and lead solder.

12 This reproduction of a "rise-and-fall" light has an "antiqued" gold cord and rich red silk shades. It is suitable for use over a desk or table, where direct light is only occasionally required.

13 The introduction of electricity resulted in the production of a vast range of bulb-holding designs that could enclose the lightbulb. This reproduction of a torchère "flame" is of the Edwardian period.

14 During the 1920s, lights were often hung from a decorative ceiling plate of brass, copper, or silvered finish. Diffusers sometimes had tinted or marbled glass. This reproduction has an attractive cut-glass, acorn-shaped bulb holder.

15 The brass bobbin on this Edwardian reproduction contains the weight to counter-balance the rise and fall of the "coolie-hat" shade. This is a typical desk light of the period. Lamps over dining-room tables and desks often had many-branched, counterweighted lights.

165

CHANDELIERS

Chandeliers (from the French word for candleholder and the Latin *candelabrum*) have been a glorious expression of extravagance and exquisite craftsmanship throughout the centuries. They continue to maintain their appeal in today's interiors, working well as a foil where modern and antique styles meet. In the seventeenth and eighteenth centuries, chandeliers were made from carved and gilded wood, brass, wrought iron, and the grandest from rock crystal. Their use and ornate design demonstrated the owner's social and financial status, but they were usually only used on formal occasions–beeswax candles, their source of lighting, being a luxury. Certain types of chandelier have long enjoyed favor: the simplest swan's-neck metal form looks perfect in a Tudor, Edwardian vernacular, or modern interior, for example. Candles have always remained the most appropriate means of lighting a crystal chandelier, but modern electric candle-flame bulbs have ensured that antique chandeliers have maintained their purpose in today's environment. Apart from a practical use, the chandelier can become a decorative device in its own right–a uniting visual focus, able to fill out an awkwardly barren vacuum in the middle of a tall room.

1 This reproduction of a simple but elegant chandelier is of a type that is usually found in grand Tudor houses. The design of its metal body is so fashioned to reflect as much candle-light as possible.

2 With its branched candles and reflecting globe, this chandelier would fit equally well in a seventeenth-century hallway or a twentieth-century formal dining room. Copies of this chandelier are available in different materials, including wood and brass. It is a good idea to disguise the chain with a casing–silk hangs best of all materials.

3 In the eighteenth century, chandeliers would only have been hung in the principal rooms and used on grand occasions. This magnificent French crystal chandelier hangs in the Swedish Room of Château de Morsan, which was built ca. 1765 in Normandy, France.

4 The decorator Frédéric Méchiche makes an extravagant statement in his Paris residence by placing two eighteenth-century chandeliers side-by-side. The Directoire style to which they belong is characterized by neoclassical manner and detailing.

5 *An Italian chandelier with characteristic "spun" branches illuminates a London dining room decorated in a Tuscany-inspired style. Such a fine piece becomes a decorative object in its own right– there is no need even to light the candles.*

6 *This classic design, with two tiers of branches, has been used since the Baroque period of the mid-seventeenth century. The addition of electric candle-flame bulbs makes it much more convenient to use.*

7 *Although this chandelier has the same proportions as 6, it is from the American Victorian period, and has the characteristic loose-beaded "necklace" and inverted "crown" of glass drops.*

8 *This magnificent chandelier, which has more decorative glass than candlepower, graces the sumptuous Music Room of Richard Jenrette's American Empire-style house on the Hudson River, in New York State.*

9 *In contrast to the fixed glass chandeliers of earlier periods, this late-nineteenth-century light has a complex system of weights and pulleys and a telescopic stem to give it versatility.*

10 *The High Victorian style of the Calhoun Mansion, in Charleston, South Carolina, is evident in the use of rich drapery, gilding, and ornamentation. A pair of gas-converted chandeliers completes the room's decorations.*

11 *English lead glass was considered most desirable for use in chandeliers. This elegant candlelit example, with its chains of glass beads, takes on an intrinsically decorative role in a Rococo Revival-style drawing room.*

WALL LIGHTS

Wall lights have historically played an important part in illuminating interiors, and the mellow light projected from the sides of a room greatly enhances its ambience. Baroque sconces had reflective brackets to maximize precious candlepower–silver for the wealthiest only, but more usually brass and, later, mirror-glass. The *girandole* wall and mirror lights in Georgian houses complemented the sophisticated interior decor of the eighteenth century. Oil and then gas lights came in an abundance of different designs, and were sold through catalogs, but when electricity reached the masses, the designs remained broadly static until the 1920s.

1 The electrified torchère takes its design from the Greek flaming symbol of life. Using this type of classical reference was popular during the second decade of the nineteenth century.

2 This is a pretty example of a carved wooden French wall light with candles. It is of a type of design and lighting method that integrates extremely well with the Empire style of the room.

3 Fashioned like a miniature ceiling-hung chandelier, this side light has a fountain of glass drops on its central shaft and two slender candleholders.

4 Here is an example of an electrified Rococo-style sconce, carved from wood. The grandest house-holds would have had silver sconces to reflect the precious candlelight.

5 The early-Georgian period saw the use of wall lights in brass, silver, and gilded or silvered wood in grander houses, and pewter or tin in poorer homes. This modernized brass version has two sets of elegant candle-flame bulbs, although three or more sets could be used.

6 The Edwardians preferred their electric lights to imitate earlier styles of candle lights. Pairs of wall brackets were a popular choice for selected rooms in the house, such as reception rooms and libraries. The invention of the material (as opposed to glass) shade helped to soften the light given out.

7 This "antique" satin-brass sconce, with its urn-shaped body and beading, echoes the dignified style of an Adam candle light, but it has been modernized with material shades and electricity.

8 By the late nineteenth century, lights could be gas- or electric-powered, and were mostly made from pewter or copper. This Art Nouveau-style reproduction wall lantern has been electrified.

9 This Edwardian design in solid cast brass has attractive pleated-silk shades. Material shades were invented by Hermann Muthesius, an Englishman of the period, to soften the harshness of carbon-filament electric light.

10 Art Nouveau design was influenced by the shapes of nature, which were often used in lighting fixtures. This reproduction in "antiqued" metal has a colored-glass shade–very popular at the time.

11 The 1920s saw a radical change in all areas of design, lighting included. Lines became leaner and sharper, with less ornamentation. This modern copy has a gleaming metal finish.

12 A feature of Victorian and Edwardian interiors was to use a pair of lights mounted as part of the overmantel mirror. These were often hinged for convenience, and they were easily converted from gas to electricity.

13 Uplighters give a pleasantly atmospheric glow to a room. This Art Deco-style wall light, which is encased in opaque glass, subtly diffuses the light up toward the ceiling.

14 Chrome swan's-neck globe wall lights were particularly popular in the 1930s. They are seen here flanking a bathroom mirror.

15 Picture lights, like this early-twentieth-century example, revolutionized the perception of the subtleties of detail and color in paintings as never before.

TABLE LAMPS

Before the appearance of the portable lamp, whether it was used in oil or kerosene, lighting had limited effectiveness and practicality, as it was circumscribed by candlepower. The invention of the relatively efficient Argand (or colza) oil lamp by Aimé Argand in Geneva, Switzerland, in 1784, allowed those who were better off to gather around a well-lit large circular table as part of the evening's social entertainment. Safe, portable light was a huge step forward, despite the smell, dirt, unreliability, and inconvenience of some lighting methods. In 1879, Thomas Edison invented the incandescent filament bulb–changing domestic lighting forever. Tiffany first produced electrified (geometric, leaded) table lamps in 1905, a time when electricity was not yet widespread. By 1920 in America, but later in Britain, electric lamps became much more common, and revolutionized the way people decorated their houses. This was because the lamps changed the way colors were perceived, defined the proportions and details of a room by illuminating every corner, and threw light in a directional path to create the *mise-en-scène*.

1

2

3

4

5

1 Of a type used in mid-nineteenth-century America and Europe, this kerosene table lamp has a classic design. The glass flue and shade allowed portability and increased safety.

2 The Victorians were particularly fond of the ornate in the furnishings of their houses, as shown in this nineteenth-century candelabrum. It is truly a work of unabashed decoration, with its extravagent bronze stag and "stalactite" glass pendants.

3 Unlike the Victorians, the Edwardians were much more traditional in design terms, preferring their lights to imitate the chandeliers and candle-sticks of earlier years. This bronze Rococo-style base is well matched by the muted tone of its pleated shade.

4 A vase, ginger storage jar, or other china vessel, can be used for the base of a table lamp. The pleated-silk shade is suitably formal for such an impressive example.

5 The animal theme of this twentieth-century vaselike lamp was inspired by the eighteenth-century Chinese blue and white export porcelain.

6 *Bernd Goeckler's New York apartment is decorated and furnished in neoclassical style, to which this slender and elegant brass column lamp is most appropriate.*

7 *This original ca. 1880 electric table lamp has a bronze base and a shade made of glass with bronze mounts. It exemplifies the favored design of an early electric lamp.*

8 *Here, an adapted French nineteenth-century vase lamp of ornate design perfectly suits the sumptuous colors and textures of its situation.*

9 *Tiffany created a type of lighting that blended well with the American and British Art Nouveau fashions of the late nineteenth century, although this lamp would suit Arts and Crafts and Gothic houses. Its bright green and golden-yellow geometric leaded-glass shade gives it a unique luminosity that greatly contributes to the atmosphere of the room.*

10 *The style of this reproduction 1920s' table lamp was influenced by the design principles of the American architect and designer Frank Lloyd Wright, who adopted geometric, clean-cut outlines.*

CANDLES

This small sample of candlestick designs illustrates the candle's potential for decorative and esthetic value. Historically, beeswax was always prohibitively expensive and, except for grand occasions, houses were illuminated with malodorous tallow candles. Despite all the advances in lighting, candles have remained in constant domestic use, being universally available, adaptable, and decorative. For today's interiors, candlelight makes an inimitable contribution to providing a convivial and romantic atmosphere.

6

8

10

7

9

11

STANDARD LAMPS

Evolved from candlestands in the late nineteenth century, the standard lamp created a new way of lighting a room, as it allowed a concentration of light to be focused on a person or an object from an intermediate (and sometimes variable) height. In addition, the standard lamp also had a profound effect on the balancing of light at all levels in a room, and could therefore be teamed with overhead lights, wall lights, and table lamps to produce different lighting effects. Another advantage of the standard lamp was that its slender dimensions did not occupy a great deal of space, and thus it could be moved around without upsetting the distribution of furniture or ornaments in a room. Decoratively, standard lamps are limited by the requirements of proportion–a stable base, long "stem," and a capping shade. However, there are certain designs that lend themselves to the lamps being placed as purely ornamental features, given the right, uncluttered setting, such as in a hallway.

1 A stabilizing tripod allowed illumination at a higher level for the lofty living hall of the medieval dwelling.

2 Medieval candles made of soft suet wax were fixed on metal-spiked cups. Instability and mess meant that a sand base was a wise precaution.

3 A neoclassical torchère-style bronze lamp makes a fine companion for a French tapestry-covered chair.

4 This modern lamp suits period or modern interiors. Gold-leaf finishing complements the neat silk shade.

5 A minimalist lamp in distressed bronze echoes a French style popular in the early years of the nineteenth century.

6 Inspired by the elegant lines of French Empire style, this modern lamp has brass casting and an acrylic bowl.

7 This reproduction standard lamp makes an interesting feature with the strong attenuated lines of its Etruscan inspiration.

8 The ebonized wood and classic gold-leaf motifs and detailing of the French Empire period come together in this dignified design.

LIGHT SWITCHES

Throughout history, lighting methods have involved the inconvenience of lighting and extinguishing each individual source separately. Not only was this time-consuming and frustrating, but it could also be highly dangerous as the fire risk of leaving a candle or lamp lit was obviously a threat. When Thomas Edison invented the incandescent electric light bulb in 1879, he presented the world with the precursor of modern sophisticated electric circuitry, which resulted in an immediacy and control of lighting that had not been previously experienced. To throw a switch and flood the room with light from different sources must have been a thrilling novelty indeed. As was expected after the proliferation of styles of lights and lamps over the years, design considerations have now even found their way into the utilitarian light switch. This is illustrated by the diversity of today's reproductions, which range from from wood to brass, and are in styles that are reminiscent of many different periods. Thus the humble light switch can be regarded as a design feature in itself and add to period authenticity.

1–4 These authentically reproduced "dolly" light switches re-create the period detail that adds character to today's renovated interiors. (1) A four-switch brass and mahogany combination. (2) A plain and simple brass switch. (3) An elegant fluted-dome switch. (4) A classic indented-brass switch.

5 Manufacturers of reproduction switches have gone to a great deal of trouble to re-create period styling. This wooden plate has been hand-polished to enhance its natural patina.

6 The sophistication of modern technology is combined with a period look in this discreet dimmer switch.

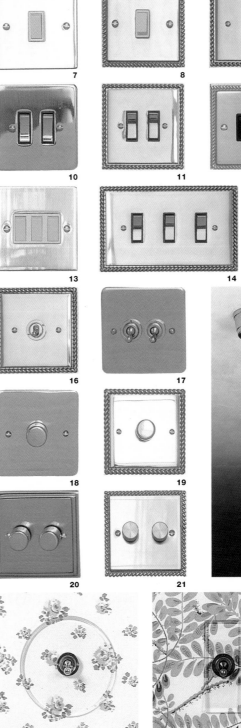

7–15 In many restored period homes, the decorations may be eclectic, which means that it is not always necessary to be a slave to authenticity. In fact, the adaptable style (and materials) of modern switch plates often makes such considerations irrelevant.

16–17 If adhering to period style is paramount, then the choice of a switch should depend on how suitable the plate material is to the interior of the room, and how many lights it will need to supply. The switch on the left has neoclassical rope molding, and is suitable for Georgian, Colonial, and Federal interiors; the one on the right is plain, and appropriate for Georgian and minimalist interiors.

18–21 Push-button and dimmer switches are a modern convenience that greatly enhance the versatility of lighting effects.

22 The ubiquitous pull switch found in British bathrooms is here given added grace by using a decorative chrome ceiling attachment.

23–24 These "invisible" Perspex wall switches are invaluable when the decorative rhythm of wallpaper needs to be uninterrupted.

DIRECTORY

Photographs used in the book are credited in parenthesis at the end of directory entries. Page numbers are followed by the photograph reference number.

DOORS

Architectural Iron Company Inc.
PO Box 126
104 Ironwood Court
Milford
Pennsylvania
18337
TEL:
(717) 296-7722
FAX:
(717) 296-4766
SEE EXTERIORS (P.187)

Baileys Home and Garden
The Engine Shed
Station Approach
Ross-on-Wye
Herefordshire
HR9 7BW
UK
TEL:
(01989) 563015
FAX:
(01989) 768172

Stockists of an extensive range of antique and traditional style fixtures and fittings, in brass and cast iron, including brackets, doorknobs, and lighting fixtures. (pp. 48-9, 8; pp. 154-5, 4)

J. D. Beardmore & Co. Ltd
17 Pall Mall
London
SW1Y 5LU
UK
TEL:
(0171) 670-1000
FAX:
(0171) 670-1010

Manufacturers and suppliers of traditional handmade ornamental brassware for doors, windows, and cabinets. A huge range of reproduction pieces from the medieval period through Elizabethan, Georgian, and Regency designs to Art Deco, including decorative grilles, and electrical and lighting fixtures. (pp. 48-9, 3, 4, 15, 16)

The Brass Knob
2311 18th Street NW
Washington, D.C.
20009
TEL:
(202) 332-3370
FAX:
(202) 332-5594
E-MAIL:
thebrassknob@juno.com
WEB SITE:
http://www.washington post.com/YP/brassknob

Suppliers of architectural antiques, including chandeliers, sconces, mantels, fireplace accessories, tiles, and ironwork.

British Gates & Timber Ltd
Castleton's Oak Sawmills
Biddenden
Near Ashford
Kent
TN27 8DD
UK
TEL:
(01580) 291555
FAX:
(01580) 292011

Makers of a range of traditional oak-ledged and boarded doors with original details and authentic hand finishes. Also supply other ranges of interior and exterior doors, frames, and accessories. (pp. 56-7, 3; pp. 64-5, 1)

Cinder Whit & Co.
753 Eleventh Ave South
Wahpeton
New England
58075
TEL:
(800) 527-9064
FAX:
(701) 642-4204
SEE STAIRCASES (P.180)

Hayles & Howe
509 South Exeter Street
Fells Point
Baltimore, Maryland
21202
TEL:
(410) 385-2400
FAX:
(410) 385-2400
SEE CEILINGS (P.179)

Hallidays
The Old College
Dorchester-on-Thames
Wallingford
Oxfordshire
OX10 7HL
UK
TEL:
(01865)340028
FAX:
(01865) 341149

Designers of period paneled rooms. Traditional wood carving and carpentry skills are used to faithfully reproduce fittings of the Georgian and Regency periods. Specialists in wood-crafted Georgian and Regency mantelpieces and brass and cast-iron fireplace accessories. (pp. 58–9, 4)

Hendricks Woodworking
PO Box 139
Kempton
Pennsylvania
19529
TEL:
(610) 756-6187

Interior and exterior doors custom-made to period designs using traditional woodworking techniques and made from solid woods. Radius woodwork for paneling, crown moldings, and arched doors is a specialty. (pp. 38-9, 9; pp. 40-1, 9)

Heritage Oak Ltd
Unit V5
Dean Clough Industrial Park
Halifax
West Yorkshire
HX3 5AX
UK
TEL/FAX:
(01422) 348231

Restoration work carried out exclusively in English oak. Doors nailed and pegged, waxed and aged. Staircases reproduced from original patterns using traditional craft methods. Paneling and flooring as well as decorative panels, wainscots, screens and traditional and period-style floors. (pp. 36-7, 3; pp. 84-5, 3, 9)

Hinges & Handles Inc.
PO Box 103
100 Lincolnway East
Osceola,
Indiana
46561
TEL:
(219) 674 8878
FAX:
(219) 674 5767

Supplies door and cabinet hardware; also does repairs and brass polishing.

House of Brass
45-47 Milton Street
Nottingham NG1 3EZ
UK
TEL: (0115) 9475430

Specialists in classic hand-finished reproduction brassware. Includes a large range of door, window, and cabinet furniture, electrical accessories, lighting, beds and headboards, locks and security devices, faucets and mixers. (pp. 48-9, 5, 6, 10-14, 19-21; pp. 64-5, 5, 6, 8, 9; pp. 74-5, 1, 2, 4; p. 173, 4, 7-21)

John Sambrook
Park House
Northiam
East Sussex TN31 6PA
UK
TEL: (01797) 252615

Specialist manufacturer of reproduction Georgian transom lights. Also Georgian metal skylights and bronze glazing bars for windows. (pp. 38-9, 2, 3; pp. 40-1, 4, 5, 6)

Looking for Ages
East Hill
Parracombe
North Devon EX31 4PF
UK
TEL/FAX: (01598) 763300

Suppliers of quality door fixtures and fittings, lighting, and other items for the period home. (pp. 74-5, 1, 2, 4)

Materials Unlimited

2 West Michigan Avenue
Ypsilanti
Michigan
48197
TEL:
(800) 299-9462
FAX:
(313) 437-3329
WEB SITE:
http://www.mat-unl.com

*Retailers of antique
architectural features,
furniture, and accessories,
including doors, hardware,
lighting, mantels, columns,
corbels, stained and beveled
glass, newel posts, iron gates,
and fencing.*

Nostalgic Warehouse Inc.

701 East Kingsley Road
Garland
Texas
75041
TEL:
(972) 271-0319
FAX:
(972) 271-9726
E-MAIL:
nostalgicw@aol.com

*Suppliers of solid-brass
reproduction doorplates,
hinges, and knobs from the
Victorian period through to
Art Nouveau and Art Deco
styles. Items are modified
from their antique originals
to function in modern
settings. Also coordinating
cabinet hardware.
(pp. 64-5, 7)*

The Original Box Sash Window Company

The Joinery
Unit 10
Bridgewater Way
Windsor
Berkshire
SL4 1RD
UK
TEL:
(01753) 858196
FAX:
(01753) 857827
SEE WINDOWS (P.176)

Samuel Heath & Sons Plc.

Cobden Works
Leopold Street
Birmingham
B12 0UJ
UK
TEL:
(0121) 772-2303
FAX:
(0121) 772-3334
E-MAIL:
mail@samuel-heath.com

*Manufacturers of marine
brassware for doors,
including knobs, handles,
knockers, letterplates, bolts,
and sockets. They also
provide a complementary
range of brass fasteners
and fittings for windows
and cabinets.
(pp. 64-5, box; pp. 148-9,
2, 3, 11; pp. 150-1, 7)*

Winther Browne & Co. Ltd

Nobel Road
Eley Estate
Edmonton
London
N18 3DX
UK
TEL:
(0181) 803-3434
FAX:
(0181) 807-0544
E-MAIL:
sales@wintherbrowne.
co.uk

*Manufacturers of fine wood
features for the period home,
including authentic-style
beams, doors, staircases,
windows, and moldings.
Available in dark oak,
light oak, gray or unstained
finishes. Aluminum
screening panels and
radiator cabinets also
available.
(pp. 104-5, 2, 8, 14;
pp. 112-13, 12-15;
pp. 116-17, 9-15, 18-23)*

Wood Factory

111 Railroad Street
Navasota
Texas
77868
TEL:
(409) 825 7233
FAX:
(409) 825 1791

*Manufacturers of
architectural millwork,
including exterior doors.*

Wood's Metal Studios

6945 Fishburg Road
Huber Heights
Ohio
45424
TEL:
(937) 233 6751

*Manufacturers of custom
wrought-iron, including locks
and latches, fences and gates,
railings, balconies, and grills,
fireplace accessories, outdoor
benches. Also carry out
metalwork repairs and
custom duplicate hardware
to authentic period designs.*

Worthington

PO Box 868
Troy
Alabama
36081
TEL:
(800) 872-1608
FAX:
(334) 566-5390
WEB SITE:
http://www.architectural-
details.com

*Manufacturers of luxury
decorative architectural
features, including columns,
capitals, moldings, mantelpieces, cartouches,
pediments, and pilasters
for interior and exterior
decoration. They also
provide technical advice
and can deliver pieces
direct to work sites.
(pp. 36-7, 5; pp. 104-5, 5)*

WINDOWS

Andy Thornton Architectural Antiques Ltd

Victoria Mills
Stainland Road
Greetland
Halifax
West Yorkshire
HX4 8AD
UK
TEL:
(01422) 377314
FAX:
(01422) 310372
E-MAIL:
email@ataa.co.uk
WEB SITE:
http://www.ataa.co.uk

*Restorers of original period
furniture, architectural
features and fittings, and
manufacturers of a broad
range of reproduction pieces.
Includes mantels, decorative
ceiling and floor tiles,
fretwork, balustrades, and
a huge selection of lighting,
including stained-glass
Tiffany domes and pendant
lights, Victorian window
lights and authentic exterior
lampposts. Also decorative
railings, gates and brass
fittings and hand-carved
copies of original wood
columns, capitals, corbels
and pediments.
(pp. 60-1, 7; p. 102, box;
pp. 104-5, box; pp. 164-5,
11; pp. 168-9, 10)*

Architectural Heritage Ltd

Taddington Manor
Taddington
Near Cutsdean
Cheltenham
Gloucestershire
GL54 5RY
UK
TEL:
(01386) 584414
FAX:
(01386) 584236
E-MAIL:
puddy@architectural-
heritage.co.uk
WEB SITE:
http://www.architectural-
heritage.co.uk
SEE EXTERIORS (P.187)

Arts & Crafts Period Textiles

5427 Telegraph Avenue
W2
Oakland
California
94609
TEL/FAX:
(510) 654-1645

*Soft furnishings and textiles
from the studio of Dianne
Ayres using turn-of-the-
century techniques,
including hand embroidery,
appliqué, and hand
stenciling. Pillows, table
linens, curtains, bedspreads,
and embroidery kits are
also available. Accepts
commissions.*

Bradley Collection Ltd
Lion Barn
Maitland Road
Needham Market
Suffolk
IP6 8NS
UK
TEL:
(01449) 722724
FAX:
01449) 722728
E-MAIL:
info@bradleycollection.
co.uk
WEB SITE:
http://www.bradley
collection.co.uk

Designers of custom-made
curtain poles, finials, and
accessories. Ranges in wood,
steel, and resin, variously
made, finished and decorated
by hand.
(pp. 74-5, box)

J. R. Burrows & Co.
PO Box 522
Rockland
Massachusetts
02370
TEL:
(781) 982-1812
FAX:
(781) 982-1636
E-MAIL:
merchant@burrows.com
WEB SITE:
http://www.burrows.com

Small company making
Victorian and Arts and
Crafts movement design lace
curtains in cotton/polyester
mix. Also hand-printed art
wallpaper.

Copycats
The Workshop
29 Maypole Road
Ashurst Wood
East Grinstead
West Sussex
RH19 3QN
UK
TEL/FAX:
(01342) 826066

Master craftsman carpenter
John Draper specializes
specializes in making exact
replica replacements for
original box sash windows.
Offers repair service and can
make exact copies of any
style window.
(pp. 70-1, 10)

Crittal Windows Ltd
Springwood Drive
Braintree
Essex
CM7 7YN
UK
TEL:
(01376) 324106
FAX:
(01376) 349662
E-MAIL:
hq@critall-windows.co.uk
WEB SITE:
http://www.critall-
windows.co.uk

Manufacturers of steel,
aluminum, and UPVC
windows and doors. Steel
windows in traditional
Georgian styles with
hinged openings for the
refurbishment of period
buildings.
(pp. 68-9, 10)

**Drums Sash & Door
Co. Inc.**
PO Box 207
Drums
Pennsylvania
18222
TEL:
(717) 788-1145
FAX:
(717) 788-3007

Manufacturers of custom-
made architectural
woodwork, especially
doors and windows.

Looking for Ages
East Hill
Parracombe
North Devon
EX31 4PF
UK
TEL/FAX:
(01598) 763300
SEE DOORS (P.174)

**The Original Box Sash
Window Company**
The Joinery
Unit 10
Bridgewater Way
Windsor
SL4 1RD
UK
TEL:
(01753) 858196
FAX:
(01753) 857827

Manufacturers of box sash
windows in traditional
designs made with pulleys
and sash cords, also
casement windows, with
single or double glazing.
(pp. 38-9, 7, 8; pp. 40-1, 3)

Pinch of the Past Inc.
109 West Broughton
Street
Savannah
Georgia
94804
TEL:
(912) 232 5563
FAX:
(912) 232 5563

Specialists in architectural
antiques and restoration.
Supplies and restores
doors, windows, and
associated hardware.
Also lighting, ironwork,
mantels, plaster ornament.
Offer reproduction custom
castings in iron, concrete,
and plaster and can restore
gold and gold leafing.

Pinecrest
2118 Blaisdell Avenue
Minneapolis
Minnesota
55404
TEL:
(800) 443 5357
FAX:
(612) 871 8956

Manufacturers of hand-
carved doors and mantels.
Custom sizes with beveled
and stained glass, wood
panels, etc. Also makes
shutters. Installation
service available.

River City Woodworks
825 9th Street
New Orleans
Louisiana
70155
TEL:
(800) 207-7738
FAX:
(504) 899-7278

Millers of custom-made
louver shutters, also beams,
flooring, and stair parts.

**Samuel Heath
& Sons Plc.**
Cobden Works
Leopold Street
Birmingham
B12 0UJ
UK
TEL:
(0121) 772-2303
FAX:
(0121) 772-3334
SEE DOORS (P.175)

**The Sash Window
Workshop Ltd**
Mayfield Farm
Industrial Estate
Hatchet Lane
Winkfield
Windsor
Berkshire
SL4 2EG
UK
TEL:
(01344) 882008
FAX:
(01344) 893034

Restorers and makers of
traditional sash windows.
(pp. 70-1, 9)

J. Scott (Thrapston) Ltd
Bridge Street
Thrapston
Northamptonshire
NN14 4LR
UK
TEL:
(01832) 732366
FAX:
(01832) 733793
E-MAIL:
100676.230@compuserve.
com

Bespoke woodworking
company since 1920,
providing sensitive
reproduction wooden
windows and doors for
period homes, from Georgian
and Victorian town houses
to country cottages. Quality
craftsmanship combined
with modern technology.
(pp. 50-1, 7; pp. 70-1, 8)

**Seekircher Steel
Window Repair**
630 Saw Mill River Road
Ardsley
New York
10502
TEL:
(914) 693 1920
FAX:
(914) 693 1912

Specialists in the repair and
restoration of all types of
steel casement windows for
commerical and residential
properties, including
period homes. Broken or
missing hardware and steel
also replaced.

**Stained Glass
Overlay Inc.**
1827 North Case Street
Orange
California
92865
TEL:
(714) 974-6124
FAX:
(714) 974-6529
WEB SITE:
http://www.sgoinc.com

*Specialists in commercial and
residential windows.*

**Weather Shield
Windows and Doors**
1 Weather Shield Plaza
Medford
Wisconsin
54451
TEL:
(800) 477 6808

*Manufacturers of dual-
shield, true-divided-light
windows and doors, made
in a choice of woods.*

**Wood Window
Workshop**
839 Broad Street
Utica
New York
13501
TEL:
(315) 732-6755
FAX:
(315) 733-0933
E-MAIL:
ker100@aol.com

*Specialist manufacturer of
custom reproduction wood
windows and doors.*

FLOORS

Albany Woodworks
PO Box 729
Albany
Louisiana
70711
TEL:
(504) 567-1155
WEB SITE:
http://www.io.com/-
webreach/albanywoods.
html

*Manufacturers of American
hardwood flooring. Can
be supplied in finished,
unfinished, naildown, or
gluedown versions. Also
make custom-made doors,
paneling, and shutters, and
provides aged beams and
pine stairparts.*

**Bruce Hardwood Floors
*(Division of Triangle
Pacific Corp.)***
16803 Dallas Parkway
Dallas
Texas
75248
TEL:
(800) 722-4647

*Manufacturers of hardwood
floors in a wide assortment
of colors and patterns
in a range of traditional,
country, and contemporary
styles.
(pp. 90-1, 5)*

Craftsman Lumber Co.
436 Main Street
PO Box 222
Groton
Massachusetts
01450
TEL:
(508) 448-5621
FAX:
(508) 448-2754

*Specialists in custom wide-
flooring, paneling, and
wainscoting in pine and
native hardwoods. Custom
milling for restoration and
reproduction work also
available.*

Fired Earth Plc.
Twyford Mill
Oxford Road
Adderbury
Oxon
OX17 3HP
UK
TEL:
(01295) 812088
FAX:
(01295) 810832
E-MAIL:
enquiries@firedearth.com

*Manufacturers of ceramic
tiles made by craftsmen
using centuries-old methods
and techniques. Over 35
different types of terra cotta
tiles. Suitable for kitchens,
dining rooms, halls,
conservatories, patios, etc.
Also reproduction early-
English delft tiles, natural
floor coverings, tribal rugs,
and kilims.
(pp. 94-5, 8)*

Francis N. Lowe Ltd
The Marble Works
New Road
Middleton-by-Wirksworth
Derbyshire
DE4 4NA
UK
TEL:
(01629) 822216
FAX:
(01629) 824348

*Specialist designers and
manufacturers of
architectural features in
natural marble, granite, and
slate for commercial and
private properties. Includes
fireplaces, floors, baseboards,
dado rails, architraves, and
intricate moldings.
(pp. 92-3, 7, 10)*

Junckers
Wheaton Court
Commercial Centre
Wheaton Road
Witham
Essex
CM8 3UJ
UK
TEL:
(01376) 534705
FAX:
(01376) 514401
E-MAIL:
mkt@juk.derxon.co.uk
WEB SITE:
http://www.junckers.com

*Leading European producer
of solid hardwood flooring,
including broad oak planking
for period homes.
(pp. 88-9, 8)*

**Stark Carpet
Corporation**
D & D Building
979 Third Avenue
New York
10022-1276
TEL:
(212) 752-9000
FAX:
(212) 758-4342
WEB SITE:
http://www.starkcarpet
corp.com

*Makers of classically
inspired carpet designs,
woven by craftsmen in the
finest wool. Includes handmade rugs made to custom
colors, sizes, and textures,
and Chinese needlepoint
rugs. Also fabric and
furniture ranges.
(pp. 96-7, 6)*

Stone Age
19 Filmer Road
London
SW6 7BU
UK
TEL:
(0171) 385-7954/5
FAX:
(0171) 385-7956
WEB SITE:
http://www.stone-
age.co.uk

*Suppliers of natural stone
flooring specializing in limestone and sandstone. Perfect
for conservatories, halls,
kitchens, and bathrooms.
(pp. 92-3, 5, 6)*

Treework Flooring
Treework Services Ltd
Cheston Combe
Church Town
Backwell
Near Bristol
BS19 3JQ
UK
TEL:
(01275) 464466
FAX:
(01275) 463078

*Manufacturers and fitters of
machined floorboards from
oak, ash, elm, and other
sustainable timbers for
restoration and new building
works. An ecological
commitment is central to
their activities. Associated
products include baseboards,
doors, and staircases.
(pp. 88-9, 7)*

Victorian Interiors
575 Hayes Street
San Fransisco
California
94102
TEL:
(415) 431 7191
FAX:
(415) 431 7144

*Designers and restorers of
authentic historical interiors
of the 1860-1915 period.
Offers a rich range of
products and services,
including decorative pieces,
floor coverings, and fabrics
from companies such as
Sanderson, Scalamandré, and
Schumacher.*

WALLS

Classic Ceilings

902 East Commonwealth
Avenue
Fullerton
California
92831
Tel:
(800) 992-8700
Fax:
(714) 870-5972

*Distributors of tin
ceilings and importers
of Anaglypta/Lincrusta
embossed wall coverings,
including ceiling patterns,
borders, and wainscots.
Ceiling moldings and
medallions also available.*

Copley Decor Ltd

Leyburn
North Yorkshire
DL8 5QA
UK
Tel:
(01969) 623410
Fax:
(01969) 624398

*Manufacturers of
architectural moldings in
hard cellular resin. Range
includes cornices, picture
rails, panel moldings,
dado rails, architraves,
and baseboards.
(p. 103, 3, 6-8;
pp. 104-5, 7)*

Crown Corporation

3012 Huron Street
Suite 101
Denver
Colorado
80202
Tel:
(303) 292-1313
SEE WALLPAPERS
AND FABRICS (P.179)

Crowther of Syon Lodge

Busch Corner
London Road
Isleworth
Middlesex
TW7 5BH
UK
Tel:
(0181) 560-7978/7985
Fax:
(0181) 568-7572
E-Mail:
crowther.syon-lodge
@virgin.net
Web Site:
http://www.crowther-
syon-lodge.co.uk
SEE FIREPLACES
AND STOVES (P.181)

Fired Earth Plc.

Twyford Mill
Oxford Road
Adderbury
Oxon
OX17 3HP
Tel:
(01295) 812088
Fax:
(01295) 810832
E-Mail:
enquiries@firedearth.com
SEE FLOORS (P.177)

Hallidays America Inc.

PO Box 731 PC
Sparta
New Jersey
07871-0731
Tel:
(201) 729-8876
Fax:
(201) 729-5149

*Specialist designers of period
paneled rooms. Traditional
wood carving and carpentry
skills are used to faithfully
reproduce designs and
fittings of the Georgian and
Regency periods. Complete
rooms with a range of
antique furniture are
showcased. Specialists in
wood-crafted Georgian and
Regency mantelpieces, and
brass and cast-iron fireplace
accessories.*

Millwork Designs Inc.

Route 4
Box 427A
Martinsburg
West Virginia
25401
Tel:
(614) 335 5203

*Specialists in reproduction
hardwood paneling,
flooring, and moldings for
restoration work in period
buildings. Available in
all hardwoods, including
walnut, Honduras
mahogany, cherry, and
quartersawn oak.*

Oakleaf Reproductions Ltd

Ling Bob
Main Street
Wilsden
Bradford
BD15 0JP
UK
Tel:
(01535) 272878
Fax:
(01535) 275748

*Reproduction wood in
traditional and period
styles, including simulated
oak ceiling beams,
paneling, and embellish-
ments, all manufactured
in rigid cellular resin,
molded and hand-stained.
Design service.
(pp. 104-5, 1, 4, 6;
pp. 112-3, 7-10;
pp. 116-17, 8, 16, 17)*

Parquet de France Inc.

54 Byram Road
Point Pleasant
Pennsylvania
18950-0156
Tel:
(215) 297-8327
Fax:
(215) 297 5854

*Manufacturers of custom-
made parquet flooring and
importers of authentic
seventeenth- and eighteenth-
century French parquet.*

Seneca Tiles Inc.

7100 South Country
Road, 23
Attica
Ohio
44807
Tel:
(800) 426-4335
Fax:
(419) 426 1735

*Manufacturers and
importers of rustic and
handmade ceramic tiles for
residential and commercial
interiors and exteriors.*

Stuart Interiors

Barrington Court
Barrington
Illminster
Somerset
TA19 0NQ
UK
Tel:
(01460) 240349
Fax:
(01460) 242069

*Specialists in all aspects of
period design from medieval
times to the eighteenth
century from concept
and design through to
manufacture and installation.
Extensive showrooms with
displays of Gothic-,
Elizabethan-, and Stuart-
style furniture, architectural
woodwork, fabrics, lighting,
pewter, and brassware, etc.
(pp. 58-9, 1; pp. 62-3, 2;
pp. 78-9, 1; pp. 82-3, 1;
pp. 108-9, 2; pp. 146-7, 1;
pp. 166-7, 1)*

Winther Browne & Co. Ltd

Nobel Road
Eley Estate
Edmonton
London
N18 3DX
UK
Tel:
(0181) 803-3434
Fax:
(0181) 807-0544
E-Mail:
sales@wintherbrowne.
co.uk
SEE DOORS (P.175)

WALLPAPERS & FABRICS

Bentley & Spens

At: Christopher Hyland
Inc.
D & D Building
Suite 1714
979 Third Avenue
New York
10022-1276
Tel:
(212) 688 6121

*Fabric and wall covering
specialists.*

Bradbury & Bradbury

PO Box 155
Benicia
California
94510
Tel:
(707) 746 1900

Wall covering designers.

Brunschwig & Fils
75 Virginia Road
North White Plains
New York 10603
TEL:
(914) 684-5800
FAX:
(914) 684-6140

Designers and manufacturers of an extensive range of more than 17,000 fabrics and 1,000 wall coverings, ranging from fine reproductions to striking contemporary New England designs. Also upholstered furniture, hand-painted lamps, and trimmings.

Classic Ceilings
902 East Commonwealth
Avenue
Fullerton
California
92831
TEL:
(800) 992-8700
FAX:
(714) 870-5972
SEE WALLS

Classic Revivals Inc.
1 Design Center Place, 545
Boston
Massachusetts
02210
TEL:
(617) 574-9030
FAX:
(617) 574-9027

Suppliers of reproduction fabric, wallpaper, carpet trimmings, and lace.

Crown Corporation
3012 Huron Street
Suite 101
Denver
Colorado
80202
TEL:
(303) 292-1313

Manufacturers of Anaglypta paints and relief wall coverings. Ranges include lightly textured patterns to heavily embossed vinyl, complemented by toning dadoes and borders. Also peel 'n' stick coverings and ranges made exclusively from recycled paper.
(pp. 168-9, 3)

Ian Mankin
US Distributors:
Agnes Bourne Inc.
2 Henry Adams Street
Showroom 220
San Francisco
California
94103
and
Coconut Company
129-131 Greene Street
New York
10012

Pioneers of the use of utility fabrics, such as calicos, butchers' stripes and tickings, used for curtaining and soft furnishings. Around 300 natural fabrics in stock.

Interior Vision in the Craftsman Style
23 Oak Shore Ct
Port Townsend
West Virginia
98368
TEL:
(360) 385-3161
FAX:
(360) 385-4874

Interior designers specializing in historic restoration of Arts and Crafts-style interiors, such as stairways, porches, wood flooring, and wainscoting. Provide on-site consultations and wallpaper and stencil installation.
(pp. 42-3, 8; pp. 84-5, 10)

Thibaut Wallcoverings
480 Frelinghuysen Avenue
Newark
New Jersey
07114
TEL:
(800) 223 0704
FAX:
(201) 643 3133

Manufacturers of historic, traditional, and Victorian wallpapers, fabrics, and borders, such as the "Historic Homes of America" and murals collections.

Tissunique Ltd
From: Quadrille
D & D Building
979 Third Avenue
New York
10022-1276
TEL:
(212) 753-2995

Wholesalers and importers of furnishing fabric and wallpapers, braids, and trimmings.

Victorian Interiors
575 Hayes Street
San Francisco
California
94102
TEL:
(415) 431-7191
FAX:
(415) 431-7144
SEE FLOORS (P.177)

Ann Wallace & Friends, Textiles for the Home
Box 16567
Saint Paul
Minnesota
55116
TEL:
(612) 228-9611
FAX:
(612) 224-1636

Makers of curtains for early-twentieth-century homes, made to order in natural fibers. Plain, appliquéd, or stenciled in linen, velvet, or cotton. Also hand-embroidered pillows and table runners. Pattern books and kits also available.

Zoffany
D & D Building
979 Third Avenue
Suite 1403
New York
10022-1276
TEL:
(800) 395-8760

Designers and manufacturers of wallpapers, fabrics, carpets, and trimmings based on authentic seventeenth-, eighteenth-, and nineteenth-century designs.

CEILINGS

Chelsea Decorative Metal Company
9603 Moonlight
Houston
Texas
77096
TEL:
(713) 721-9200
FAX:
(713) 776-8661
WEB SITE:
http://www.thetinman.com

Specialists in traditional pressed-tin ceilings, walls, and cornices. Tin sheets are fashioned to traditional decorative designs ranging from the Victorian period to Art Deco.

Classic Ceilings
902 East Commonwealth
Ave
Fullerton
California
92831
TEL:
(800) 992-8700
FAX:
(714) 870-5972
SEE WALLS (P.178)

Felber Ornamental Plastering Corp.
PO Box 57
1000 Washington Street
Norristown
Pennsylvania
19404
TEL:
(610) 275 4713
FAX:
(610) 275 6636

Sculptors, mold-makers, and period-ceiling designers.

Hayles & Howe
509 South Exeter Street
Fells Point
Baltimore
Maryland
21202
TEL:
(410) 385-2400
FAX:
(410) 385-2400

Ornamental plasterers involved in the restoration and conservation of plaster-work in historic and listed buildings. Specialists in antique scagliola. Also moldings, cornices, niches, columns, and capitals.

Raymond Enkeboll Designs
16506 Avalon Boulevard
Carson
California
90746
TEL:
(310) 532-1400
FAX:
(310) 532-2042
WEB SITE:
http://www.enkeboll.com

Makers of an extensive array of architectural features in carved wood, including capitals, corbels, moldings, and inlays. Available in hard maple or red oak.
SEE ALSO WALLS (P.178)

STAIRCASES

Cinder Whit & Co.
753 Eleventh Ave South
Wahpeton
ND 58075
TEL:
(800) 527-9064
FAX:
(701) 642-4204

Restorers and creators of replica and custom-designed exterior and interior cedar wood-turned porch posts and newel posts, balustrades, spindles, and rails for staircases.

D. S. Nelson Co. Inc.
115 Airport St Quancit Point
North Kingston
Rhode Island
02852
TEL:
(401) 267-1000
FAX:
(401) 295-4756
WEB SITE:
http://www.dsnelson.com

Designers and manufacturers of custom-made curved staircases in wood, metal, and glass. Complete design service available.
(pp. 80-1, 1)

Robert Coles Furniture and Architectural Joinery
Church House
Broad Street
Congresbury
Avon
BS19 5DG
UK
TEL:
(01934) 833660

Designers and manufacturers of hand-crafted wood furniture and architectural features, including staircases.
(pp. 78-9, 6; pp. 84-5, 7)

Spiral Manufacturing Inc.
17251 Jefferson Highway
Baton Rouge
Louisiana
70817
TEL:
(504) 753-8336
FAX:
(504) 753-8351
WEB SITE:
http://www.spiralstair.com

Manufacturers of wood spiral, curved, and straight stairs and suppliers of stair parts and metal spiral kits.

Stair Specialist Inc.
2257 West Columbia Ave.
Battle Creek
Michigan
490157
TEL:
(616) 964-2351
FAX:
(616) 964-4824

Manufacturers of custom-made wooden circular staircases.

Stairways Inc.
4166 Pinemont
Houston
Texas
77018-1106
TEL:
(800) 231-0793
FAX:
(713) 680-2571

Manufacturers of spiral staircases in any size in wood, brass, and aluminum. Supplied as single unit or in kit form.

Stuart Interiors
Barrington Court
Barrington
Illminster
Somerset
TA19 0NQ
UK
TEL:
(01460) 240349
FAX:
(01460) 242069
SEE WALLS (P.178)

Treework Flooring
Treework Services Ltd
Cheston Combe
Church Town
Backwell
Near Bristol BS19 3JQ
UK
TEL:
(01275) 464466
FAX:
(01275) 463078
SEE FLOORS (P.177)

Winther Browne & Co. Ltd
Nobel Road
Eley Estate
Edmonton
London
N18 3DX
UK
TEL:
(0181) 803-3434
FAX:
(0181) 807-0544
E-MAIL:
sales@wintherbrowne.co.uk
SEE DOORS (P.175)

Wood Factory
111 Railroad Street
Navasota
Texas
77868
TEL:
(409) 825-7233
FAX:
(409) 825-1791

Manufacturers of architectural millwork, including parts for staircases.

The Woods Co.
610-B 5th Avenue
Chambersburg
Pennsylvania
17201
TEL:
(717) 263-6524
FAX:
(717) 263-9346

Manufacturers of wide-board flooring milled from antique lumber. Also offer stair-parts, moldings, and special millwork. Woods available include antique oak, yellow and white pine, and chestnut.

Worthington
PO Box 868
Troy
Alabama
36081
TEL:
(800) 872-1608
FAX:
(334) 566-5390
WEB SITE:
http://www.architectural-details.com
SEE DOORS (P.175)

FIREPLACES AND STOVES

Acquisitions (Fireplaces) Ltd
Acquisitions House
24-26 Holmes Road
London
NW5 3AB
UK
TEL:
(0171) 482-2949
FAX:
(0171) 267-4361
E-MAIL:
sales@acquistions.co.uk
WEB SITE:
http://www.acquistions.co.uk

Manufacturers of reproduction Victorian and Edwardian fireplaces and accessories. Includes cast-iron, wood, and marble surrounds, inserts, grates, fenders, coal buckets, hand-painted, and embossed tiles to Victorian and Edwardian designs. All fireplaces suitable for solid-fuel or decorative fuel-effect fires.
(pp. 120-1, 1; pp. 126-7, 1, 3; pp. 130-1, 4, 10; pp. 132-3, 7)

Adams Co.
PO Box 268
Dubuque
Indiana
52004
TEL:
(319) 583-3591
FAX:
(319) 583-8048

Makers of fireplace accessories.

Aga-Rayburn

US distributor:
Aga Cookers Inc.
Alliance Shipping Group
Lake Park Drive 325
Smyrna
Atlanta
Georgia
30080
TEL:
(770) 438-9150

Manufacturers and retailers of traditional cast-iron stoves. Aga, Rayburn, and Coalbrookdale cooker models can be run from oil, gas, solid fuel, or off-peak electricity. (p. 136, 1; pp. 158-9, 5)

Amazing Grates Fireplaces Ltd

61-63 High Road
East Finchley
London
N2 8AB
UK
TEL:
(0181) 883-9590
FAX:
(0181) 365-2053

Makers of quality British-made mantels faithfully following original eighteenth- and nineteenth-century designs. Marble, stone, and slate specially selected by their stonemasons, including Carrara and Cremo marbles, Portuguese limestone, and green Verde Dolomite. Also supply grates and gas fire inserts. (pp. 120-1, 5, 8; pp. 138-9, 7)

Architectural Salvage Inc.

1215 Delaware St
Denver
Colorado
80204
TEL:
(303) 615-5432

Suppliers of a broad range of original antique architectural items for the period home, including fireplaces and accessories.

Architectural Salvage Warehouse

212 Battery Street
Burlington
Vermont
05401
TEL:
(802) 658-5011

Suppliers of reclaimed antique mantels. Also doors, windows, hardware, baths.

Artefact Architectural Antiques

790 Edison Furlong Road
Furlong
Pennsylvania
18925
TEL:
(215) 794-8790

Stockists of an extensive collection of eighteenth- and nineteenth-century architectural antiques, ranging from carved mantels and newel posts to stained-glass panels and brass, copper, bronze accessories.

Baxi Heating Ltd

Brownedge Road
Bamber Road
Preston
Lancashire
PR5 6SN
UK
TEL:
(01772) 695555
FAX:
(01772) 695410
WEB SITE:
http://www.baxiheating.co.uk

Manufacturers of gas and solid-fuel heating appliances. (pp. 138-9, 4)

Bisque Radiators

15 Kingsmead Square
Bath
BA1 2AE
UK
TEL:
(01225) 469244
FAX:
(01225) 444708

Extensive range of stylish radiators in a variety of colors and finishes. Heated towel rails, classic pieces, modern steel tubes, hot coils, and panel heaters. Made to measure by Arbonia of Switzerland. (p. 137, 5)

Chesney's Antique Fireplace Warehouse

194-202 Battersea Park
Road
London
SW11 4ND
UK
TEL:
(0171) 627-1410
FAX:
(0171) 622-1078
E-MAIL:
sales@antiquefireplace.co.uk
WEB SITE:
http://www.antiquefireplace.co.uk

Maintains an extensive stock of antique and reproduction marble and stone fireplaces Incorporating eighteenth- and nineteenth-century English and Continental designs. Also offer a bespoke masonry service and can undertake designs in marble and stone. Install grates, hearthstones, and gas-effect fires. (pp. 120-1, 4; pp. 124-5, 4, 6; pp. 126-7, 4; pp. 134-5, 4)

The Chimney Pot Shoppe

1915 Brush Run Road
Avella
Pennsylvania
15312
TEL/FAX:
(412) 345 4601

Importers of antique chimney pots in a range of colors and styles.

The Chiswick Fireplace Company

68 Southfield Road
Chiswick
London
W4 1BD
UK
TEL:
(0181) 995-4011
FAX:
(0181) 995-4012

Specialists in Victorian, Edwardian, and Art Nouveau original fireplaces, marble, stone and wood mantels, and comparatively rare cast-iron registers. Also baskets and grates and radiator covers. Offer a restoration and installation service for most types of fireplace and custom-made gas fires to suit all grates. (pp. 132-3, 4; pp. 134-5, 8)

Creative Tile Marketing Inc.

222 SW 15th Road
Miami
Florida
33129
TEL:
(305) 858-8242
FAX:
(305) 858-9926

Representatives of suppliers of ceramic tiles for fireplaces, also sinks, toilet bases, and vanities. Ranges in porcelain, natural stone, and limestone.

Crowther of Syon Lodge

Syon Lodge
Busch Corner
London Road
Isleworth
Middlesex
TW7 5BH
UK
TEL:
(0181) 560-7978/7985
FAX:
(0181) 568-7572
E-MAIL:
crowther.syon-lodge@virgin.net
WEB SITE:
http://www.crowther-syon-lodge.co.uk

Stockists of fine antiques for gardens and interiors. Specialist items include Georgian architectural features, such as oak and pinewood paneling, stone and marble chimney pieces. Offer a complete paneling service. Also antique garden ornaments. (pp. 100-1, 4; pp. 108-9, 4, 7; pp.118-19, 6; pp. 124-5, 3)

Dick's Antiques

670 Lake Avenue
Bristol
Connecticut
06010
TEL:
(860) 584-2566
FAX:
(860) 314-0296

Antique items including mantels.

Dovre Castings Ltd
Unit 1
Weston Works
Weston Lane
Tyseley
Birmingham
B121 3RP
UK
TEL:
(0121) 706-7600
FAX:
(0121) 706-9182
E-MAIL:
enquiries@dovre.co.uk
WEB SITE:
http://www.dovre.co.uk

Manufacturers of traditional cast-iron gas, electric, multi-fuel, and wood-burning stoves in a range of enameled colors.

Easy Heat Inc.
31977 US 20 East
New Carlisle
Indiana
46552
TEL:
(219) 654-3144
FAX:
(219) 654-7739
WEB SITE:
http://www.easyheat.com

Manufacturers of electric-resistance radiant heating cables and systems for floor warming, snow and ice melting, pipe tracing, roof and gutter de-icing and other radiant heating applications.

Emsworth Fireplaces Ltd
(The Robert Lyman Collection)
Unit 3
Station Approach
Emsworth
Hampshire
PO10 7PN
UK
TEL:
(01243) 373431
FAX:
(01243) 371023
E-MAIL:
info@emsworth.co.uk

Producers of fine reproduction English and French style mantels available in solid timber: pine, mahogany, oak, white painted, and other wood finishes to order and in a choice of 90 different marbles.
(pp. 124-5, 2; pp. 128-9, 7; pp. 130-1, 1, 7)

Faral Radiators
Tropical House
Charlswood Road
East Grinstead
West Sussex
RH19 2HJ
UK
TEL:
(01342) 315757
FAX:
(01342) 315362

Suppliers of radiators, towel rails, and accessories. Also a range of die-cast aluminum, steel-column, and cast-iron radiators. (p. 137, 2)

Flamewave Fires
The Farmyard
Pearson's Green
Brenchley
Tonbridge
Kent
TN17 7DE
UK
TEL:
(01892) 724458
FAX:
(01892) 724966
E-MAIL:
nod@flamewavefires.co.uk
WEB SITE:
http://www.flamewavefires.co.uk

Manufacturers of Tortoise convection fires and importers of the All Black range of stoves.
(p. 136, 4)

Franco Belge
Dovre Castings Ltd
Unit 1
Weston Works
Weston Lane
Tyseley
Birmingham
B121 3RP
UK
TEL:
(0121) 706-7600
FAX:
(0121) 706-9182
E-MAIL:
enquiries@dovre.co.uk
WEB SITE:
http://www.dovre.co.uk

Manufacturers of traditional stoves, distributed by Dovre Castings. (p. 136, 3)

Marble Hill
Fireplaces Ltd
70-72 Richmond Road
Twickenham
Middlesex
TW1 3BE
UK
TEL:
(0181) 892-1488
FAX:
(0181) 891-6591

Producers of reproduction fireplaces, including English stone mantels to Victorian and Georgian styles and a range of stone mantels in Louis XV and XVI styles, hand-crafted in France. Stockists of a large range of antique French chimney pieces.
(pp. 120-1, 7; pp. 122-3, 1)

Nevers Oak Fireplace
Mantels
312 N Hwy 101
Encinitas
California
92024
TEL:
(760) 632-5808
FAX:
(760) 749-3990

Makers of hand-carved wooden mantels in a range of woods, including ash and poplar.

Robert Aagaard & Co.
Frogmire House
Stockwell Road
Knaresborough
North Yorkshire
HG5 0JP
UK
TEL:
(01423) 864805
FAX:
(01423) 869356

Manufacturers of reproduction hand-carved mantels, made to authentic designs and emulating original processes. Fire surrounds in choice of woods based on originals dating back to the seventeenth century, complemented by granite, hand-painted tiles. Offer fireplace restoration and design service.
(pp. 128-9, 4)

Stone Manufacturing Co.
1636 West 135th Street
Gardena
California
90249
TEL:
(310) 323 6720
FAX:
(310) 715 6090

Specialist manufacturers of fireplace accessories, including custom-made pieces. All items are individually handcrafted and come in a variety of finishes.

Stovax Ltd
Falcon Road
Sowton Industrial Estate
Exeter
Devon
EX2 7LF
UK
TEL: SALES
(01392) 474000
FAX:
(01392) 219932
E-MAIL:
info@stovax.com

Manufacturers of finely reproduced nineteenth-century cast-iron fireplaces. Hand-cast and finished with period detail, the range embraces fireplaces for solid-fuel and gas-effect fires from the Victorian, Georgian, and Art Nouveau periods. Also extensive range of decorative hearth and fireplace tiles and fireplace surrounds in wood and cast iron.
(pp. 86-7; pp. 94-5, 1, 2, 6; pp. 116-17, 4)

THS Distribution
53-55 High Street
Uttoxeter
Staffordshire
ST14 7JQ
UK
TEL:
(01889) 565411
FAX:
(01889) 567625

UK importers of several makes of multi-fuel stoves.
(p. 136, 5)

Temco Fireplace Products
301 South Perimeter Park Drive 227
Nashville
Tennessee
37211
TEL:
(615) 831-9393
FAX:
(615) 831-9127
WEB SITE:
http://www.hearth.com/temco

Suppliers of vent-free gas fireplaces and logs; vented gas and wood-burning fireplaces.

Walney Ltd
108 West Walnut Street
North Wales
Pennsylvania
19454
TEL:
(215) 699-0566
FAX:
(215) 699-2611

Manufacturers of radiator cabinets and tubular steel column radiators in range of colors. Radiator cabinets come in a range of grilles and wood veneers. Traditional brass radiator valves also available, plus range of bathroom units for basins, in wood or ceramic.
(p. 137, 3)

BATHROOMS

American Standard
1 Centennial Plaza
PO Box 6820
Piscataway
New Jersey
08855-6820
TEL:
(732) 980-6000
FAX:
(732) 980-3335

A world leader in bathroom design and manufacture using quality materials and internationally renowned designers. A wide range of traditional-style baths and basins, shower fittings, faucets, and other accessories.
(pp. 142-3, 6; pp. 144-5, 4; pp. 148-9, box)

Antique Plumbing
7240 West 38th Ave
Wheat Ridge
Colorado
80033
TEL:
(303) 403-8531
FAX:
(303) 403-0886

Suppliers of original-finish period bathrooms fixtures, such as clawfoot tubs, pedestal sinks, and toilets, and resurfaced antique fixtures. Also reproduction antique faucets and shower surrounds.

Baileys Home and Garden
The Engine Shed
Station Approach
Ross-on-Wye
Herefordshire
HR9 7BW
UK
TEL:
(01989) 563015
FAX:
(01989) 768172
SEE DOORS (p.174)

Barber Wilsons & Co. Ltd
(Including Barwill Traditional and Contemporary Water Fittings)
Crawley Road
Westbury Avenue
Wood Green
London
N22 6AH
UK
TEL:
(0181) 888-3461
FAX:
(0181) 888-2041
E-MAIL:
100127.1551@compuserve.com

Range of faucets ideal for those seeking to re-create an authentic period look. Each fitting is manufactured to an original design from a portfolio stretching back to 1905 when the Company was founded. Choice of finishes: inca brass, chrome, nickel, satin, and polished brass. (pp. 148-9, 1, 5, 10; p. 156, 1, 2)

Black Country Heritage Ltd
US distributor:
Waterworks
29 Park Avenue
Danbury
Connecticut
06810
TEL:
(203) 792-9979
FAX:
(203) 731-5495

Producers of every conceivable bathroom accessory and low-energy towel warmers in three ranges: Edwardian England, 1920s New York, and Art Deco styles. Handmade in solid brass with antique gold-, polished- or satin-nickel-, and chrome-plate finishes. (pp. 150-1, 2, 3, 5, 6, 8, 9, 11)

Brass & Traditional Sinks Ltd
Devauden Green
Chepstow
Monmouthshire
NP6 6PL
UK
TEL:
(01291) 650738
FAX:
(01291) 650827
E-MAIL:
sales@sinks.co.uk
WEB SITE:
http://www.sinks.co.uk

Leading suppliers of traditional and modern fireclay sinks.
(pp. 150-1, 10)

Caradon Plumbing Solutions
Launton Road
Alsager
Stoke-on-Trent
ST7 2DF
UK
TEL:
(0870) 8400035

Manufacturers of a full range of bathroom products made from vitreous china. Also steel and acrylic baths, faucets, fittings, and accessories. Makers of Twyford and Doulton bathroom ranges and Mira showers.

Chadder & Co.
Blenheim Studio
Lewes Road
Forest Row
East Sussex
RH18 5EZ
UK
TEL:
(01342) 823243
FAX:
(01342) 823097
WEB SITE:
http://www.pncl.co.uk/chadder

Specialists in antique and traditional baths, showers, toilets, and accessories, featuring hand-cast metal, ornate brackets, chrome, nickel, and antique gold pipes, and porcelain handles.
(pp. 146-7, 2)

Czech & Speake
244-254 Cambridge Heath Road
London
E2 9DA
UK
TEL:
(0181) 980 4567
FAX:
(0181) 981 7232

Designers of stylish kitchen sink mixers and accessories for bathrooms and kitchens in traditional designs. Includes an Edwardian range, also towel rails, shower hoses, mahogany toilet seats. Metalware in chrome, nickel, and no-tarnish brass.
(pp. 142-3, 9; pp. 150-1, 4; p. 156, 4, 5)

Doulton
Caradon Plumbing Solutions
Launton Road
Alsager
Stoke-on-Trent
ST7 2DF
UK
TEL:
(0870) 8400035

(pp. 146/7, 6)
SEE CARADON PLUMBING SOLUTIONS ENTRY ABOVE

Lefroy Brooks

10 Leonard Street 2N
New York
10013

*Quality English bathroom
ware and accessories,
including an Edwardian
range. Faucets made in solid
brass, and cast, polished, and
assembled entirely by hand.
Items include cast-iron
baths, towel warmers,
shower rails.
(pp. 142-3, 5, box;
pp. 146-7, 7; pp. 148-9, 4;
pp. 150-1, 12)*

Pipe Dreams of Kensington Ltd

72 Gloucester Road
London
SW7 4QT
UK
TEL:
(0171) 225-3978
FAX:
(0171) 589-8841

*Antique baths, basins, and
accessories in Art Deco,
Victorian, and other styles.
(pp. 92-3, 8; pp. 142-3, 2,
8; pp. 144-5, 5, 6)*

Samuel Heath & Sons Plc.

Cobden Works
Leopold Street
Birmingham
B12 0UJ
UK
TEL:
(0121) 772-2303
SEE DOORS (p.175)

Stiffkey Bathrooms

Stiffkey
Wells-Next-Sea
Norfolk
NR23 1AJ
UK
TEL:
(01328) 830460
FAX:
(01328) 830005

*Restored bathroom fittings
and period sanitaryware,
all reconditioned and in full
working order. Includes
Victorian shower baths,
marble basins, and
Edwardian towel warmers.
Stockists of a vast range
faucets and shower mixers,
and other original and reproduction accessories, such as
mirrors and soap dishes.
(pp. 146-7, 4)*

Water Front Ltd

9 The Burdwood Centre
Station Road
Thatcham
Berkshire
RG19 4YA
UK
TEL:
(01635) 872100
FAX:
(01635) 872200
E-MAIL:
waterfront@btconnect.com
WEB SITE:
waterfront.ltd.uk

*Manufacturers of classic
quality bathroom accessories
in a range of finishes.
(pp. 150-1, 1)*

The Water Monopoly

16/18 Lonsdale Road
London
NW6 6RD
UK
TEL:
(0171) 624-2636
FAX:
(0171) 624-2531

*Feature quality antique
baths and basins and period
accessories. Items date from
seventeenth century to the
Victorian era. Recommended
suppliers of suitable period-
style fabrics, flooring, and
other features to complement
their sanitaryware.
(pp. 142-3, 1, 7)*

Watercolors Inc.

Garrison-on-Hudson
New York
10524
TEL:
(914) 424-3327

*Suppliers of traditional and
contemporary bathroom
accessories in brushed and
polished nickel, chrome,
brass, gold, and baked enamel
in a range of colors. In
addition to washbasin and
shower sets, provides
mirrors, shelf units,
and armchairs.
(pp. 148-9, 6-9; p. 156,
7, 8)*

KITCHENS

Aga-Rayburn

US distributor:
Aga Cookers Inc.
Alliance Shipping Group
Lake Park Drive 325
Smyrna
Atlanta
Georgia
30080
TEL:
(770) 438-9150
SEE FIREPLACES AND
STOVES (p.181)

Harcourt Designs Ltd

4 Harcourt Road
Redland
Bristol
Avon
BS6 7RG
UK
TEL:
(0117) 9756969
FAX:
(0117) 9756675

*Designers and fitters of
kitchen furniture with a
range of made-to-measure
units in pine, hardwood, or
composite materials which
can be finished in stain,
colorwash, or with painted
decoration. In addition, free-
standing furniture in any
wood and constructions such
as conservatories and porches
can be designed, built, and
fitted.
(pp. 154-5, 8)*

Landsowne Kitchen Sinks & Taps

Amana
280 200th Trail
PO 8901 Amana
Indiana
52204-0001
TEL:
(319) 622-5511
FAX:
(319) 622-2158

*Manufacturers of high
quality, fine fireclay ceramic
kitchen sinks combining
classic and durable design
with up-to-date
manufacturing processes.
The sinks are complemented
by a range of faucets in
nickel, brass, and chrome,
and wood draining boards.
(pp. 154-5, 6)*

Neff (UK) Ltd

Grand Union House
Old Wolverton Road
Wolverton
Milton Keynes
MK12 5TP
UK
TEL:
(01908) 328300
FAX:
(01908) 328399

*Innovative built-in appliances
for kitchens. Manufacturers
of single and double-ovens,
cooker hoods, hobs, fridges
and freezers, dishwashers,
washing machines, and
microwaves using recyclable
materials where possible.
(pp. 158-9, 9)*

Rencraft Ltd

Unit 9
Chart Farm
Styants Bottom Road
Seal Chart
Sevenoaks
Kent TN15 0ES
UK
TEL:
(01732) 762682
FAX:
(01732) 762535

*Manufacturers of the
Wooden Kitchen range of
traditional, hand-crafted
kitchen units, available in
solid pine, solid pine for hand
painting, or in rustic-English
oak. Unit doors are paneled
and hung on butt-hinges and
drawers are comb-jointed.
(pp. 42-3, 4)*

Romsey Cabinetmakers

Greatbridge Business Park
Budds Lane
Romsey
Hampshire
SO51 0HA
UK
TEL:
(01794) 522626
FAX:
(01794) 522451

*Designers and makers of
bespoke kitchens. Styles and
finishes reflect a range of
periods and are available in
painted finishes or solid
wood: oak, cherry, and ash.
Also for bedrooms and
bathrooms.
(pp. 56-7, 8; pp. 154-5, 9)*

SieMatic Corporation
Two Greenwood Square
3331 Street Road
Suite 450
Bensalem
Pennyslvania
19020
Tel:
(215) 244-6800
Fax:
(215) 244-6822

US branch of this German manufacturer's range of fitted kitchens. A broad range of styles and designs, from classic farmhouse and country kitchens with hand-painted traditional features, to high-tech 1990s stainless steel units.

Underwood Kitchens Ltd
Lawn Farm Business Centre
Grendon Underwood
Buckinghamshire
HP18 0QX
UK
Tel:
(01296) 770043
Fax:
(01296) 770412

Manufacturers of hand-crafted kitchens in solid English oak and elm, Canadian maple, European beech, and limed ash. Styles include traditional American, Edwardian elegance, and incorporate hand-painted finishes and dark granite worktops.
(p. 157, 5)

LIGHTING

The Antique Lamp Shop
600 King's Road
London
SW6 2DX
UK
Tel:
(0171) 371-0077
Fax:
(0171) 371-3507
SEE CHRISTOPHER WRAY
LIGHTING ENTRY BELOW

American Period Lighting Inc.
3004 Columbia Ave
Lancaster
Pennsylvania
17603
Tel:
(717) 392-5649
Fax:
(717) 392-3557

Specialists in handcrafted traditional and period lanterns, postlights, and chandeliers for interiors and exteriors.

Architectural Iron Company Inc.
PO Box 126
104 Ironwood Court
Milford
Pennsylvania
18337
Tel:
(717) 296-7722
Fax:
(717) 296-4766
SEE EXTERIORS (p.187)

Arroyo Craftsman
4509 Little John Street
Baldwin Park
California
91706
Tel:
(626) 960-9411
Fax:
(626) 960-9521

Arts and Crafts movement-inspired lighting. Elegant table, wall, and ceiling lamps incorporating design principles of Gustav Stickley and Frank Lloyd Wright for interior and exterior use.
(pp. 52-3, 11; pp. 170-1, 10)

Bradley Collection Ltd
Lion Barn
Maitland Road
Needham Market
Suffolk
IP6 8NS
UK
Tel:
(01449) 722724
Fax:
(01449) 722728
E-Mail:
info@bradleycollection.
co.uk
Web Site:
http://www.bradley
collection.co.uk
SEE WINDOWS (p.175)

Brook Grove Antique & Custom Lighting
21412 Laytonsville Road
Laytonsville
Maryland
20882
Tel:
(301) 948-0392
Fax:
(301) 926-4023

Suppliers of restored antique lighting. Replacement glass shades also available.

Chelsom Ltd
Heritage House
Clifton Road
Blackpool
Lancashire
FY4 4QA
UK
Tel:
(01253) 831400
Fax:
(01253) 698098

Designers and manufacturers of a wide range of stylish lighting fixtures: table and floor lamps, corridor, bathroom, architectural, and exterior lighting. Including reproduction Georgian and Regency lanterns. Restoration of period fixtures including the manufacture and source replacement of glasses, crystals, and fabric shades. Also do custom-made pieces.
(pp. 52-3, 10, 12, 13; pp. 164-5, 7, 10, 13; pp. 168-9, 5-9, 14; p. 172, 4-8; p. 173, 5)

Christopher Wray Lighting
591-593 King's Road
London
SW6 2YW
UK
Tel:
(0171) 736-8434
Fax:
(0171) 731-3507
E-Mail:
christopher-wray@dial.
pipex.com
Web Site:
http://www.christopher/
wray.com

Manufacturers and retailers of decorative lighting for interiors and exteriors. Includes reproduction Gothic, Tiffany, Art Deco, and classic styles for table, ceiling, and walls, spotlights, picture lights, lanterns, and a wide range of shades, bulbs, switches, and other accessories.
(pp. 164-5, 8, 12, 15; pp. 168-9, 13, 15; p. 173, 6, 22)

Classic Lamp Posts
3645 NW 67th Street
Miami
Florida
33147
Tel:
(800) 654 5852
Fax:
(305) 836 1296

Manufacturers of reproduction period lighting posts for entrances, walkways, courtyards, etc.

Conant Custom Brass Inc.
266-270 Pine Street
Burlington
Vermont
05401
Tel:
(802) 658-4482
Fax:
(802) 864-5914
E-Mail:
wholesale@conantcustom
brass.com
Web Site:
http://www.conantcustom
brass.com

Manufacturers of a range of lighting in a choice of 16 different finishes. Custom-made commissions and brass restoration, including paint removal, nickel stripping, polishing, lacquering, gold leafing, retinning, rewiring, etc. Specialize in gas and early-electric lighting fixtures and stock antique lamp parts.
(pp. 48-9, 9, 22; pp. 168-9, 11)

Faubourg Lighting Inc.
PO Box 709
Hazelhurst
Missouri
39083
Tel:
(601) 894-9090
Fax:
(601) 894-5195
E-Mail:
faubourg@netdoor.com

Manufacturers of copper, gas, and electric lighting fixtures.

Forbes & Lomax Ltd
205b St John's Hill
London
SW11 1TH
UK
TEL:
(0171) 738-0202
FAX:
(0171) 738-9224

Manufacturers of light switches and sockets in brass, Perspex, including "invisible" clear Perspex plates and a painted socket range. Also dimmers, push plates and one, two, three, and four-gang switches.
(p. 173, 23, 24)

Gaslight Time
5 Plaza Street West
Brooklyn
New York
11217
TEL:
(718) 789 7185
FAX:
(718) 789 6185

Suppliers of original restored Victorian and period lighting from the 1850s to the 1930s. Wall and floor lamps, chandeliers, wall sconces, including gas-burning fixtures.

Hamilton Litestat Group
R. Hamilton & Company Ltd
Quarry Industrial Estate
Mere
Wiltshire
BA12 6LA
UK
TEL:
(01747) 860088
FAX:
(01747) 861032

Manufacturers of decorative electrical accessories with rocker, dolly, or push switches, dimmers, power sockets, and connection units.
(pp. 50-1, 7; p. 173, 3)

Light Power
59A Wareham Street
Boston
Massachusetts
02118
TEL/FAX:
(617) 423-9790
WEB SITE:
http://www.intexp.com/lightpower

Restorers and sellers of authentic antique brass and crystal chandeliers. Also sconces, inverted domes, and a range of lighting pieces and fixtures from the 1860s to the 1940s, incorporating Victorian, neoclassical, and Art Nouveau styles.

Lighting by Hammerworks
6 Fremont Street
Worcester
Massachusetts
01603
TEL/FAX:
(508) 755-3434
WEB SITE:
http://www.hammerworks.com

Specialist manufacturers of handmade Colonial reproduction lighting fixtures in copper, brass, and tin. Includes wall lanterns, postlights, candlestands, and chandeliers and hand-forged hardware, including strap hinges and H hinges. They also accept custom commissions.

McLean Lighting Works
1207 Park Terrace
Greensboro
North Carolina
27403
TEL:
(910) 294-6994
FAX:
(910) 294-2683

Suppliers of antique and reproduction eighteenth- and nineteenth-century lamps, lanterns, postlights, chandeliers, and foyer lights.

Metro Lighting & Crafts
2216 San Pablo Avenue
Berkeley
California
94702
TEL:
(510) 540-0509
FAX:
(510) 540-0549

Makers of handcrafted lamps and fixtures in the Arts and Crafts and Art Nouveau style. Includes sconces, chandeliers, and table lamps in solid copper or brass with glass and mica shades.

Newstamp Lighting Company
(Division of N. E. Stamping & Fabricating Works Inc.)
227 Bay Road
PO Box 189
North Easton
Massachusetts
02356
TEL:
(508) 238 7071
FAX:
(508) 230 8312

Manufacturers of all types of lighting fixtures in metal, glass, and plastic. Reproductions, rewiring, and new fixtures made by skilled craftsmen.

Olivers Lighting Company
Udimore Workshops
Udimore
Rye
TN31 6AS
UK
TEL/FAX:
(01797) 225166

Makers of a unique range of quality reproduction electric switches, sockets, and accessories. Backplates crafted by hand in a choice of woods and finishes, including antique mahogany and oak. Available by mail order only.
(p. 173, 1, 2)

The Saltbox
3004 Columbia Avenue
Lancaster
Pennsylvania
17603
TEL:
(717) 392-5649

Manufacturers of authentic reproduction North American period chandeliers, hall lanterns, and postlights. Pieces are handcrafted in heavy copper, solid brass, tin, and pewter. Many are exact copies of original designs from the eighteenth century onward. Also solid redwood reproduction lampposts.

Stephen J. Malaney
The Stone House
28 East Market Street
Middleburg
Pennyslvania 17842

Expert tinsmith.

Stiffkey Lampshop
Stiffkey
Wells-Next-Sea
Norfolk NR23 1AJ
UK
TEL:
(01328) 830460
FAX:
(01328) 830005

Suppliers of unusual and antique lamps and shades, from elegant library lamps to Victorian gasoliers and ornate candelabrum. Includes reproduction polished brass table, wall, and ceiling lamps.
(pp. 164-5, 14)

Victorian Lighting Works
251 South Pennsylvania Avenue
PO Box 469, Center Hall
Pennsylvania
16828
TEL:
(814) 364 9577

Manufacturers of polished or lacquered solid-brass light fittings. Includes pendants, chandeliers, wall lights, backplates, and lamp shades.

EXTERIORS

Architectural Heritage Ltd

Taddington Manor
Taddington
Near Cutsdean
Cheltenham
Gloucestershire
GL54 5RY
UK
TEL:
(01386) 584414
FAX:
(01386) 584236
E-MAIL:
puddy@architectural-heritage.co.uk
WEB SITE:
http://www.architectural-heritage.co.uk

Stockists of one of the widest ranges of antique garden ornament, statuary, urns, fountains, and seats. On display in the grounds of a sixteenth-century manor. Also antique paneled rooms and period chimney pieces in oak, pine, and mahogany.
(pp. 50-1, 5; pp. 120-1, 2)

Archadeck

2112 West Laburnum Ave.
Suite 100
Richmond
Virginia 23227
TEL:
(888) 687-3325
FAX:
(888) 358-1878

Manufacturers of bespoke decks, gazebos, and porches.

Architectural Iron Company Inc.

PO Box 126
104 Ironwood Court
Milford
Pennsylvania
18337
TEL:
(717) 296-7722/(800) 442-4766
FAX:
(717) 296-4766

Restorers of cast and wrought iron, specializing in ironwork of every type, from gates, railings, and seats to architectural decoration. Also make and supply new iron crestings, finials, newel posts, and caps and firebacks.

Architectural Salvage Warehouse

212 Battery Street
Burlington
Vermont 05401
TEL:
(802) 658-5011
SEE FIREPLACES AND STOVES (p.181)

Baileys Home and Garden

The Engine Shed
Station Approach
Ross-on-Wye, Herefordshire
HR9 7BW
UK
TEL:
(01989) 563015
FAX:
(01989) 768172
SEE DOORS (p.174)

Chilstone

Victoria Park
Fordcombe Road
Langton Green
Kent
TN3 0RD
UK
TEL:
(01892) 740866
FAX:
(01892) 740867
E-MAIL:
chilstone@hndl.demon.co.uk
WEB SITE:
http://www.greatbritain.co.uk/chilstone

Specialists in stone building and features for house exteriors and gardens. Includes porticos, window surrounds, pilasters, and balustrades, and a wide range of ornamental garden urns, seats, sundial plates, statues, and sculpted water features.
(pp. 50-1, 4; pp. 52-3, 9)

Classic Garden Ornaments Ltd

83 Longshadow Lane
Pomona
Illinois
62975
TEL:
(618) 893-4831

Manufacturers of garden planters made of reconstituted limestone in Arts and Crafts movement and traditional designs.

Cinder Whit & Co.

753 Eleventh Ave South
Wahpeton
ND 58075
TEL:
(800) 527-9064
FAX:
(701) 642-4204
SEE STAIRCASES (p.187)

Country Designs

PO Box 774
Essex
Connecticut
06426
TEL:
(860) 767-1046

Suppliers of a collection of complete building plans for outbuildings: garages, barns, sheds, and studios. Also for cottages.

Knight & Gibbins Ltd

Windham Road
Sudbury
Suffolk
CO10 6XD
UK
TEL:
(01787) 377264
FAX:
(01787) 378258

Designers of traditional house bells in late-Georgain and early-Victorian style. Hand cast-brass bells with a choice of solid and veneer mahogany or oak mounts. Mains electricity run.
(pp. 48-9, 23)

Vande Hey's Roofing Tile Co. Inc.

1565 Bohm Drive
Little Chute
Wisconsin
54140-2533
TEL:
(414) 766-0156

Designers, manufacturers, and installers of roof tiles in eight styles and 60 standard colors. Can custom-color to match tiles for restoration work on period properties. Handcrafted floor tiles and patio pavings produced in any design and finish.

Samuel Heath & Sons Plc.

Cobden Works
Leopold Street
Birmingham
B12 0UJ
TEL:
(0121) 772-2303
FAX:
(0121) 772-3334
E-MAIL:
mail@samuel-heath.com
SEE DOORS (p.175)

Traditional Line Ltd

143 West 21st Street
New York
10011
TEL:
(212) 627-3555
FAX:
(212) 645-8158

Architectural restoration service for interior and exterior woodwork.

Walpole Woodworkers Inc.

767 East Street
Walpole
Massachusetts 02081
TEL:
(508) 668-2800

Manufacturers of authentic reproduction Wiliamsburg all-cedar fencing and gates. Also arbors, pergolas, and small outbuildings. Accept custom commissions.

West Virginia Split Rail

PO Box F
Buckhampton
West Virginia
26201
TEL: (800) 624-3110

Manufacturers of pressure-treated Appalachian pine split rail, stockade, picket fencing, and gates.

OF SPECIAL NOTE

Stephen Mack

Stephen Mack Associates
Chase Hill Farm
Ashaway, Rhode Island
02804
TEL: (401) 377-8041

Stephen P. Mack is a nationally renowned architectural and interior designer and expert in the restoration and reconst-ruction of seventeenth- and eighteenth-century structures and their environments.
(pp. 88, 2; pp. 122, 4, 5; pp. 128, 2, 3; pp. 152)

GLOSSARY

acanthus Foliage ornament based on the serrated leaves of the *Acanthus spinosus* plant, native to the Mediterranean. Often used for *scrolling foliage.

Adam style *See* pp. 16–7.

aedicule An opening or niche framed by two columns or *pilasters carrying an *entablature and *pediment.

aegricanes Heads or skulls of rams or goats, sometimes hung in *swags-and-tails in Greek and Roman ornament.

anthemia Floral motifs based on the flower of either the *acanthus or the honeysuckle.

arabesques Stylized, interlaced foliage patterns of Near Eastern origin, based on laurel leaves. In Western ornament often combined with *strapwork.

arcading A range of arches supported on *pilasters or columns.

architrave Lowest part of an *entablature. Also a collective term for the moldings around a window, door, panel, or niche.

Art Nouveau *See* p. 33.

Arts and Crafts *See* pp. 30–1.

balusters Small posts or colonnetes used in rows to support a handrail. Together they form a **balustrade** (as on the side of a staircase or a terrace).

Baronial style Late-nineteenth-century mock *Gothic style of architecture based on *medieval designs of eccelestiastical buildings and castles.

Baroque *See* pp. 10–1.

baseboards The wooden boards fixed to the base of an internal wall at the junction of the floor and the wall; often molded or chamfered along the top.

bead moulding A molding consisting of rows of small, convex or semicircular (bead-like) shapes.

bead-and-reel A molding comprising alternating, bead-like and cylindrical shapes.

Beaux Arts A strand of late-nineteenth- and early-twentieth-century *classicism, particularly prevalent in America and based on the teachings of the influential École des Beaux Arts in Paris.

brattishing A cresting, usually of leaf or floral forms, or miniature battlements.

broken pediment *See* *pediment.

bucrania Skulls of oxen or bulls, hung with garlands; like *aegricanes, often incorporated into *swags-and-tails.

cantilevered A method of supporting a horizontal projection, such as a step(s), balcony, beam, or canopy, with a downward force at only one end–usually through a wall into which the one end is keyed.

capital The top or head of a column or *pilaster (*see* *Orders).

cartouche A decorative panel consisting of a round, oval, or scroll-shaped frame with either a plain or decorated center.

casements *See* pp. 68–9.

castellated Topped or crested with battlement-like, alternating projections and indents.

caulicolae The *fluted stalks of *acanthus leaves.

chamfered Cut or planed to an approximately 45 degree angle.

checker pattern A geometric "counterchange" pattern consisting of regularly spaced squares of alternating color.

chimney breast The part of a wall that contains the fireplace and projects into a room.

chinoiserie Western adaptations of Chinese furnishings, artefacts and styles of ornament.

clapboarding Overlapping wooden boards applied as the external covering to wood-framed walls.

classicism Post-*medieval revivals of the principles and forms of Ancient Greek and Roman architecture and ornament.

closed-string A staircase in which the sides of the steps are covered by a sloping member (a string) which supports the *balusters.

Coade stone An artificial cast stone made in London from the 1770s onward, mostly used for masonry.

coffered ceiling A ceiling that has been divided into compartments (coffers) by exposed beams or by plaster moldings.

Colonial Revival A late-nineteenth- and early-twentieth-century revival of *Colonial-style architecture and decoration.

Colonial style *See* pp. 14–5.

consoles Ornamental brackets in the form of scrolls or *volutes.

corbel A stone or timber block projecting from the top of a wall and used to support a beam or part of the ceiling.

Corinthian A Classical *Order.

cornice A plain or decorative molding (crown molding) used to cover the join between the walls and the ceiling.

crockets Small leaf carvings used in *Gothic architecture.

cyma recta An S-shaped moulding.

cyma reversa An S-shaped molding in reverse.

dado Lower section of a wall (*see* pp. 116–7).

dentils Decorative moldings made up of regularly spaced, square-shaped blocks.

diaper patterns Collective term for patterns used in Western and Oriental decoration, consisting of a geometric framework (*latticework or *trelliswork). often embellished with decorative motifs.

dog grate A metal basket used in a hearth for burning coals.

dogleg A type of staircase (*see* p. 77).

Doric A Classical *Order.

"drab" A brownish-grayish-green paint popular during the first half of the eighteenth century.

egg-and-dart A molding comprising alternating egg and arrow shapes.

Empire style *See* pp. 18–9.

encaustic tiles Earthenware tiles patterned with inlays of colored clays.

en suite Designed or decorated to match other objects, surfaces, or materials.

entablature The top of an *Order, made up of an *architrave, a *frieze, and a *cornice.

faux marbre French for "fake marble." A technique for simulating the appearance of marble using paints and glazes.

Federal style *See* pp. 18–9.

field The center section of a wall (*see* pp.114–5).

fielded A raised center part of a panel.

finial A carved, cast, or molded ornament on top of a spire, gable, or post. Also used on furniture and the ends of curtain rod ends. Typical forms include acorns, arrowheads, and pinecones.

fireback A fixed or freestanding iron plate at the back of a hearth, protecting the wall and reflecting heat into the room.

firedogs Pairs of raised metal bars used to support burning logs in a hearth.

flat-painted A surface covered with one or more uniform, opaque coats of paint.

flocked wallpaper A type of wallpaper with a raised textured pattern formed by sprinking fine particles of wool (or other fibers) over the paper.

fleur-de-lis A stylized three-, or sometimes five-, petal lily motif, widely used since the early Middle Ages.

floorcloth A floor covering made from linseed-oil-stiffened canvas, and then painted or stenciled with patterns.

fluting A row of parallel, vertical, concave grooves.

"flying" stairs A staircase in which the flight or flights of stairs are *cantilevered from the wall(s) of the stairwell, and have no *newel.

foliate Leaflike.

fretwork Carved or painted geometric patterns (such as *Greek key patterns) consisting of bands of horizontal and vertical lines.

frieze The section of wall from the ceiling or *cornice down to the top of the *field.

gable The part triangular-shaped section of a wall directly under the end of a sloping roof.

girandole A convex mirror.

Gothic *See* pp. 8–9.

Gothic Revival A nineteenth-century revival of *medieval Gothic architecture, ornament, and decoration.

gougework Patterns and motifs chiseled into wooden surfaces.

Greco-Roman Collective term for the classical architecture, ornament, and decoration of Ancient Greece and Rome.

Greek key A border pattern of regularly repeated, interlocking lines, originating in classical Greek architecture.

grisaille A monochromatic, *trompe l'oeil technique in which figures and patterns are rendered three-dimensionally in shades of black, gray, and white.

grotesques Decorations based on Ancient Roman wall paintings. Typical motifs include animals, birds, and fishes, set within *foliate scrolls or panels.

guilloche A form of decoration or ornament made up of interlacing curved bands, sometimes forming circles embellished with floral motifs.

herringbone Geometric pattern consisting of alternating diagonal lines, and resembling the spinal and rib structure of the herring fish.

Italianate A 19th-century style of architecture based on the rural buildings of northern Italy and the palaces of the Italian *Renaissance, typified by low roofs, bracketed overhanging eaves, entrance towers, *arcaded porches, and *balustrated balconies.

Ionic A Classical *Order.

Jacobean An historical period embracing the reigns of James I and Charles I of England

jambs The straight, vertical sides of a doorway, an arch or a fireplace–in the latter, flanking the hearth and sometimes in the form of *pilasters.

key stone The central stone in the curve of an arch.

lath-and-plaster A network of thin slips of wood (laths) covered with layers of flat plaster.

latticework A grid pattern of open diamond shapes used for leading in late-sixteenth-century glazed windows. Also worked in stone or wood as an architectural and furniture embellishment, and used as a pattern on ceramics, fabrics, wallpapers, and metalwares.

limewash An early form of paint, made from lime putty, water, linseed oil, and pigments.

linenfold A carved pattern resembling vertical folds in linen, and mostly applied to wall paneling and doors.

marquetry See pp. 90–1.

medallions Circular or oval decorative devices, often bearing a portrait or other motifs and imagery.

medieval See pp. 8–9.

Middle Ages Historical period extending from the fall of the Western Roman Empire in the 5th century A.D. to the beginning of the Renaissance in the fifteenth century. The *Medieval period.

millefleurs A dense floral pattern (French for "a thousand flowers"), originally used on medieval pictorial tapestries. Favored flowers, naturalistically depicted, include roses, anemones, pinks, columbines, and violas.

modillions Projecting, bracket-like ornaments used in a *cornice, and similar in appearance to small *corbels.

mortised-and-tenoned A method of joining two pieces of wood, in which a hole (a mortise) is cut into one piece to house a projection (a tenon) shaped in the other.

mosaic A pattern made from small pieces of stone, ceramic, or glass, much used in classical and Oriental architecture.

moldings Decoratively contoured strips of wood, plaster, or stone.

mullions Vertical bars (of stone or wood) used to divide windows and other openings. Also fixed or hinged, vertically divided windows.

neoclassical A style of architecture, ornament, and decoration that began in the mid-eighteenth century, and based on interpretations of classical Greek and Roman precedents. See pp. 16–23.

newel Post at the end of a staircase, often attached to the handrail and string (see *open-string). On circular staircases, the central post around which stairs curve, and which supports the narrow side of the steps.

ogival arch Pointed arch formed by pairs of serpentine-shaped reversed curves.

open-string A staircase in which the side or sides of the treads and steps are not enclosed by a string (see *closed-string), and are thus visible.

Orders The architectural components that constitute the basis of classical Greek and Roman architecture. Each Order consists of a *column, usually rising from a *plinth, topped by a *capital, and supporting an *entablature. The Greek and Roman Orders are Doric, Ionic, Corinthian, Composite, and Tuscan.

Oriental Collective term used for Eastern ornament and decoration. Includes Arabian, Chinese, Indian, Japanese, Persian, and Turkish.

overmantel The decorative treatment of the wall area above a fireplace, often incorporating a painting or mirror.

parquetry See pp. 90–1.

paterae An oval or circular motif based on dishes used in religious ceremonies–often with a central flower and/or *fluting. Similar to *rosettes.

pedestal The supporting base for a column, or an artifact such as a statue or vase.

pediment A low-pitched (triangular-shaped) *gable across the top of a *portico, door, window or fireplace. When the top of the triangular shape is omitted, or left open, it is called a *broken pediment.

pelmet Fabric-covered wooden fitting, or a stiffened section of fabric, fixed above a window and designed to conceal the curtain pole and the tops of the curtains.

piano nobile The principal floor of a large house or villa, containing the reception rooms.

picture rail A *molding on upper part of a wall, sometimes defining the top of the *field or the bottom of the *frieze, and used to hang pictures.

pier glass A tall, narrow, often ornately framed mirror traditionally hung between two windows.

pilaster A flat, rectangular classical column fixed to a wall. Often used to frame a doorway, or as the *jambs of a fireplace.

polychrome Multicolored.

Pompeiian A style of architecture, ornament, and decoration found in, and inspired by, the Ancient Roman town of Pompeii, rediscovered in southern Italy through a series of archaeological digs starting in the mid-eighteenth century.

porphyry A fine-grained rock, either dark red, purple, gray, or green, and flecked with crystals.

portico A roofed entrance, usually supported by columns.

portieres Curtain designed to be hung over an archway or door.

purlins Horizontal members of the wooden framework of a roof.

quarries Panes of diamond-shaped glass, supported by *latticework leading, in six-teenth-century glazed windows.

quarry tile An unglazed floor tile made from fired clay.

rectilinear In a straight line, or lines, and bounded by straight lines.

Regency See pp. 20–1.

Renaissance A term used to describe the movement in art, architecture, design, and ornament that originated in Italy in the late fifteenth century and spread across Europe during the next 200 years. At its heart lay a revival (and re-interpretation) of the architecture and ornament of Ancient Greece and Rome.

rosettes Circular, formalized floral ornament. See *paterae.

roundels Circular shaped ornament, either plain or containing decorative motifs.

sash window A window formed with sashes–glazed wooden frames which slide up and down in grooves by means of counterbalanced weights. The standard type has two sashes, and is known as a "double-hung" sash.

scrolling foliage A pattern or form of ornament consisting of scrolling, curving, or trailing plant forms, such as grapevines or *acanthus.

side lights Panes of glass on either side of a door.

slips The fascia panels often installed between the opening of a hearth and the *jambs and the *frieze of a mantelpiece.

spandrels The approximately triangular-shaped spaces between an arched opening and any linear *moldings surrounding it.

stenciling A technique for applying patterns to a surface by dabbing paints, glazes, or dyes through cutouts made in a stencil–a thin card often made of oiled paper, but sometimes wood, metal, or plastic.

strapwork Form of ornament consisting of twisted and interlaced bands (similar to strips of leather or ribbons). Sometimes combined with *grotesques, and often studded with *rosettes, or faceted, jewel-like forms–the latter known as jeweled strapwork.

stucco A fine cement or plaster made from sand, slaked lime, and gypsum. Mostly applied to walls and moldings. From the nineteenth century, generally known as render.

swagged-and-tailed Lengths of fabrics, or strips of carved, molded, or painted motifs (of flowers, fruits, vegetables, leaves, or shells), hung in horizontal loops (swags), and allowed to hang or trail down at the ends (tails).

tongue-and-groove A method of jointing wooden boards, in which the edge of one board has a tongue, or lip, that fits into a groove cut into the edge of the adjacent board.

tracery An ornamental arrangement of intersecting ribwork, forming a pierced pattern. Often employed in the upper part of *Gothic windows.

transom The horizontal component running across the top or middle of doors or windows.

transom light See pp. 40-1.

trelliswork A criss-cross support for plants, and geometric patterns based on this botanical accessory. Notably popular in *Medieval, *Regency, and *Arts and Crafts decoration.

trompe l'oeil French for "trick of the eye." A decorative technique in which paints are applied to a flat surface to create the appearance of three-dimensional scenes or objects. See *grisaille.

Tudorbethan A late-nineteenth- and early-twentieth-century hybrid style of architecture, combining elements of English Tudor and Jacobean prototypes.

vaulted Arched, as in an arch-shaped roof or ceiling.

Venetian window A window with an arch-top center section flanked by two narrower rectangular sections. Also known as a serliana.

vergeboard A flat wooden board, often carved, that seals the space between the roof and wall on a *gable end.

volute A spiral, scrolling form, shaped like a ram's horn.

wainscoting Alternative name for wooden wall paneling.

wall-strings Diagonal or inclined timbers attached to the wall of a stairwell, into which one or both sides of the steps of a staircase are secured.

wattle-and-daub An early method of wall construction in which thin branches or *laths (wattles) are fixed to a wood frame and roughly plastered over with mud or clay (daub).

wavescrolls Undulating, linear, wavelike patterns.

winding stairs See *spiral stairs.

INDEX

ACKNOWLEDGMENTS

I would very much like to thank the team at Mitchell Beazley for all the long hours, dedication and skill they have committed to this book: to Julia North for running the project, and for procuring and sifting myriad examples of period fixtures and fittings from numerous manufacturers; Christopher Sparks for the substantial and complex task of hands-on layout and design; Suzanne Woloszynska for contributing; Judith More and Janis Utton for overseeing, respectively, content and design; Karen Farquhar for production control; Bruce Darlaston for US rights; and, last but by no means least, Arlene Sobel for the expertise of her text editing and American "translation," and her unflagging patience and good humor. Thank you.

Together with the publisher, I would like to thank the numerous manufacturers of reproduction architectural fixtures and fittings on both sides of the Atlantic for supplying us with so many examples of their products. You will find their names and addresses in the Directory, on pages 174–87.

Together with the publisher, I also wish to thank all the homeowners, architects, interior designers, museums, trustees, and architectural salvage companies who so kindly opened their doors to our photographers.